T0117118

ALSO BY WILLIAM G. OUCHI

*Theory Z: How American Business Can Meet the Japanese
    Challenge*
*The M-Form Society: How American Teamwork Can
    Recapture the Competitive Edge*
Organizational Economics (with J. B. Barney)

Making Schools Work

**A Revolutionary Plan
to Get Your Children
the Education
They Need**

William G. Ouchi

With Lydia G. Segal

Simon & Schuster

New York   London   Toronto   Sydney   Singapore

SIMON & SCHUSTER
Rockefeller Center
1230 Avenue of the Americas
New York, NY 10020

Copyright © 2003 by William G. Ouchi
All rights reserved,
including the right of reproduction
in whole or in part in any form.

SIMON & SCHUSTER and colophon are registered trademarks
of Simon & Schuster, Inc.

Designed by Karolina Harris

Manufactured in the United States of America

10   9   8   7   6   5   4   3   2   1

Library of Congress Cataloging-in-Publication Data
Ouchi, William G.
   Making schools work : a revolutionary plan to get your children
 the education they need / William G. Ouchi with Lydia G. Segal.
       p. cm.
   Includes bibliographical references (p.) and index.
   1. School improvement programs—United States. I. Segal,
 Lydia G., date. II. Title.

LB2822.82.O93 2003
371.2'00973—dc21   2003050585

ISBN-13: 978-1-4391-5045-0

ISBN-10: 1-4391-5045-1

For information regarding special discounts for bulk purchases,
please contact Simon & Schuster Special Sales:
1-800-456-6798 or business@simonandschuster.com

Acknowledgments

*T*his book is the product of a research team that at its largest included twelve members. Primary among these were Professors Bruce Cooper of Fordham University and Lydia Segal of John Jay College. Professor Cooper led the budgetary analyses of the school districts, and Professor Segal did the same on the accountability analysis. Both made broad contributions to the work as a whole. Cooper modestly declined co-authorship, but his impact on the book was great. Other members of the team included Carolyn Brown, Elizabeth Galvin, Tim DeRoche, John Gabree, Bernice Tsai, Jim Mirocha, Jicky Thantrong, Kristina Tipton, and a few undergraduate students at UCLA. Carolyn Brown, both a Ph.D. candidate at UCLA and an experienced former public school teacher and principal, was particularly crucial in instructing me on the subtleties of the classroom. Tim DeRoche played a major role in the analysis of school budgets. On our school visits, Bernice Tsai proved to have the keenest eye in the group. Stephanie Kagimoto was and is indispensable to me. She did most of the scheduling of the hundreds of interviews, arranged flights and hotels for everyone, and typed all of the taped transcripts.

Mike Strembitsky, the great innovator, has spent hours educating me during several visits in both Los Angeles and Edmonton over a period of ten years, and I will be forever grateful to him. Mike is a man of great decency, warmth, and courage, and I hope that he'll approve of my description of his unprecedented impact on the way that public schools are run.

I am a professor in a graduate school of management, not a school of education. I serve on the boards of directors of companies, and for years I served as a management consultant to businesses, along with my teaching. I initially became seriously engaged in the idea of revolutionary change in public school systems as a founding board member of a Los Angeles citizens' reform group. First known as LEARN, and now as The Alliance, these stalwarts have never wavered from their mission: to save the children by revolutionizing their failing schools. LEARN was founded in 1990 by Helen Bernstein, Richard Riordan, and Robert Wycoff, along with ten others. In turn, the three founders were the teachers' union president, the future mayor of Los Angeles, and the ARCO president. What a group. Because we understood that school reform is all about politics, we hired the talented speaker pro tem of the California state assembly, Mike Roos, as president. Today, The Alliance is ably led by President Howard Lappin, and I have the privilege of sharing the co-chair duties with the deeply wise and fabulously persistent Virgil Roberts.

My experience with politics deepened when Mayor Richard Riordan asked me to join his government from 1993 to 1995. I had the privilege of serving him as senior advisor, and then as his chief of staff. What I learned has equipped me with political X-ray lenses, although I'm still only an intermediate-level observer rather than an expert. Now, when I view any complex situation, I am more likely to see the underlying political structure that previously would have been invisible to me. Dick Riordan also gave me a permanent commitment to children and to public education, along with an absolute refusal to accept anything short of the best quality education for all children. He is a great inspiration and always will be.

The collecting of hundreds of interviews and thousands of pages of documents does not make a book. Ann Dilworth, who is both a close friend and a richly talented person—as well as a perfectionist—forced me through more than two dozen drafts of an outline before the structure of an argument emerged. Once the structure had begun to take shape, Ann commented that I now needed to find my writer's *voice*. I searched for it high and low, and finally found it in Hawaii. It had been on vacation since my last book, keeping company with my father, who returned it to me with his usual good humor and his always positive outlook. Mark Chimsky helped me to give the outline sharpness, and then my literary agent Michael Carlisle had me revise it yet again—and then persuaded Simon & Schuster to publish the book.

My very able editor, Robert Bender, would be a rare gift to any writer. He gave me on-target advice about writing while always encouraging me. I hope to work with him again. The manuscript was greatly improved by the expert copyediting of Ann Adelman.

The financial support for this project was difficult to find. My outlook comes from the world of business rather than education, and traditional education foundations found my approach either heretical or off-center. Instead, I found intellectual venture capital to get me started. The first, critical grants came from Peter Bing and from the Frank and Kathrine Baxter Family Foundation and its president, Stacey Bell. Major gifts also came from the John M. Olin Foundation, as well as the National Science Foundation (Grant #0115559), which had also funded the research for my first book, *Theory Z*. The Thomas B. Fordham Foundation and the Anderson School of Management at UCLA also provided important support. The Foundation for Research in Economics and Education and its chairman, J. Clayburn LaForce, ably administered part of the funds for me.

Introductions to key superintendents and others came through Frank Baxter, Michael F. Brewer, Eli Broad, Janet Brown, Veronica Davey, Senator Dan Inouye, Nikki Irvin, Dan Katzir, Gerard and Lilo Leeds, Robert Lipp, Donald McAdams, Joseph Rice, Richard Riordan, Susan Sclafani, Janet Sisler, William E. Simon, Jr., and Monsignor Lloyd Torgerson. I gained great insight into the issues facing school districts through conversations with Anthony Bryk, Ramon Cortines, Harry Handler, Eric Hanushek, Paul Hill, Senator Ted Kennedy, Frank Macchiarola, and Marc Tucker.

I had my earliest introduction to the teacher's point of view from my sister, Carol S. Ouchi, and from my late mother, Shizuko Nakano Ouchi. Both were lifelong public school teachers. My wife, Carol K. Ouchi, supported me through the endless travel to gather data and the long days and nights of writing. She has been my partner and my support for nearly forty years. Our children and their spouses, Sarah and Vince Tsai, Jenny and David Gallon, and Andrew Ouchi, dropped by often to lend moral support. When my energy waned, I was invariably revived by my grandson, Ethan Tsai. Good friends Carl and Rena McKinzie endured literally dozens of dinners during which, I'm afraid, I could talk of little but this project.

The draft of the book was read by several experts, each of whom offered wise counsel, and I am grateful to each of them: Patrick Bassett, Norman Bradburn, Veronica Davey, Chester Finn, Harry Handler, Antonia Hernandez, Sonia Hernandez, Dan Katzir, Donald McAdams, Clinton McKinzie, Carol S. Ouchi, Diane Ravitch, and Christina Warden.

I am grateful to all of these people, and to the many who

gave their time to be interviewed or to help us to find data. I alone wrote every word in this book, though, and I accept full responsibility for any and all errors.

William G. Ouchi
Santa Monica, California

To the memory of my mother, Shizuko Ouchi, and to my sister, Carol Ouchi. Both were career-long public school teachers who gave me the highest respect for the profession of teaching.

We are to regard the mind not as a piece of iron to be laid upon the anvil and hammered into any shape, nor as a block of marble in which we are to find the statue by removing the rubbish, nor as a receptacle into which knowledge may be poured; but as a flame that is to be fed, as an active being that must be strengthened to think and feel—to dare, to do, and to suffer.

—MARK HOPKINS, INDUCTION ADDRESS AS PRESIDENT
OF WILLIAMS COLLEGE, 1836

Contents

Part One:
What Makes a
School Great? ✔

1

The Best Schools in America— Problems and Solutions

Welcome to the Goudy School: Where the Future Dies Early.
— Chicago Schools: Worst in America *(1988)*

*T*he year was 1988, and William Bennett was secretary of education. Americans were furious over the continued failure of their public schools. To galvanize the nation's attention on this issue, Bennett visited the city of Chicago and declared that its public schools were the worst in the nation, and he singled out one school as the city's worst failure, and thus, by inference, *the worst school in America:* the Goudy Elementary School, prekindergarten through 8, located in Uptown/Edgewater. Uptown/Edgewater is a blue-collar, immigrant neighborhood on the far north end where twenty-six languages are spoken every day. The teachers, students, and families were devastated by the negative publicity. Within the year, the Illinois legislature moved quickly to pass a new law that gave local control to individual schools to free them from the shackles of the massive, top-down bureaucracy of the superintendent's central office.

Fourteen years later, under the leadership of Principal Patrick Durkin, Goudy has risen like a phoenix. Goudy has an

3

official capacity of 850 students, but today it is packed with 938 children, all of them from the neighborhood. Ninety-eight percent of the students are from low-income homes and thus qualify for free or reduced-price lunches under a federal program; 41 percent are classified as limited-English-proficient. On the Iowa Test of Basic Skills used in all Chicago schools, reading scores have risen from the 14.9th percentile to an astounding 56th— above the state and national averages. Math scores have also sky-rocketed, from the 24.7th percentile to the 63rd. This in a school that has a student population that is 29 percent Hispanic, 28 percent Asian-Pacific, 22 percent white, and 21 percent black (I sometimes refer to students as black or Hispanic and other times as African-American or Latino. In each case, I'm using the form that the school district uses in its official reports). Virtually every eighth grader from Goudy takes the test to enter one of Chicago's elite test-in high schools like Northside College Prep, Lane Tech, Lincoln Park, or Whitney Young.

How did Patrick Durkin produce this miracle? Our study shows that he, like the other successful principals described here, relied on a set of management principles that I call the Seven Keys to Success. He used his freedom to custom-design a school that would exactly fit the needs of his unique population of students. No other school in America has precisely the same situation, and thus no other school should be quite like Goudy. Understanding that, the principal set out to craft the right school for his children.

Patrick Durkin is an entrepreneur. That is, he's the opposite of a bureaucrat—he doesn't follow rules blindly, he keeps his eye focused on his main goal, which is to see that his students succeed. He operates under another rule: that it's easier and better to ask forgiveness from the central office after taking action than to ask permission beforehand. He expects to be held accountable for results. Durkin knew what to do with his newfound freedom allowing local control. He focused everyone on student achievement, not complaining about the poor children who were in the neighborhood, but seeking to do right by every last one of them. To accomplish this task, he delegated most of the decisions to his teachers, who chose their own approach to teaching reading and math.

Durkin moved quickly to take control of all of the money that the new law allowed him to use at his discretion. He and his teachers decided, for example, to place an intense focus on reading, with everyone spending ninety minutes on reading in small classes of no more than twenty, and he added a teaching aide to every class in grades 1 through 4. Durkin also made sure that every teacher felt accountable for the progress of his or her students. He instituted a system in which every student is tested on reading level when he first enrolls, and then is measured for progress.

To help the students from China, Mexico, Africa, the West Indies, Poland, Albania, Cambodia, Vietnam, and Bosnia who have trouble with reading, he added two reading recovery teachers who tutor each child one-on-one. His teachers did their own research and imported a program from New Zealand that in six or seven weeks can help a child who is in danger of falling behind in reading. Today, virtually all of the children are reading by the end of first grade.

In order to put the resources in grades K–4 where they were most needed, the teachers decided on larger class sizes in the later grades. In one fifth-grade class, for example, thirty-two children are intent on their work—and they are not distracted when visitors enter the classroom. An eighth-grade class has thirty-four children eating a late lunch at their desks, because there is no other place. Breakfast and lunch are served in the auditorium, which then is closed for another reading program for groups of twenty at a time. Goudy has no new buildings, but it needed space for these newly created activities, so the former book storage room and the teachers' office space were converted to that use. Durkin designed teachers' desks that would fit along one wall in the wide hallway. The small library is full to overflowing, and it has received donations of 25,000 brand-new books from the Starbucks Corporation over the past few years.

Principal Pat Durkin loves his school. That's clear to any visitor. He's the kind of principal who insists on taking visitors to see every single class in the building. He knows in detail what is going on in each class and what progress the students are making. The teachers are visibly fond of him and each one greets him warmly. He knows most of the students by name. Even the reading recovery teachers, who work in what was formerly the school's safe—which still has the impregnable steel door—have smiles for the principal. Because Pat Durkin has the freedom to choose his own teachers, he has only teachers who share his passion for the school's mission, and the results speak for themselves. Goudy Elementary has become more than just a school—it's become a community of learners that includes teachers, students, and families.

If the worst school in America can become one of the best, then every school can be a success. Pat Durkin, please note, did not make a wholesale change in his teachers or his students. The *only* changes that he made were in the way the school was organized and managed. If you had to change all of your school district's teachers to improve it, you'd be understandably gloomy about the future. The good news in this book, though, is that you don't have to change the teachers or the students—you only have to change the way that your schools are managed, and that is entirely within the realm of the possible. If the same teachers and the same students can go from the cellar to the penthouse as at Goudy, then it can be done elsewhere. For those who believe that an inner-city school made up of immigrants from homes in poverty cannot achieve at high academic levels, Goudy proves otherwise. Every school in America can and should be this good, and you can help to make them so. Before we get on with the process of how to do this, though, let's briefly review some of the troubles that our schools face today, and let's identify the reasons that most of them are still in the cellar.

REPORTS FROM THE FRONT LINES
IN THE EDUCATION WARS

Our schools are failing—everyone knows it.[1] School board meetings have become battlefields as angry parents are on the attack and central office bureaucrats strap on their helmets and hunker down. In New York, the state legislature has admitted that the New York City schools are failing and, in desperation, has given control to Mayor Mike Bloomberg. *The New York Times* reported on July 11, 2002, that only 29.5 percent of the city's eighth graders passed the state English test, lower than the year before and lower still than in 1999, when the current test was first used. The really bad news, according to the newspaper, is that students in Rochester, Syracuse, and Buffalo are doing even worse. In New England, the *Boston Globe* reported in February 2002 that the charter school movement to secede from the public system has grown to the point that it now is battling increasing opposition from public school officials.

In April 2002, Governor Mark S. Schweiker of Pennsylvania assumed control of the failed Philadelphia school district and hired several private firms to manage this system in which more than half the students cannot pass basic reading and math tests. Several months later, Philadelphia hired former Chicago superintendent Paul Vallas to turn its district around. On July 10, the *Pittsburgh Post-Gazette* carried the front-page headline: "Foundations Yank City School Grants." The paper quoted William Trueheart, president of the Pittsburgh Foundation: "It's clear the school system is in a crisis." *Education Week* reported in March that the Detroit Board of Education had to "abruptly adjourn" its meeting amid "emotional chants and songs of protesters" and that the Dallas Board of Education called a sudden recess due to a scuffle with a speaker and then located observers to a separate room to watch the remainder of the meeting over closed-circuit television.

Our nation also has a persistent gap in educational attainment between races. While 93 percent of white students graduate from high school, only 63 percent of Hispanics and 87 percent of blacks do so. Writers such as Jonathan Kozol have argued that this gap is a result of embedded racism, which leaves students of color with underfunded, abandoned schools.[2] He may be right, but we have found many schools that are successfully educating poor minority students—thus demonstrating, as we'll see, that good management of a school can overcome all kinds of obstacles.

We are in the midst of a rising national debate over K–12 education as more and more parents reach the point where they won't take it any more. They've lost confidence in the ability of school boards and superintendents to fix the problems and have turned to mayors and governors to get the job done. But what will these politicians do that hasn't already been tried? In other words, why are the schools failing, and what needs to be fixed?

THREE COMMON BUT INCORRECT THEORIES ABOUT THE FAILURE OF OUR SCHOOLS

There are three basic theories that we hear from education experts, school officials, and the press to explain the failure of our schools: first, the teachers aren't any good, and they are the source of the failure; second, the students, especially minority students, just aren't able or willing to learn; and third, we have to spend more money on our schools to improve them. All three of these theories are wrong. Instead, I offer to you the management theory. Consider this: when a business is failing, the owners don't blame the customers, the front-line employees, or the budget—they go after the management and shake *them* up. There's nothing wrong with the students or the teachers, and most (though not all) school systems already have enough money to do the job well. It's the management of school districts that needs to be changed. I have visited 223 schools in nine school systems and have carried out a carefully designed study of the management systems in all of them. I found that some entire districts are succeeding wonderfully while others are failing. What separates the successes from the failures is not different teachers, students, or money—it's their approach to managing the schools.

Teacher-bashing has become the favorite sport of politicians and superintendents who don't know what to do about the schools—and are looking for someone to blame. Their criticisms don't hold water, though. Scholars such as Dr. Eric Hanushek of the Hoover Institution and New York University education historian Dr. Diane Ravitch observe that while teacher preparation is better than ever, student scores have not improved.[3] This leads to the conclusion that the fundamental problem is not the teachers.

Others will argue, although in guarded tones, that the basic problem is the students. These critics believe that public schools in suburban areas with mostly white students are doing fine, but that urban schools with mostly minority students are the ones in trouble. At bottom, these people believe that African-American and Hispanic students either can't or won't learn, that it's hopeless to try to improve their schools. The result of this attitude has been chronicled by Jonathan Kozol in his devastating critique, *Savage Inequalities* (New York: Crown, 1991). Kozol points out that schools of mostly minority children in East St. Louis (Illinois), New York City, and other cities never have a chance to succeed because they are prejudged to be inevitable failures.

To these people I say, let me tell you about the View Park Prep Charter School in Los Angeles. View Park is 99 percent African-American and 1 percent Latino, in grades K–7. In the most recent Stanford 9 standardized tests, its fifth graders scored on the average in the 77th percentile in language, the 78th percentile in spelling, and the 81st percentile in math—better than any of the four elementary schools in Beverly Hills. View Park (and other similar schools we've found across the nation) isn't widely known to parents, but it should be. Schools such as this are living proof that the problem is not with the children. The key question is, what is it that makes View Park Prep a great school, and how can we make every school—including those in Beverly Hills—just as good?

Another argument, especially from school district officials and the leaders of teachers' unions, is that the fundamental problem is money—we aren't spending enough per child on education. After investigating this allegation, I now believe that we've been fed a line of baloney by self-serving bureaucrats who seek to shift the blame for their failures to mayors, governors, and the public.

Consider these facts in the Los Angeles Unified School District as an example: the annual operating budget per student for 2001–02 was $9,889. On top of that, the district budgets $2,810 per student for school construction and renovation and $375 per student for debt service. Add it all up, and it's a total of $13,074 per student per year.[4] By comparison, a study by the *Los Angeles Business Journal* shows that for twenty-five private schools in Los Angeles, the average annual tuition is only $7,091, and our research shows that the 298 Catholic schools in the city spend an average of $2,500 per student in elementary schools and $5,100 per student in high school.[5]

In New York City, the operating budget is a whopping $11,994 per student. Add to that the annual budget of $2,298 per student for school construction and renovation and debt service, and the total spending is $14,292 per student per year. That amount doesn't even include bus and subway fees, which come out of the mayor's budget. Both New York City and Los Angeles spend more than the average tuition of $11,246 for the 851 independent day schools that are affiliated with the National Association of Independent Schools.

The problem is not that there isn't enough money in public schools. School districts like New York City and Los Angeles have already raised teacher pay, they've reduced class size, they've bought the latest reading books and computers, yet nothing seems to work. The salespeople for new approaches keep coming and the school boards keep buying, but things don't get any better.

Everyone is looking in the wrong place, focusing on the wrong things. It's a classic case of missing the forest for the trees. The research that went into this book will show you that it's the way schools are *managed* that makes the difference. Here's just one example of how good management makes for a good school: have you ever wondered why some schools have lots of good teachers—even the ones who are new to teaching—while other schools seem to have few good teachers? It's the management. Good management both attracts dedicated teachers and creates the environment in which all teachers do their best every day.

THE RESEARCH FOUNDATIONS OF THIS BOOK

In order to get a good overview of schools, we need to look at them in two ways: first, at several school districts so that we can compare them to each other; and second, at several schools within each district.[6] Our basic guess, drawn from studies of business, was that school districts that are run in a very special way that allows principals to be entrepreneurs—managers who take the initiative rather than taking orders—would be more successful. In order to test this idea, we needed to choose a range of school districts—from some that give principals very little leeway to others in which individual schools have all of the decision-making power. You may have read lots of research about the management of schools, but few people have studied the way that the school districts are organized and managed. We've found that it's the management of the entire district that is the important factor, the one that determines whether each school will have the local autonomy that it needs to adjust to its specific circumstances, or not. If the district is run properly, all of the schools in it will be successful. If not, all schools will suffer, and only those few principals who are willing to buck the central office will succeed. In time even they will tire of the conflict and will retire early or burn out.

In order to create our sample, we chose four types of school systems. First, we selected the three largest and, by reputation, most centralized, top-down districts in the United States: New York City, with 1.1 million students; Los Angeles, with 723,000 students; and Chicago, with 435,000 (all in 2001). We took several measurements to determine whether they were truly centralized. Next, we chose three little known but very successful school districts, all of which had turned themselves around supposedly by creating lots of entrepreneurs—Edmonton, Canada, with 81,000 students; Seattle, Washington, with 47,000; and Houston, Texas, with 209,000. Here, too, we measured them and found that all three are successful because of the radically different way that these districts are run.

The third set of schools consisted of the three largest Catholic school districts in the United States. These were Chicago, with about 128,000 students; New York City, with approximately 115,000 students; and Los Angeles, with approximately 103,000. We chose these Catholic school districts because they are often said to be loosely affiliated networks of schools in which each school has great local autonomy. We wanted to find out if that is a correct perception, and if so, we wanted to see what the greater autonomy does for a typical Catholic school.

Finally, we selected a group of six independent schools— one in each of our six cities—because independent schools, as their name implies, have the ultimate in local freedom—they report to no higher authority. Now we had a range—from schools that are believed to have almost no freedom to be entrepreneurial to those that have complete freedom to rise or fall on their own decisions.

We visited at least 5 percent of the schools in each district, more than 5 percent in the small districts. For example, we visited sixty-six public schools in New York City and forty-one in Los Angeles. In all, we visited 223 schools. In each case, we interviewed the principal, gathered information on student performance and on how the school was managed, and had a tour of classrooms. Along the way, I had the rare chance that few parents ever have to ask lots of experienced principals and teachers how to spot a good school and a good classroom. In this book, you'll learn everything that I learned on those subjects.

Finally, we visited the headquarters of each school district several times. We interviewed the chancellor or superintendent and other top officials. We spent a great deal of time understanding the budgets, the accountability systems, and the achievement of students. We talked to the inspector general in every district that has one, along with the internal auditor, in order to find out which kinds of school districts have more waste and corruption, and which have less.

What we've seen are some entire school districts that are succeeding and others that are failing. The picture is one that provokes in me a strong emotional reaction, because I now know that any school superintendent who follows certain management principles can create success—and that there is no excuse for not making every school a success. I have boiled down these lessons into an essence of seven key elements that distinguish successful schools and school districts, and in this book I pass them along to you so that you can help your school to be successful. Let's review them in summary form, and then we'll expand on each one in the chapters to follow.

THE SEVEN KEYS TO SUCCESS

Successful school districts are the ones that have learned how to keep several important elements in balance. For example, they give teachers and principals the freedom to be entrepreneurs, to identify and solve their own problems with their own unique solutions, while at the same time collecting information on what is going on and intervening when necessary. This is impossible to do in a traditional, old-fashioned school district—which unfortunately means most school districts. To build a really top-flight school district, you have to embrace dramatic changes in how things are run. What is called for, and what the successful districts have done, is to uproot the existing top-down way of doing things and replace it with huge, revolutionary change.

THE SEVEN KEYS TO SUCCESS

1. Every principal is an entrepreneur
2. Every school controls its own budget
3. Everyone is accountable for student performance and for budgets
4. Everyone delegates authority to those below
5. There is a burning focus on student achievement
6. Every school is a community of learners
7. Families have real choices among a variety of unique schools

Let's review each of these seven elements.

1. Every principal is an entrepreneur

An entrepreneur is the opposite of a bureaucrat. Bureaucrats, especially good ones, know the rules backwards and forwards and always follow them. In a routine, stable situation, that's a good thing. When confronted with the nonroutine, though, bureaucrats cannot act until a higher-up gives them a new rule that they can follow. In schools, where each day brings new and previously unknown situations, bureaucracy is deadly. Bureaucracy is not limited to large, urban school districts. Even small, suburban districts can become rulebound. Bureaucracy flourishes wherever customers have no choice. Bureaucrats act the way they do because they can get away with ignoring customers. Don't blame the people who work in those kinds of organizations, because if you worked there, you'd probably act like a bureaucrat, too. Do blame the organization and its managers—they know better, and it's up to them to see that customers matter, especially those customers, namely, students who have no choice but the public schools. In business, health care, and education, you will find bureaucracy in both large and small organizations.

Every school district, even old-fashioned, top-down, rule-bound school districts, has a few entrepreneurs. And in successful school districts, everyone is an entrepreneur in spirit and in behavior. Usually, an entrepreneurial principal in a bureaucratic district is viewed by the central office as a renegade, an outlaw, and a troublemaker. She fights for her teachers and students every day, hangs way out there taking chances with the central office, and gets no thanks from above for her accomplishments.

2. Every school controls its own budget

It's now considered politically expedient to be in favor of local neighborhood control for schools, rather than central office dictatorship. Almost every school district has adopted school-based management, school-site management, local school councils, or something similar. Your superintendent surely claims to be granting great leeway to each school to make its own decisions. Chances are, though, that he's lying to you. Fortunately, when you know what to ask, it's easy to tell the difference between talk and action concerning neighborhood control.

Ask your principal how much money he has in his budget this year. We did this at every school that we visited. In the top-down, old-fashioned districts, more than 90 percent of the principals gave us a puzzled look in response. They didn't know how much money their school had! At one high school in Los Angeles, the principal asked if we really needed to know the budget numbers. When we said that we did, she went to her assistant principal for administration and came back with the answer: "It's $50 million this year." We expressed doubt that it was that high and suggested that she look it up on the school district Web site. She did and reported that the number was actually $21 million! "But it doesn't really matter," she continued, "because I only control $32,000."

You might find this alarming, but she didn't. Most principals around the nation don't care what their budget is because they aren't allowed to decide how to spend it. Most of the control lies in the central office, which sends the schools teachers, aides, paraprofessionals, nurses, custodians, guards, and so on. The central office does not send the money to a school and allow it to decide whom to hire. It does the thinking for the principal. Which would be okay except that the bureaucrats in central don't know nearly as well as the principal what the school actually needs.

When your superintendent claims at parent meetings or in the newspapers that he or she has established local school parent councils and has decentralized the management of the district, smile sweetly and ask him what percent of the budget each principal controls. You'll be aghast at the answer. Ignore everything that you hear about local control except how much money is subject to local control. Follow the money—that's where the control lies.

3. Everyone is accountable for student performance and for budgets

"Accountability" has become one of the most overused words in all of education. Politicians demand school accountability, superintendents vow to demand it, and businesspeople who become involved in school reform often conclude that it's at the root of the whole problem. To these people, accountability means getting tough on teachers. It's really just another form of teacher-bashing, and it misses the point.

Accountability should mean openness, so that everyone from parents to teachers to the community at large gets regular, understandable, and credible accounts of what is going on in the schools. Three categories of reports matter most: student performance, budget performance, and customer satisfaction. Budgets are the key input to schools and student performance is their key output.

In a successful school district, the superintendent knows exactly how much progress each school is making, knows from annual questionnaires how the students, parents, and employees in each school rate the principal's leadership, and knows which principals are using their money wisely. The principal in a great school will usually be able to tell you exactly which teachers are delivering good student progress in each subject, and which ones are not. She will have a plan for helping the teachers who need it and for removing the few teachers who won't improve. In a truly accountable district, there is a third element of accountability: customer satisfaction. In Edmonton, Canada, for example, and in Santa Monica, California, every parent, student, and teacher fills out a questionnaire each year and rates the teachers, the principals, and the superintendent! With these three pillars of accountability in place, it's prudent to grant local autonomy to each school.

4. Everyone delegates authority to those below

My image of private school headmasters has always been one of benevolent despots. Not any more. As Arthur Powell says in his book on independent schools, "the days of despotic but benevolent heads are largely over. Since the 1960s considerable power has been dispersed . . . downwards to middle-management administrators and faculty."[7] Perhaps the independent schools have been forced into this change because they too have a more diverse and complex body of students and must give teachers more freedom to make adjustments. In any case, these schools are remarkable for the extensive autonomy that they give to their teachers.

Great public school districts do much the same. They take great care selecting and training each teacher and each principal because they delegate so much power to those people.

5. There is a burning focus on student achievement

If you focus only on decentralization, you'll get a decentralized district, but with low student achievement.

17

You've got to focus on student achievement.
—*Angus McBeath, Superintendent, Edmonton Public Schools*

I didn't say that this would be easy, only that it would be good—and worth any amount of effort that it takes. Commitment to student achievement is like school-based management—everyone is for it, but almost no one really does it.

Having a burning, monomaniacal commitment to student achievement takes more than oratory. It takes hard, hard work. It also requires an underlying belief that every student can learn and that, if the school does its job correctly, every student *will* learn. Think about it for a moment, and you'll realize why I conclude that so few schools really have this commitment. If every child does not learn, does not make a full year's progress in the core academic subjects every year, if you believe that every child can learn, then the school, not the child, is at fault.

A focus on student achievement should produce a different set of activities in each school, depending on the local circumstances. For example, let's consider the Jose Clemente Orozco Community Academy, 718 students in grades 6–8. Located in the Pilsen neighborhood of Chicago, Orozco Academy when we visited it was 97 percent Mexican, 1.9 percent Puerto Rican, with one white student, one black student, one Cuban student, and three other Hispanic students. More than 98 percent of the students qualify for the free lunch program. In seven years, Principal Rebeca De Los Reyes has built a team of teachers and parent volunteers who have changed the school by focusing on student achievement. They've implemented a once-monthly Saturday program with workshops for parents and academics for their children so that parents will have the focus too. They've changed the daily schedule to block scheduling, with periods of varying length, which enable teams of teachers to plan together every day and permit a more effective focus on language arts. They've mandated school uniforms, with 100 percent compliance with this step to instill discipline in the classrooms. They've instituted additional support programs for students who are learning English as a second language. The school had three Family Reading Nights last year, and was able to free eighteen half-days for teacher training, a necessity nowadays when major advances in teaching methods are taking place.

The result? From 1992 to 2000, the average standardized reading test score has risen from the 22.7th percentile to the 44.4th. The average mathematics score has risen over that period from the 30.7th percentile to the 57.5th. Principal De Los Reyes received the Outstanding Leadership Award for 2000, and she deserved it.

6. Every school is a community of learners

Every good school is, first and foremost, a community of learners. In a school that is a community, there is a consistent set of shared beliefs about what the school should be in order for its children to succeed. In a school that is divided into conflicting cliques, children suffer because they are presented with inconsistent expectations and incompatible demands.

In a unified school community, scarce resources still must be allocated among competing demands, but these decisions do not lead to outbreaks of fighting among the adults over the basic values of the school—because those issues have been openly confronted and resolved. What does it take to transform an ordinary school into a true learning community? It's not magic—it's plain, old-fashioned hard work.

First: the school must reach out to the outside community that it serves and put in the time and the work that it takes to understand what the community wants and needs for its children—and then come up with a plan that meets those needs. This doesn't mean compromising or having winners and losers. It means continuing to debate the issues until the school locates that space where the many competing demands intersect.

Second: each teacher is part of a vertical team that unites, say, grades K–3 or the teachers of science in grades 7–9. Teachers are in horizontal teams, too, so that the teachers of different subjects in the tenth grade meet together once a week or twice a month to coordinate with each other. Thus all of the adults in the school are part of a learning community. Now they're ready to bring the children into this community.

We'll also take a look at the Catholic schools of the inner cities. These schools serve the poor on painfully small budgets—yet many of them succeed magnificently at their task. They do so by creating famously strong learning communities, and we'll see how they do it.

7. Families have real choices among a variety of unique schools

All of the successful school districts in our study, whatever their size, racial composition, and location, permit families to choose whichever public school they feel is best for their children. In a sense, they've found a way to have the proven power of competition—but within the public school system. If a school cannot attract enough students to remain viable in these systems, it's reduced to a program rather than a school, and the principal is removed and replaced by a program director, who then reports to another, successful principal. Once the school is restored to health, a new principal is appointed and the school regains its independence. In other cases, the superintendent has a variety of means through which to give close supervision to a school that is in trouble. In some instances, a failing school is simply permitted to go out of business.

Combine this competitive system with the entrepreneurial freedom given to each principal, and you have schools that very quickly adapt themselves to the precise needs of the families whom they serve. The result is the opposite of cookie-cutter schools: it's schools that are as different from each other as a rose is from a gardenia. Let a thousand different flowers bloom, and let each family choose the one that best meets its needs.

IT TAKES ALL SEVEN OF THE KEYS TO SUCCESS TO MAKE A DISTRICT WORK WELL

The Seven Keys to Success are not a cafeteria of ideas on school reform from which you can choose the two or three that most appeal to you. History and experience show that such a piecemeal approach won't work. Allan Odden and Carolyn Busch, for example, demonstrate in their book *Financing Schools for High Performance* that reformers who have implemented only school-based management committees have failed. Instead, they urge those bent on real change to implement a broad array of elements in their blueprints for revolution.[8]

You will ultimately have to conduct your revolution step by step, but you'll also want to put before your larger school community the comprehensive outlines of your entire plan. You can overcome the skeptics with a well-developed, systemic approach to school reform, and this book will show you how to do it.

As you travel down the road to revolution, also remember to pack your humility. For, although you have armed yourself through deep study with a good deal of knowledge about how to improve the schools, you still won't know as much as the teachers and principals know. The professionals have a deep knowledge of how best to educate children. Left alone, they will continue to be mired in the status quo. You bring an intense focus on student results and a commitment to changing whatever needs to be changed. By yourself, you might concoct utopian ideas that will never be implemented. As the educational historians David Tyack and Larry Cuban have noted, the utopian dreams of generations of school reformers litter the roadside to true revolution.[9] But if you work together, you can make revolutionary change succeed.

2

Three School Districts That Have Won the Revolution

*E*dmonton (Canada), Seattle, and Houston are three school districts that have successfully turned themselves around—and all three did it by implementing the basic elements that I've named the Seven Keys to Success. All three were drowning in bureaucracy and mismanagement. Parents were angry, teachers were frustrated, and community leaders were demanding change. All three responded by reinventing themselves. They didn't try to patch what was there. Instead, they used hard-headed common sense and an unflinching dedication to change everything that stood in the way of success for students.

The revolution began in Edmonton thirty years ago, when new Superintendent Mike Strembitsky—a hog farmer (with 3,000 hogs!) and teacher who was not yet forty—took over and stayed for two decades. The Edmonton public schools are the most mature form of the Seven Keys to Success—and the most successful. In about 1995, the revolution spread to Seattle and Houston, and by the year 2001, both U.S. cities had fully established all of the Seven Keys, too. Both also have problems that are still being ironed out, as Edmonton had, but as they gain experience with this new approach, they'll continue to improve.

Make no mistake—what we are talking about here is not improving the existing system, nor is it gradual change. It is revolution. In the case of Edmonton, the best summary comes from teachers' union president Karen Beaton, who has words of praise for what former superintendent Mike Strembitsky achieved:

> He turned the entire concept of the district upside down!
>
> As far as I am concerned, decentralization is a wonderful thing, because it gave teachers the opportunity to be empowered and to have a role in making decisions about their schools. . . . It used to be that someone else, somewhere at Central, would decide what books I should be using and send them to me. It would be a surprise to me when the books arrived! Under decentralization, they send the money to the school, and now the teachers have decisions to make for themselves.

Let's take a look at one example of what the change has meant in each of these pioneering school districts. See if you can recognize your city and your school in these stories of what is possible. If not, see if you can dream about what your school could become.

JASPER PLACE—THE SWISS WATCH OF HIGH SCHOOLS

Jasper Place is a large comprehensive high school in Edmonton, Alberta. It accommodates all kinds of students in one of its three programs. Among the 2,140 students, about half are college-bound. Another 276 are in special education programs, and many of those are profoundly challenged. The remaining students, about 35 percent of the total, are bound for work after high school graduation and are part of the Career and Technology Studies program. Eighty students are enrolled in off-campus home schooling but participate in some activities at the school.

Of the seventeen high schools in the Edmonton public school system, Jasper Place ranks fourth or fifth in average test scores on the diploma examinations. That is a good record because the top three schools are primarily for the college-bound, while Jasper Place is for everyone.

Principal Bruce Coggles is a friendly, mild-mannered man who is a good listener—and who remembers everything that he hears. He's the "watchmaker" who has painstakingly assembled several different programs and teachers into a smoothly working whole. He takes particular pride in the success of the school's programs for severely challenged special needs children. It's clear that Coggles respects his teachers and looks after their morale. He's part of every important decision, but he leaves it largely to the teachers to make the choices about where the school's money should be spent on educational programs.

In Edmonton, because families have freedom of choice, a weak school won't be able to attract many students. If a school declines to the point that it can't cover its expenses with the per-student money, the principal is removed and the remaining teachers and facilities are assigned to a strong principal. Otherwise, the school is simply closed, and all the staff are moved to other, more successful schools. That's how Jasper Place took over a failing middle school, grades 7–9, several years ago.

It's apparent that even in this large comprehensive school no child is allowed to get lost. For instance, Rod Dean, a veteran teacher with strong student handling skills, is assigned each year to the "resource room," an empty classroom that has no students at the start of the school year. Over the course of a year, he picks up twelve to fifteen students, the "square pegs" who don't quite fit in any of the school's "round holes," including many street kids who are very disruptive in class. Rod Dean's counseling skills with these young people are so good that he makes them successful in school. Coggles is free to use his budget for someone like Dean because the Seven Keys to Success give him that freedom.

The per-pupil budgeting system in Edmonton provides more money for special needs pupils, and Jasper Place offers a first-rate program that attracts many families. A blind student or one with Down's syndrome, for example, comes with an extra allocation of $12,000 per year. The families, in turn, are free to take the money and go to any public school they choose. Unlike most U.S. schools, Jasper Place *wants* to attract more special needs students.

The PASS program (Programming for Academic Student Success) was started for those students who are likely to become dropouts. They're the ones who struggle in class, become discouraged, and as a result dislike school. PASS students begin the year in two classes of twenty-five students each—no additions permitted once school begins. All of these students have had poor attendance records in the past, but no one misses school in this program. If a student is absent, the teacher calls his home right away. Due to the stable membership, each class becomes cohesive and supportive. As the students start to experience success, they begin to like school. Most important of all, they start to feel good about themselves. Almost no one drops out of PASS, and last year more than half these students passed their diploma exams—out of a group that previously would never have attempted to take the exam.

Bruce Coggles will only accept teachers who want to teach in PASS, and they receive no extra pay. The team of teachers meets every Thursday to discuss students and to plan. The program works in part because it has a unique class schedule—and in Edmonton, each school can schedule classes as it wishes, so long as the total teaching time is within the union contract.

In Jacinda Rolph's tenth-grade math PASS class, the students are intent, bent over a test, calculators at work. Their faces are contorted in concentration, and there is a fair amount of grunting and groaning over the more difficult questions. Ms. Rolph announces that anyone who has finished the test may quietly come up to her desk and see his score on last week's test. Nine students leap up and form a line. Their faces show apprehension as their turns come, followed either by big smiles or frowns of concern. Most, though, have smiles. You need only to see how much the students care to know that this class is a success.

The faculty enjoys a lovely dining room, with chandeliers, wood paneling, and comfortable chairs. Next to it is a private meeting room. Six PASS teachers are having lunch together and discussing how best to approach the problems of various students. Their conversation addresses attendance problems, schoolwork, and family situations. The team of teachers, as a group, obviously has thorough knowledge of all the students and how they are coming along in every aspect of their development.

Jasper Place, always looking for a way to attract students, also offers an unusual English as a Second Language program targeted at noncitizens. About sixty students from Korea, China, and Japan are enrolled. Each pays about $9,000 per year in tuition to Edmonton Public, of which slightly more than $7,000 goes to Jasper Place—well above the $5,100 per pupil that the school receives for other students. The foreign students also enrich the education for everyone in relatively remote Edmonton.

Jasper Place has a unique two-day rotational schedule instead of the typical five-day, Monday-through-Friday schedule. Students do half of everything on day 1, and the other half on day 2. That way, Monday classes don't get cut disproportionately by the holidays that mostly fall on that day. The first period of each day is 1 hour and 20 minutes, followed by a period of 2 hours. Lunch is next, then another period of 1 hour and 20 minutes. The final period of the day goes for 2 hours and 20 minutes. Because each day of the week can be a day 1 or a day 2, there are signs posted everywhere to remind everyone which day it is! Once again, the freedom to innovate allows the school to do whatever works best for the students.

As we walk through the school, we ask directions of a teacher who happens by. He offers to show us the way and asks what we are studying. I explain, and ask if local control is important from a teacher's point of view. "Oh, I really think it is," he replies, "because you get a lot more control of what goes on in your department, rather than having everything come from downtown and being told what to do."

How about the regular academic program, which accounts for half of the students at JP? In Sharon Zylstra's twelfth-grade biology laboratory, the twenty-eight students are gathered around lab tables. It is a regular biology class, not Honors, Advanced Placement (AP), or International Baccalaureate, but it is impressive. Ms. Zylstra has prepared little cards about half the size of an index card. Each has on it the abbreviation for one of the proteins that make up DNA. The students start by decoding the DNA sequence and then creating an RNA sequence. Next, they take all of the proteins from four grass plants and use them to assemble the protein sequence sequence for two cows. Then they take all of the cards that make up the proteins for the two cows and reassemble them to make the sequence for one human. According to Ms. Zylstra, once they've done this exercise they all "get it," and they never make a mistake in decoding DNA again.

The third major program at Jasper Place is Career and Technology Studies. In the old days, it was only for those who were preparing for work rather than for college, but it has reinvented itself from an old-fashioned business education curriculum into three modern strands that prepare the students for today's world.

Harvey Duff is department head of Computer Studies, which occupies a beautiful, newly renovated space with ample hardware. In addition to the department head, the staff includes a curriculum coordinator, a senior local area network administrator, and a junior technician. They are supplemented by local college students who teach part time. Eighty-five percent of the graduates of the three strands will go on to some form of education: university, two-year technical college, or private training perhaps in the Novell or Windows systems; 15 percent will go directly into the workforce. All of this has been created purely as a local school initiative since 1995, with all of the funds allocated out of the school's budget—over which it has great freedom.

Think for a moment about the large number of small details that make Jasper Place the success that it is. Consider all the intricate pieces that smoothly mesh into a working whole—like a Swiss watch. Try to imagine how closely the principal and the staff have to coordinate, how many details they have to oversee to make the school run well. Now ask yourself whether they could do this if they had to ask the central office for permission each time they needed to do something that departed from the norm.

Down the hall from Computer Studies is a privately operated day care center for children of the teachers and other employees, as well as for the community at large. The school leases space to the private operator of the center, who, in turn, provides practical work experience for some of the high school students.

It is day two of our visit to JP, and at eight-thirty in the morning, students from the Commercial Foods department are at work in the large kitchen, which is outfitted with huge soup kettles, a meat locker, and spacious food preparation tables. Len Hallowes is the head teacher for the 140 students in the program, which grew out of an old-fashioned Home Economics program. The emphasis today is on commercial food preparation in which taste, presentation, and visual appeal of the food are emphasized. The students are introduced to the basics of commercial cooking—many of them will go on to a two-year cooking program at a technical college, while others will enter a three-year apprenticeship program to become journeyman chefs. The Commercial Foods students prepare the seven to nine hundred meals that are consumed each day by fellow students, faculty, and staff. Their kitchen and the attached dining room are sparkling clean, their equipment is first-rate, and their instructors are experienced. This is not a neglected corner of the school, it's a centerpiece.

The rooms of the Beauty Culture program look like a high-end beauty salon, complete with reception desk, a display of Paul Mitchell hair products for sale, and two large rooms, each equipped with about twenty chairs, wash basins, and dryers. A visitor can't help but be impressed that the "classroom" looks as good as any commercial boutique, not a sparsely outfitted, forgotten area of the school. The 240 students, all girls at the moment, sign up in tenth grade to learn grooming and hairstyling skills. Of the twenty or so who continue through twelfth grade, all find jobs immediately upon graduation. A beautician who is starting out earns about $26,000 in Edmonton, and a ten-year veteran who is good at cutting hair can earn $90,000 a year, according to Head Teacher Felice Lynge.

The forty students in the welding program can all look forward to apprenticeships and then to good-paying, high-skill jobs after graduation. Their shop looks professional, as does their instructor. The program is serious about its instruction, and the students take pride in their work. The demand for graduates is so strong that, according to the teacher, he could graduate twice the number each year and all would find good positions.

Principal Bruce Coggles makes trade-offs every day. One of these is that the English teachers have to take on more students than they do at other schools. In return, Jasper Place has funding for a Career Counseling Center, where every student and his or her parents must come to work through a plan for what comes after high school. For many of the students, the plan is to go to university. For others, the center offers aptitude tests that help the students to discover their options. Each student, though, gets individual attention, and every parent knows it and appreciates the attention.

Coggles is held accountable for student achievement, budget performance, and customer satisfaction at Jasper Place. In some ways, the three forms of accountability are intertwined in Edmonton Public. For example, Jasper Place does not simply receive an allocation of money for each student enrolled. It has to *earn* that money by showing that each student attends and completes courses. The central office sends the school a list of about sixty students each year and audits their attendance, course completion, and final marks. Any hint of "cooking the books" is likely to trigger a full-scale audit of the school.

If an Edmonton school runs a budget deficit, it has to pay back that money to the district over a period of years. When Bruce Coggles arrived at Jasper Place, it had an accumulated deficit of $500,000. Some staff positions were left unfilled, and everyone had to tighten their belts, remember to turn out the lights, and save every penny until it was paid back. Finally, every student, parent, and employee at the school fills out a questionnaire each year in which they rate all aspects of the school, including the performance of the principal. Teachers are asked if they have adequate opportunity to influence the decisions that affect their work.

Looking back at the history of Jasper Place, Edmonton superintendent Angus McBeath sees a school that has succeeded because it has a determined focus on student achievement and an entrepreneurial principal who is held accountable for results:

> Jasper Place had a terrible reputation at one point and it was kind of a grunt school in an unattractive part of Edmonton. It was not a school where people sent their kids if they were doctors, lawyers, or upper professional people.
>
> The school decided to rebrand itself, but not by tossing out its traditional clientele. They made a decision to say, These are our clientele—we celebrate and respect them and let us make sure that we provide them the very best education. And so consistently, I think, the respect for the clientele was huge.
>
> In most education systems people like good kids—the

more middle class the better. Our belief is, as our former superintendent Mike Strembitsky used to say, parents send us the best kids they have—they don't keep the good ones at home! So these are the kids that we have. So let's not blame the kids any more. Let's not use poverty as a reason for kids' achievement.

So I think that Jasper Place has got a first-class principal—absolutely you need a first-class principal. You have to hold a principal accountable, but you also have to give them the flexibility. Sometimes even to do the odd thing that would make your heart stop beating!

In Edmonton Public today, 87 percent of first graders, 88 percent of seventh graders, and 92 percent of twelfth graders score at or above grade level on the Alberta Provincial standardized test. The once-bad reputation that Edmonton Public had with the community has been turned around.

In fact, the change of attitude toward the public schools is so great that they have been gaining market share in recent years. According to Mike Strembitsky, after the public schools had adopted the new management system, they won over five thousand students from the Catholic system. Keeping in mind that the Edmonton Catholic schools receive the same funding as the public schools do, that's a major competitive achievement. Now, here's the topper: Edmonton Public has taken over several private schools, including two of the largest ones, which asked to join the public school district. Can you imagine that happening in New York City, Philadelphia, or Dallas?

One of the private schools that has joined Edmonton Public is the Millwoods Christian School, grades pre-K through 12. Millwoods joined in the 2000–01 school year. According to the new principal, Del Bouck, a former minister, enrollment at the twenty-one-year-old school had dropped to about two hundred students and financial pressures were mounting. The former principal rarely visited a class except to evaluate a teacher.

Although it was a difficult decision for the Calvary Community Church, which owned the school at the time, they took the step because they knew that their school needed a stronger academic program, and they knew that Edmonton Public gave all schools lots of autonomy. Today, after intensive marketing as a public school, Millwoods has 615 students and it's full. In fact, it's looking for new space so that it can grow. Says Principal Bouck: "I gotta tell you, I love being part of Edmonton Public, because you always feel the support."

All Millwoods students pay a fee of from $450 to $950 to the church, which continues to own the building and which staffs the religious instruction classes. Full scholarships are available to any who qualify on the basis of need. All of the other staff, though, are employees of Edmonton Public. The teachers and the principal were evaluated by the public school district after the changeover. Two of the teachers were not accepted. The school uses the same Alberta curriculum as all public schools, with the addition of classes in religious study.

Millwoods also has 190 students on home study. Edmonton Public gives the school about $4,000 for each of these students. The school, in turn, makes $1,000 per child available for books and materials, but their parents must turn in receipts to get the reimbursement. The home-schooled children come in to the school to participate in athletics, computer instruction, and other specialized classes. Says Principal Bouck, "A lot of the home educators are people who were here when it was church-run, became dissatisfied, and left. Our goal now is to get them back."

Several of the principals we interviewed described the parents in Edmonton the way Principal Bouck does: "Parents are very strong in voicing their opinion here. They know what they want. We give them choice." Perhaps that's a good lesson to all parents everywhere. Public schools can be great. They don't have to be mediocre and they don't have to be unresponsive. A truly great public school system can hold its own against any and all competitors. Today, there are almost no independent schools left in Edmonton, so popular are the public schools. Still, Edmonton Public has to stay on its toes because it competes against the 35,000-student Catholic schools. Superintendent Angus McBeath doesn't fear competition, though, he relishes it:

> I also like the fact that in Canada we have public competition. So we have sitting next door to us another system that our kids can go to. The Catholic system is publicly funded—they can go to the Catholic system. They also have the right here to have charter schools. They can also go to private schools where two-thirds of their expenses are paid for by the government.
>
> There are next to no private schools. We put them out of business. We have thirty alternative programs. Two of Edmonton's largest private schools joined us. We've gained market share, and that's the game. We play that game twenty-four hours a day. We want 100 percent of the kids!
>
> The thing is, you are allowed to go out of business in the public sector. We've had a number that went out of business or slowly declined to the point where either the school board decides to close them or the parents close them by moving. The parents vote with their feet.
>
> We have a small central staff. We can't afford more. All of the central maintenance staff have to sell their services to the school. All of the consultation staff, plus the reading specialists, social workers, and psychologists.

Accountability at Jasper Place and the other schools in Edmonton Public is part and parcel of the overall system of local school autonomy. You may be surprised to hear this, but local school freedom makes financial accountability better, not worse. As McBeath puts it:

> Just think about giving ninety-two cents on every dollar to the schools. Just think about how many eyes are on

the money. They don't steal money in this organization—trust me.

When we paid our utilities centrally, we had a guru from Europe who was exhorting our people to save energy. And we didn't save. We got rid of the guru and we gave the utilities money to the schools. The first year we saved $2 million. And do you know what we said they could do with the money? They could spend it on programs. We never swooped in and took it. You can only take a school's surplus once and they'll never have another one.

The changes that Mike Strembitsky put into place beginning in 1973 and supported until his retirement in 1994 have lasted to this day. Superintendent McBeath notes:

We had a long-serving superintendent, Dr. Strembitsky, who had sufficient tenure that he was able to manage the change process politically, year after year, until it was so integrated into the system that when he left, his successors were not able to nor inclined to dismantle what had become a fundamental operating system in the district. The benefits were so widely distributed in the minds of principals and parents and teachers and others that there was no appetite to change the basic operating system.

SEATTLE ADOPTS THE SEVEN KEYS TO SUCCESS

In 1954, the United States Supreme Court issued its historic decision in Brown v. Board of Education. The court found that schools that were segregated by race could not provide an equal education for all. Years later, school districts across the country finally began to comply, often by resorting to forced busing of students to achieve desegregation. In many cities, white residents fled the urban center in order to enroll their children in suburban schools. Seattle was one of those cities. In Seattle, public school enrollment fell from nearly 100,000 students in 1962 to 39,087 for the 1989–90 school year.[1] This decline was the result of three factors, which had a similar effect on urban districts everywhere: the "baby bust," the onset of suburbanization, and the forced busing in urban areas in the 1970s. Those who remained, both black and white, were angry at the school district, frustrated about the decline of their schools, and frightened that their children would be the ones to suffer.

By 1990, test scores were dropping, there were frequent fights in schools, and there was no money. The Washington State legislature, led by Governor Gary Locke (who at the time was a state legislator), commissioned an evaluation by an outside consulting firm. The resulting report created an uproar.[2] It criticized the superintendent and the board for a failure to provide leadership and accused the superintendent of spending his time trying to keep one step ahead of the board.[3] The report went on to say that schools had little flexibility to alter the mix of resources in a way that would most benefit students, because the money was allocated in an inflexible manner, with a fixed number of teachers and other staff per student.[4]

The business community formed "Step Forward" to find and support new, revolutionary candidates for the school board. The teachers' union, following a scandal at the top, elected a new president who vowed to be part of the solution. In 1995, several reform-oriented business groups formed The Alliance for Education. The business reformers had been inspired in part by a similar group in Houston that had formed to revolutionize the schools. With all of this community support, the new school board hired an executive search firm to find a visionary leader for the Seattle schools.

In June 1995, the reformers recruited retired Army General John Stanford, an African-American, from his post as county administrator of Fulton County, Georgia, to become the new superintendent. Their charge to Stanford was, in effect: "Whatever we're doing—change it!"

John Stanford moved to an apartment building in Seattle, where he met investment banker Joseph Olchefske in the elevator one evening. In short order, Olchefske agreed to become chief financial officer, working with Stanford. The two men had heard of the success in Edmonton, and off they went to meet Mike Strembitsky. Together, they started the revolution in Seattle. Three years later, John Stanford died of leukemia. Joseph Olchefske became superintendent and vowed to continue the fight for change. On April 14, 2003, reporter Linda Shaw of *The Seattle Times* reported that Olchefske would resign at the end of the school year. Olchefske had been under criticism for moving too slowly to close small schools and reduce central office expenses, though the weighted student formula that he and John Stanford implemented appears to be widely accepted in Seattle. Olchefske's superintendency lasted for nearly 6 years, longer than the average of 2.5 years for urban superintendents. The rest is history, but history in the making, so new is the revolution in Seattle.

As always, our acid test is student achievement. Seattle, like other districts, uses a variety of standardized tests. One of these is the Iowa Test of Basic Skills, which is also used by two of the other districts in our study, the Chicago public schools and the New York City Catholic schools. On this test, Seattle students in 2002 averaged in the 59th percentile in reading and the 65th percentile in math. Elementary students gained six points in reading and eight points in math scores from 1996 to 2001. This is higher than either Chicago Public, with the 38th percentile in reading and the 43rd percentile in math, or the New York Catholic schools, which score in the 51st percentile in reading and the 51st percentile in math. As the schools have improved, enrollment has rebounded to 44,831. Although Seattle does not measure customer satisfaction at each school as in Edmonton, the district takes an annual survey of more than 1,000 parents and community members to measure their perceptions of the schools.

As we'll see later in the book, Seattle today has many excellent schools that have soared with their newfound freedom. Some other schools, though, are still in the early or middle stages of transition—and transition can be difficult. No school more clearly illustrates both the need for change and the difficulty of change than James A. Garfield High School, in the historically African-American section of town.

When Susan Derse took over as principal in 2001, she was the third principal in three years. The racial tensions that accompanied forced busing in Seattle were strongly felt at Garfield, which then had a 95 percent black student body. It declined to as few as 800 students but today is back to 1,720—47 percent white, 34 percent black, 12 percent Asian, and 7 percent Hispanic and other. When the school had hit bottom during the 1980s, the school board came up with the idea of "saving" it by making it a magnet school to attract gifted students. As a result, the school now has a huge array of Advanced Placement (AP) courses and produces each year more National Merit semifinalists than any other school in the state of Washington.

However, the school had become a camel—only 6 percent of the black students were passing the state tests in math and reading, while 80 percent of the white students passed. Teachers had formed two conflicting camps, one which taught the neighborhood black students, and the other which taught the AP courses to the whites and Asians. There can be no clearer example of the harm that can result from a central office that tells each school what to do without really understanding the local situation.

Principal Derse, to her credit, is not cowed. She applied for this job knowing the situation and relishes the challenge. "I want to be here. This is the right challenge for me. I want to leave my legacy here, not in a rich neighborhood." Why, given the problems, does Susan Derse think that she can succeed where so many others have failed? Because the Seattle public district is adopting the Seven Keys to Success:

> This district is struggling to move from a centralized, controlling bureaucracy to a more flexible, responsive system. . . . Joseph Olchefske, our Superintendent, understands, and so do the people close to him, but the middle-level people in headquarters don't want to change.

Principal Derse is using her local school autonomy to make change happen—and fast. She's brought together a committee of eighteen teachers, parents, students, classified employees (such as teaching aides and security staff), and administrators who represent all of the previously warring factions, and has them all in a dialogue with one another to decide as a unified community what they want their school to become. They've already agreed that every student—African-American, Asian, white, and Hispanic— will be in a college preparatory program. Their goals are to break the glass ceiling for underrepresented minorities; to set high expectations for every student; and to provide high levels of support for them. She's used $53,000 of her budget to put textbooks in the hands of every child. The local Rotary Club is raising funds for college scholarships for African-American students, and new programs have started in parent training, mentoring by local college students, and study tables during free periods.

Susan Derse will be held accountable for her students' results and her budget performance by Superintendent Olchefske. Although principals and teachers in Seattle have tenure, they can be and are let go for poor performance. In 2000–01, Olchefske got everyone's attention by terminating the employment of a few principals—and he had the support of the school board and of the community of Seattle. The Seattle approach to principal accountability is in some ways more severe than in Edmonton, but both systems work. It's easy to believe that Seattle, a district that has the gumption to hire a principal who is so clearly independent-minded and determined to have local school autonomy, is a district in which this principal and this school will succeed.

HOUSTON—THE BEST SCHOOL DISTRICT IN AMERICA?

Texas students are required to take a "high stakes" exit examination in grades 10, 11, or 12 in order to graduate. The results in Houston are dramatic to the point of straining the limits of credibility—but they're true. On April 18, 2002, the Houston Chronicle reported that 85 percent of Houston's tenth graders had passed the test, up from only 50 percent passing in 1994. Houston students also take the Stanford 9 standardized test, which is taken by the students at two other districts in our study—the Los Angeles Unified School District and the Los Angeles Catholic Schools. The Los Angeles Catholic students did best with an average reading score in the 53rd percentile in 2001. The Houston public schoolers at the 42nd percentile beat their Los Angeles counterparts in the 33rd percentile by a wide margin. In 2002, the Houston Independent School District (HISD) became the first recipient of the new Broad Prize in Urban Education.

Houston has its critics. Parents, though, seem very satisfied. Teachers are widely respected, as evidenced by the fact that Houston, almost alone among urban districts, managed to fill every single teaching position with a regular, credentialed teacher in 2001–02. Los Angeles, by comparison, has 9,500 teachers who lacked full credentials in that school year.

At 209,000 students, the Houston Independent School District is the largest in Texas and sixth largest in the United States. Ninety percent of the students are minorities, and 86 percent of elementary students qualify for free or reduced-price school lunches. The demographics are strikingly similar to those of the Los Angeles Unified School District (90 percent minority and 82 percent of elementary students on free lunch program). Houston, though, has gone through revolution, just as Edmonton and Seattle have.

The Houston story is told in dramatic fashion in a book by a former school board member, Donald R. McAdams, published in 2000. His opening paragraph foreshadows the battles that awaited the small band of reformers:

> Within six months we had bonded as a small band of warriors determined to do whatever necessary to turn the district upside down. The superintendent, Dr. Joan Raymond, had a different opinion.[5]

The year was 1989, and the reformers had just been elected to the school board. One of the hardy band was Rod Paige, at the time dean of the School of Education at Texas Southern University. On June 18, 1990, the board adopted its "Declaration of Beliefs and Visions" over the opposition of Superintendent Raymond, according to McAdams.

Raymond was soon gone, and reform was on. Progress was halting, though, as opposition to change arose both from central office personnel and from some parents. Another superintendent came and went. And then, on February 22, 1994, the board members persuaded their board president, Rod Paige, to become superintendent.

Paige moved to cement relationships with the business community of Houston, creating the Houston Business Advisory Council, which worked with the Board of Education through its chairman, Harold Hook, who was chairman and CEO of the American General insurance company. Hook went on to advise Paige on solid business practices that could be implemented in the school district, and Hook created perhaps the best management training program for principals in the United States.

The revolution then picked up steam, according to Bob Stockwell, who is now chief academic officer of the Houston district: "When Paige became the Superintendent in 1994, that's when things really began moving."

The essence of the revolution is summarized by Leonard Sturm, who is chief financial officer of the district: "We decided that if we're going to hold people responsible, we should let them decide how to spend the money." The leadership had planned to slowly phase in a revolutionary new budgeting system—30 percent the first year, 30 percent more the second year, and the remaining 40 percent the third year. Once the change had begun, though, it picked up its own momentum. Says Dr. Kaye Stripling, who is now superintendent, "We did 30 percent in 2000–01. The principals then came and said, 'Can't we chop the dog's tail off all at once?' So this year, 2001–02, we're going to 100 percent. There's been some pain. Some schools had to cut some programs."

Much of that pain, as in Seattle, was felt at the smaller schools in wealthier neighborhoods, which lost some money as schools in poor neighborhoods gained. There was a very vocal outcry from some of them: wealthy parents complained that they were paying all the taxes and not getting back enough. Houston is an independent school district, which means that the money comes not from the state but from property taxes levied by the school board. What really enabled Houston to turn the corner and get the support of the public? Here's the opinion of Bob Stockwell: "Paige kept the tax rate flat for five years. When people saw the tax rate flat while student achievement started to rise, they said, okay, it's really doing something now."

Finally, there was another key source of inspiration and of confidence. Says Dr. Stripling: "We have sent teams and teams of people to Edmonton."

Houston isn't perfect; at least, not yet. Graduation rates are low at 44.8 percent of first graders eventually graduating from high school, according to our calculations. By comparison, the graduation rates are 55.5 percent in New York City, 51.8 percent in Los Angeles, and 41.3 percent in Chicago. Edmonton and Seattle again stand out, with graduation rates of 63 percent and

66.4 percent, respectively. These may sound low to you, but that is because most school districts report a "graduation rate" that actually calculates only the percentage of ninth or tenth graders who graduate. That isn't what parents want to know. Parents want to know how many *first* graders eventually graduate. The national average is 88 percent, but for these larger, urban districts, it's typically a good deal lower. On the other hand, our statistics are only rough estimates because school districts do not actually report which students entered in the first grade, track them as they change schools and school districts, and then calculate how many eventually graduate. So we had to make rough estimates based on the numbers of students who were in first grade twelve years ago, and the numbers who graduated last year. Perhaps in the future enough parents will demand this critically important information that school districts will report it. One wonders how they can manage their schools without it today. *Houston Chronicle* reporter Zanto Peabody raised these issues in an April 3, 2003 article that is rare for its attention to the problem. Ask your local newspaper to investigate, too.

Houston also has a "race gap"—white and Asian students have higher test scores than black and Hispanic students. However, the gap is getting smaller there: in the past three years, it has closed by 4 points in reading and by 6 points in math for Houston students. Meanwhile, the reading and math gaps in Los Angeles are exactly the same over the past four years. In Seattle, the reading gap is unchanged in the past three years, and the math gap has actually gotten worse by 2 points.

Rice University professor Linda McNeil has been harshly critical of the reforms in Texas, including those in Houston. McNeil argues in her book *Contradictions of School Reform* that the pressure on principals to raise student scores on standardized tests has been so intense that it has caused many teachers to simply "teach to the test" rather than teaching what they feel is best for students. She fears that the same kinds of pressures will ultimately afflict schools throughout the nation as parent pressure for school performance continues to mount.[6] There are education experts across the nation who worry that the increasing emphasis on standards and testing will end up doing more harm than good. On the other side of the argument are those who say that although standards can be misused, having no standards at all is far worse. Some observe that "teaching to the test" isn't necessarily a bad thing—and point out that the Advanced Placement tests have long required exactly that, yet students and parents demand more AP courses.

It's not easy for most of us to make sense out of the technical arguments and the heated politics that surround the testing issue. Perhaps the best advice is that you take standardized test results seriously—but with a grain of salt. Don't rely solely on any one standardized test to judge whether your district is improving or declining. Do ask which other districts use the same test, and what their scores are, so that you can make your own comparisons. Ask whether your district uses the same fixed pool of questions year after year, or whether it uses different questions each year, so that teachers can't drill the students on the questions that they're likely to see on the test. In evaluating the overall progress of your district, look at standardized tests, the dropout rate from kindergarten through twelfth grade, the percentage of graduates who go to four-year colleges, the percentage who enter two-year colleges, and other measures such as teacher qualifications and training of principals.

In any case, the most important thing about the Houston schools is what they have done with their newfound freedom. Virtually every school is a "magnet" school with a distinctive program and character.

Take, for example, the Michael E. DeBakey High School for Health Professions. Principal Dr. Charlesetta Collins-Deason has a big goal to achieve on a small budget. She's preparing high school students for nursing school, medical school, and other health-related professions. As a result, they need lots of tough academic courses so that they can get into good colleges and lots of small, expensive-to-teach science laboratory courses to prepare them for the premed curriculum.

You're right—no public high school can afford to do all of that. No normal high school, that is. In Houston, though, the aim is not "normal" schools. The goal is supernormal schools, each one uniquely designed to achieve a specialized task for its special group of students. Principal Collins-Deason not only has the autonomy to design her staffing and curriculum to reach her goals—she's expected to do it. And because principals in Houston gave up tenure a few years ago in exchange for higher pay, she'd better do it! Like other Houston principals, she has a set of goals, called "dials," each year. Last year, she made all fourteen of her dials and received a large bonus. Every school is also required to hold a parents' meeting and explain its accountability rating each year.

Michael DeBakey High School has a very highly specialized curriculum. Its goal is not to be a comprehensive high school. The student who wants to pursue a broad array of electives will not find them at DeBakey, but the student who wants the best possible high school preparation for medical school will find it here.

The school has a diverse mixture of students: 40 percent of the 688 students in grades 9–12 are African-American, 26 percent are Hispanic, 23 percent are Asian, and 13 percent are white. Every student must have four years of English, science, math, social studies, and health science, and at least three years of one foreign language, plus computer science and word processing. That means that virtually all of the courses are required, and every class is full.

DeBakey uses its freedom to innovate in other ways. This year, for example, the principal chose to eliminate an assistant principal position and to use the money to hire a business manager. To weed out the 1,200 applicants each year, she uses the Otis-Lennon School Abilities Test, used by several independent schools, but no other Houston public school.

The results: in a typical year, 98 percent of the students will go to college, and ten of them will win full tuition scholarships to the University of Houston and to Baylor College of Medicine. The 170 graduating seniors of the class of 2000 were awarded a total of $8 million in college scholarships—an average of $47,059 per student.

Michael E. DeBakey High School is what the revolutionaries of Houston were fighting for. Now that you understand what it takes, you'll look at your district with new eyes, and you'll see what needs to change and what should not change. Most important of all, you've now seen three living examples of how it can be done, proof that an entire district can turn itself upside down for its children.

In Edmonton, the change began with a hog farmer turned educator who stayed long enough to change the culture of a district. In Seattle, it took an outraged community, political leadership from the state legislature, and a transition from General Stanford to Joseph Olchefske. In Houston, like Seattle, the school board formed a partnership with the business community and the board was taken over by a group of revolutionaries. The only constant is that ordinary people cared enough to keep pushing until things changed for the better. There is no other secret formula. In other words, it's up to you.

THE PLAN OF THIS BOOK

Now it's time to lay out in more detail just what each of the seven critical Keys to Success really means and what each one looks like in various school settings. Along the way, I'll share with you some of the colorful characters that we met, the real and difficult situations that schools face, and the great successes that will warm your heart and bring a smile to your face.

In each chapter in Part Two, I'll emphasize what *you* can do to make a difference in your school and in your school district. You may wonder whether just you and a few other parents, businesspeople, or teachers can really make a difference. Here is my reply, a remark by Margaret Mead that is also the inspiration to The Alliance, the Los Angeles citizens' group that is pressing for revolutionary change in that city's schools:

> Never doubt that a small group of thoughtful committed citizens can change the world. Indeed, it's the only thing that ever has.

One of the things that I enjoyed most about visiting schools was the chance to learn how to spot a good classroom and a good school. It reminds me a lot of the process that a medical resident goes through in learning to become a radiologist. You've probably had the experience of having a radiologist show you your X-ray and say something like, "See here? You can see it very clearly." I'm always too embarrassed to tell my doctor that it all looks like one big gray cloud to me. A trained radiologist, though, can identify important information in that same X-ray.

An experienced teacher or principal can stand right next to you in a classroom, and she or he will see dozens if not hundreds of important details that you don't notice. This book will teach you what I've learned about how to be an astute observer. After all, your goal is to be influential in improving your school, and you can't influence something that you can't see.

Finally, I've spent more than ten years as a volunteer school revolutionary. I've been alternately helped, inspired, lied to, and misled by school district bureaucrats. I've talked with union leaders, parents, and school reformers from around the country. I've learned something about the tricks, the spins, and the head fakes that they will throw at you when you try to make things improve. I want to teach you, based on my experience, what to expect and how to be effective in your school and your school district. Above all, I want to encourage you to keep at it, even when you're discouraged, tired, and frustrated. Don't give up.

Remember this quotation from Gabriela Mistral, the Chilean poet and Nobel Laureate:

> Many things can wait; the child cannot. Now is the time his bones are being formed; his mind is being developed. To him, we cannot say tomorrow; his name is today.

Part Two: The Seven Keys to Success ✔

3

Key #1: Every Principal Is an Entrepreneur

*E*very principal can be an entrepreneur, though not all principals are. Some are strong enough to become entrepreneurs even in centralized, anti-entrepreneurial systems, but they're rare. In this chapter, we'll see what true entrepreneurs look like, what they do, and what they can accomplish. Then, we'll see the opposite: school systems that defeat all but the hardiest principals, that throw cold water on the flames of entrepreneurial drive. You choose which you'd rather have.

It is 7:50 A.M. at the Mabel Wesley Elementary School, located in the Acres Homes housing projects area of Houston. The one-story building sprawls over a large lot surrounded by a chain-link fence. The nearby homes are old and tired-looking, but inside, the school is as bright and clean as the kitchen of a five-star restaurant. Not fancy or elaborate, but clearly a place that takes pride in itself. The principal, Dr. Sandra Cornelius, arrived two years ago. She had cut her administrative teeth as assistant principal at Wesley School under the legendary principal Thaddeus Lott. After Dr. Lott retired and the school had a dip in performance, Dr. Cornelius was called back up to the major leagues as principal, and the school is on track again. Dr. Cornelius is an educational entrepreneur. She listens, and she leads. She sets high expectations for teachers, students, and families. Above all, she does what's best for her children, not what the rules say she's allowed to do.

The 816 children in grades pre-kindergarten through 5 are lined up at the doors to their classrooms. On entering, each child hands her homework to the teacher, who is standing at the door. One of these teachers is Mrs. Haugh. Her four-year-old students have chanted in unison the days of the week, the months of the year, and numbers up to 100. They have big, happy smiles on their faces. Wesley is a uniform school—the students are all in white tops; navy bottoms—pants, shorts, or skirts; white socks; and white or black shoes. Most of the children are African-American, and a very few are Hispanic; there are no white students. The children clearly like Mrs. Haugh. This is a very warm classroom, yet the teacher is fully in command—it's not easy to control twenty-two four-year-olds who are full of life and jumping around!

The classroom is roomy, with a big carpeted area and a large linoleum area. There are little desks in groups of four or six and two large, kidney-shaped tables, one with computers and the other where the teacher sits across from four to six students at a time for lessons. The walls are decorated with pictures that the children have colored for Halloween.

In one corner there is a math center with a desk, a chair, and various things for the children to spread out, count, and arrange. There is reading material everywhere, a screen with an overhead projector, and more drawings by the children all over the walls, along with calendars and a variety of hand-drawn posters and instructions. The room is a rich environment for the students.

Another teacher comes by and smiles at the children,

admonishes one of them to stand properly, and gives several of them hugs or pats and a big smile.

I ask Mrs. Haugh if she feels respected and appreciated as a teacher.

Yeah. Look what Dr. Cornelius gave me—a tin of cookies with a ribbon. I think that she thinks the way to our happiness is through our stomachs!

Next is Ms. Rutledge's kindergarten class. Although it is only October and the school year has just begun, several of the five-year-olds are reading. The children at the kidney-shaped table are doing letters, numbers, colors, and writing out words.

Dr. Cornelius drops by. She points out that each student's work is graded each day, even in kindergarten. The students know their grades for the day, but they soon learn that they are not competing with the student sitting next to them. They are competing with themselves, and they are focused on their own progress. The school, she says, is very "driven." They know where each student is, and they know what each student needs.

Next is the classroom of Mrs. Harris—first grade, nineteen students. Mrs. Harris is an expert at teaching the phonics-based Reading Mastery system that the school uses in pre-K, kindergarten, and first grade. It is a very high-intensity class. She has four students sitting with her in a corner of the room, and she moves them very rapidly through the Reading Mastery material. Each child has many opportunities to read out loud and gets immediate feedback from the teacher.

Mrs. Harris sits just inches away from her four reading students. She watches each one of them like a hawk. She is energized and motivated, and her intensity is infectious.

There are books everywhere in this first-grade classroom. It looks almost like a library. There are of course the Reading Mastery books. Then there are plastic bins with the science journals published by Harcourt, other series by McGraw-Hill, several bins of general reading books, and another full bookcase. There are Math Advantage books on a table, along with more reading and language books. In addition, books with titles like *There Is a Clean House for Mole and Mouse* and *More Spaghetti* are available, nine or ten copies of each. Down on the other end of the side table is the SRA Reading Laboratory 1A with Power Builders and then a whole set of Harcourt reading books with titles like *Where the Clouds Go* and *Starlight, Starbright*. There are about ten copies of each of these books. There is also a Scholastic Guided Reading Program with a whole set of workbooks.

On the other side of the room are more bins with the McGraw-Hill National Geographic Society and the McGraw-Hill Science in Texas series. There are spelling books and bins where the children keep their daily workbooks and their writing. Each one has been corrected by the teacher with a red pen. Then there are phonics practice books, more math books, maps rolled up above the blackboards, and cutout letters hanging from the ceiling. Maps of the continents are also hanging from the ceiling, and lots of student work is on the walls.

Late in the afternoon, Ms. Harris's third-grade class has started a science project in which the students have planted seeds of green beans in either pumice, sand, or potting soil. Later, they will compare the growth rates of each plant. Now, though, the students are reciting in unison, much in the style that took place in Mrs. Haugh's pre-kindergarten class early this morning. The third graders are reciting the days of the week, the months of the year, and the number of days in a week, month, and year. Then they recite their multiplication tables, their code words for mathematics concepts, the names of the fifty states, the seven continents, and on and on. The chanting is not desultory or reluctant. It is joyful and enthusiastic. It is a wonderful scene.

In Ms. Gauthier's fourth-grade class, the students have silently read a passage of three paragraphs and are writing their answers to several questions about it. Next, they will practice cursive handwriting. One little boy looks over his shoulder and gives a big smile, though he's really not supposed to notice visitors.

How about the academic results? Mabel Wesley is a Texas State Exemplary School, with 99 percent of third and fourth graders and 100 percent of fifth graders getting passing scores on the TAAS state test in 2001 in both reading and math. Out of 182 Houston elementary schools, Wesley ranks twelfth on the standardized Stanford 9 reading test—by far the highest ranking for any school that has predominantly low-income families (at Wesley, 82 percent of students qualify for a free or reduced-price lunch). The school has a budget of $3,800 per student per year (the district spends $5,558 per student per year, but, as in all school districts, local schools do not get all of the money), and Principal Sandra Cornelius controls 90 percent of it. She and her teachers decide how to staff the school, what materials to buy, and what schedules to arrange. Mabel Wesley is a unique school, but it's only one among many distinctive public schools in Houston.

The Houston Independent School District (HISD) is a district of 288 different flowers. Each school is unique, and virtually every school is a "magnet" school, which implies both the independence to be unique and an obligation to offer subjects and a focus that are unique in some way. The district hasn't always been that way, though. It wasn't that way in 1974, when Dr. Thaddeus Lott became the third principal to serve at Mabel Wesley Elementary. When Dr. Lott arrived, Wesley was a neglected, poor black school in a city that had not a single "high-profile" school for black students.

Thaddeus Lott, an entrepreneur of the first order, was determined to create a school in which every child would succeed. After extensive research and experimentation, he settled on what was then a new and innovative reading program. Reading Mastery was based on research on early childhood development, and it called for each teacher to follow a phonics-based, strictly "directed" approach to teaching reading. The approach was unusual then and is still controversial among some teachers today, but at Mabel Wesley School, it worked.

After Mabel Wesley had become successful with its approach, which included not only the Reading Mastery system but also student discipline, constant teacher training, and development of up-to-date information on the progress of each student, the Houston school district adopted a systemwide reading approach. At the time, the district was a traditional one, with a top-down approach. It required that all schools adopt a new reading system, with no leeway for Mabel Wesley. Thaddeus Lott, though, was not about to deny his students the approach that was working for them, and he sought a way to keep Reading Mastery.

By the 1990–91 school year, Mabel Wesley was a raging success, and its students were setting state records. Houston officials would not believe that these poor, black students could do so well, and they accused the school of cheating on the state tests. The central office sent an audit team to perform a surprise inspection at the school. The team marched in unannounced, locked the teachers and students out of their classrooms, and searched for evidence of test-tampering. Unable to find any evidence of wrongdoing, they made the children retake the state test under the supervision of inspectors. The students did even better than they had before.

On June 6, 1991, with the community furious at the treatment the school had received by the auditors, ABC's *PrimeTime* aired an exposé of the district's rough tactics. Mabel Wesley, though, had established its success if not its independence.

In 1995, Texas passed its law to permit the formation of charter schools, so Dr. Lott applied for permission from the state to become the first charter school. As a charter school, he continued to report to the Houston school district and to be a part of it, but he had freedom to choose his teachers, curriculum, and teaching materials. The district bureaucrats, however, refused to buy the books Dr. Lott requested, and he refused to give in. So he simply made his own copies for each teacher and each student.

Today, Dr. Lott is a much-respected retired educational leader within the Houston Independent School District. His unique school continues in its winning ways under a new principal. Most important of all, all schools in Houston increasingly reflect the first of our seven essential elements—every school principal is an entrepreneur.

WHY ENTREPRENEURSHIP IS AN ESSENTIAL INGREDIENT FOR A SUCCESSFUL SCHOOL

Let's consider for a moment what an entrepreneur is—and is not, why schools need entrepreneurs, and how every principal can use the four tools of an entrepreneur.

According to Merriam-Webster's *Collegiate Dictionary,* an entrepreneur is "one who organizes, manages, and assumes the risks of a business or enterprise." The key idea here is that the leader of any organization sees to it that the customers get served not by her doing it herself, but by organizing the employees in a way that makes the best and most efficient use of their individual time and talents. In a typical elementary school, for example, there might be 350 students and twenty or so staff. The students will fall into a variety of small sub-groups, each of which needs a somewhat different teaching approach. The teachers and other staff will each bring unique skills, and they should be thoughtfully organized in a way that allows each one to be at their best.

In a typical school, the principal manages, but she does not have the power to organize a school, and she takes few risks because risk-taking is discouraged. In a centralized, top-down school district, the central office has a standard table of organization that dictates how many teachers, counselors, assistant principals, and front-office clerks each school will have. In many districts, the teachers' union has negotiated contractual provisions that further limit the principal's discretion. A principal is not free to deviate from these bureaucratic and contractual requirements.

An entrepreneur is a principal who has the freedom to organize her school in whatever way will work best for both students and staff. That is to say, an entrepreneur is a problem-solver rather than a rule-follower. That doesn't mean entrepreneurial principals must be renegades or loose cannons. It means that they are focused on solving every problem that stands in the way of student achievement.

How can every principal be more of an entrepreneur? It's by following a simple, four-step process. Remember that many business entrepreneurs fail because they lack a disciplined process, even though they may have great energy and desire to succeed. Here are the four steps:

FOUR STEPS TO BECOMING AN ENTREPRENEUR

Step 1: Analyze your customers
Step 2: Design a staffing plan that fits your needs
Step 3: Arrange the schedule to fit the plan
Step 4: Choose teaching materials to fit the students

Step 1: Analyze your customers

Before designing a school program, the principal must know who the students are—and what unique needs each one of them has. This means performing a data-based analysis of the student body. For example, when I was involved in training reform-oriented principals and teachers in Los Angeles in the early 1990s, I encountered this problem. A principal said that her school had an annual turnover (called the transiency rate) of about 70 percent each year among its students. She felt that effective education was impossible in this setting.

Our program taught her that her first step in improving her school was to design on educational plan for it. But before she could do this, she needed to analyze the data that she already had—to find out who her students were. With our guidance she did the analysis and found that her school had two distinct sub-populations of students. One-half of the students were from the neighborhood, and most of them remained in that school from kindergarten through sixth grade. The other half of the students were from undocumented immigrant families, and most remained for only a few months. One group had very low turnover and the other group had extremely high turnover—over 100 percent per year—and on the average, the turnover was 70 percent.

Each of the two sub-groups of children in this school had very different educational needs, but all were being treated the same, to their mutual detriment. Once the principal saw this insight, she and her teachers were able to plan two different approaches, one suited to the needs of each child.

Step 2: Design a staffing plan that fits your needs

Staffing includes defining which positions the school will have, choosing the teachers and staff who will fill those positions, and organizing departments, teams, academies, and schools-within-a-school. If all of these elements are dictated by a central office that is far from the neighborhood, the school will find that it is handcuffed in its attempts to give the students what they need. If the principal in each case is granted the authority to behave like an entrepreneur, the staff will be custom-fitted to the needs of the school community.

In most cities, the assignment of teachers is not left entirely up to the principal, even though the principal is held accountable for their performance. In New York City, for example, each school must have a formula-driven number of teachers, and the union contract requires that teachers be assigned to schools by the central office, which allows them to choose based on their seniority, without any input from the principal. If 75 percent or more of the teachers in a school vote to select teachers locally, the union seniority system may be bypassed. Similar union-bypass systems are in place in Los Angeles for LEARN schools and school-based management schools, and in New York City for school-based options schools. Most schools in these cities, though, are hemmed in by the union contract. In other cities, including Chicago, Houston, Seattle, and Edmonton, the decision on which teachers to hire is up to the principal, with virtually all principals following the practice of asking teachers to participate in the selection process.

Choice of teachers is critical to the success of any school for two reasons. First, a successful school must be a community in which the teachers form a cohesive team. Imposing new teachers on a team will almost always have disruptive effects. Second, the teachers and the principal are attuned to the subtle differences that distinguish a good teacher from a bad one. Although minimum district standards for teacher preparation are important, they aren't enough.

We've relied on the research by Dr. Eric Hanushek of Stanford University. He's studied this matter in depth, and here's the summary of his analysis:

> Study after study demonstrates the importance of the classroom teacher. Estimates suggest that in a single school year an average student with a good teacher can progress more than a full grade level faster than an average student with a poor teacher. The same also holds for disadvantaged students. . . . No single set of teacher characteristics, teacher behaviors, curricular approaches, or organizational devices (such as team teaching) guarantees a high probability of success in the classroom. . . . For that reason, detailed central regulations and directives on the nature of the instructional process and the characteristics of school personnel are bound to be wasteful and perhaps even self-defeating.[1]

Step 3: Arrange the schedule to fit the plan

The Seven Keys to Success taken together comprise an integrated system. And the variety of schedules uncovered in our study is enormous.

Here are but two examples of what a true entrepreneur can accomplish when he has the power to design the schedule.

- In Los Angeles, St. Thomas the Apostle School serves 315 inner-city students in grades kindergarten through 8. Principal Vincent Donahue, who hails from New Jersey, felt that the standard school year of 180 days was not enough, given his school's goals. So, in 2000 he got the approval of more than 75 percent of the parents to lengthen it to 190 days. That worked well, so he went back to the parents and extended the school year to 200 days. One hundred forty applicants took the test to qualify for one of the 36 places in the 2001–02 kindergarten class.

- At the Baruch College Campus High School, one of New York City's public schools, some teachers teach twenty-one periods per week while others teach only eighteen periods so that they can meet with ten to twelve student advisees. The goal is to make sure that every student is known by the faculty as a whole person.

The lesson that emerges is that a flexible schedule enables a school to combine its teachers and students in ways that make the most of everyone's time. It may be tempting for the central office to have every school follow an identical structure of periods, days, and months, but to be rigid about schedule is to deny a school one of its most important tools for student success. We visited successful schools that have two-day "weeks," three-day weeks, and even six-day weeks (day six might be a Monday, a Thursday, or any day of the week). The idea that every school must have seven periods a day, five days a week, is too standard-ized to work for every child.

Another important aspect of staffing a school is the contin-ued professional development of the teachers and other staff. Many educators would assert that a principal's most powerful tool is control over his or her own professional development budget. After all, it's the teachers who are managing the educa-tion of children. Investing in the continuous improvement of their skills and the maintenance of their enthusiasm has to be as important an investment as there could be. In too many districts, the central office controls these professional development funds, with the result that the district offers dried-out, misdirected con-tinuing education courses that miss the target of what teachers need and want.

Step 4: Choose teaching materials to fit the students

The choice of books and materials is much more than a matter of taste. The case of Mabel Wesley School illustrates what a difference this can make. The Houston school district had cho-sen one approach to teaching reading in the early grades, but Dr. Lott had reached the conclusion that for his specific group of children, a different approach would be better. He had in mind a total approach that combined phonics-based books, specially trained teachers, and a method of teaching that stresses lots of reading out loud, reciting, and unison chanting out loud by the entire class. Another method might have worked just as well, but perhaps not. Let's take a closer look at Dr. Lott's decision.

There is a great deal of debate in some quarters about how young children should be taught to read. Two of the major con-tenders for the method of choice are "phonics," or the learning of letter and word sounds, versus "whole language," which empha-sizes reading entire passages and books to build comprehension. Many, perhaps most experienced educators would say that the debate is silly, that every classroom should use both, or as it is also known, the "balanced literacy" approach. The important point, though, is that the balance between the approaches that will work best will vary from student to student. Only the teachers are well-informed enough about each child to find just the right balance, and they need the local school autonomy to let them do it.

Nonetheless, some school districts have mandated a single series of books and materials that must be used by all teachers to teach reading or math. This may be a necessary measure if the district is seriously failing and if many teachers lack the necessary training. One hopes, though, that as each school rights itself, it will win back the freedom to choose the materials that are best suited to its specific groups of students.

Equally controversial was Dr. Lott's choice of a method of teaching literacy in which the teacher reads a "script" provided by the publishing company, with appropriate prompts for the students. Some parents and some experienced teachers criticize this "direct instruction" method as robotic and an insult to trained teachers. On the other hand, in a district like the Los Angeles Unified School District, where one fourth of the classroom teachers lack full credentials, many new teachers have no experience, and the use of a rival method of phonics-based direct instruction, Open Court, is producing dramatic gains in the early grades—though critics point out that it doesn't meet the needs of all children equally well.

As for the reading out loud, the chanting in unison, and the constant hearing of words, these make Mabel Wesley unique. What purpose does all the out-loud activity serve? Dr. Shelley Harwayne, whose District 2 in New York City is known across the country for its superb teachers, offered the following insight in an interview: "There is an old saying among educators that a child is ready to read when he or she has had 1,000 books read to them."

A thousand sounds like a lot of books (it doesn't have to be 1,000 *different* books, though). Dr. Harwayne observes that it's really only one book a day from age two through age four, and the child is ready to read by age five, when school begins for most children. Interestingly, a similar opinion comes from Dr. Reid Lyon, who is chief of the Child Development and Behavior branch of the National Institute of Child Health and Human Development in Washington, D.C. Dr. Lyon, speaking at a Silicon Valley conference—the New Schools Summit 2002—pointed out the direct connection between hearing someone else read and learning to read: "If you don't have awareness of the sounds, phonics training will not work."

Dr. Lyon went on to observe that middle-class parents are very good reading teachers, and that the typical middle-class child receives about 3,000 hours of this in-home preparation before beginning school at age five. When a parent reads to her child, she is pointing out letters, letter sounds, and word sounds. A child from a low-income home, by comparison, receives only about one tenth that amount of preparation for reading. The students at Mabel Wesley School are figuratively bathing in the sounds of words all day long, and it's working.

On the tough South Side of Chicago, Principal Lee Brown runs the Shoop Academy, pre-kindergarten through eighth grade. Shoop Academy has 760 children, of whom 94 percent qualify for free lunch, and 99 percent are African-American. Principal Brown says, "Our kids should be reading when they leave kindergarten—and they are." Sound familiar? Five years ago, Lee Brown happened to be watching the *Oprah Winfrey Show* when Oprah described a kindergarten in Houston that was using direct instruction—and the children were reading and writing. Brown hopped on a flight to Houston the next week and spent a full day at the Mabel Wesley Elementary School.

Since that time, Shoop Elementary students have risen from 13.7 percent scoring at or above national norms in reading to 23.8 percent at that level. In math, the increase has been from 12.0 percent to 43.7 percent. Lee Brown still has to fight for her school's independence because her Chicago school district does not employ the Seven Keys to Success. Entrepreneurship in the Chicago system is not yet expected, and it doesn't come naturally. An unusual leader can be an entrepreneur anywhere, but the goal of a school system should be to create a climate in which even the ordinary principals can be entrepreneurs. An entrepreneurial principal in a middle-class school may well settle on an approach that is different from that at Mabel Wesley or Shoop, and that is our message: children are not stamped out of cookie cutters, and schools should not be, either.

ARE ENTREPRENEURS BORN THAT WAY, OR CAN EVERY PRINCIPAL BE ONE?

Edmonton, Seattle, and Houston have each faced this challenge. Each has had a similar experience, summarized by Edmonton innovator Mike Strembitsky:

> If people do not know how to manage, they never will unless they are given an opportunity. And so the first thing is that you have got to give them a chance. The second is that you do so within a controlled context. And one of the things that we have learned through our experiences is not to judge people's behavior under the old set of rules as to how they will behave when you change the rules. We couldn't recognize the behavior of most of them under the new system!

In Seattle, the principals who were already entrepreneurs used their new freedom to develop truly responsive, custom-designed schools for their communities. Those few who were too tired or too rigid mostly took early retirement when the new system was adopted. The majority of principals learned to be more entrepreneurial. Some of them are struggling, some are making steady progress, and some have surprised themselves and others by turning into full-fledged innovators.

ENTREPRENEURSHIP IS THE OPPOSITE
OF BUREAUCRACY

If you are still not sure whether a school district made up of entrepreneurs is a good idea, consider the alternative. That is an old-fashioned, top-down bureaucracy in which the central office does the strategic thinking for all of the principals and teachers and expects them to do as they are told. Parents in these systems are rarely consulted—they are *handled* by the public relations staff. The three traditional districts that we studied—New York City, Los Angeles, and Chicago—are largely of this old-fashioned type, although all three have new superintendents who are locked in a battle to bring about change.* There is substantial cause for optimism about the new leadership in each of the three behemoths, but it would be going too far to say that any of the districts is as good as its students deserve. As you read about the problems and the progress in these three big districts, keep in mind that bureaucracy is not confined to big districts. Several parents have told me hair-raising tales of small, wealthy suburban school districts that are just as rigid and nonsensical as these big urban ones.

New York City—The biggest and best—and worst

The New York City Department of Education has 1.1 million students in nearly 1,200 schools. As of 2002, there are 78,162 teachers, 12,774 school-site administrators, and 19,202 paraprofessionals such as teachers' aides; 25,500 people report to the Chancellor's Office, although most of those are assigned to individual schools. The numbers are huge, reminiscent of the tons of beef and millions of hamburger buns used by McDonald's each year.

---

*The New York City schools adopted a new structure in late 2002. The 32 local community districts and the 10 special purpose and high school districts were replaced by 10 regional districts. Whether this change will have any effect at all on the degree of autonomy of each school is not yet clear.

Diane Ravitch has chronicled in *The Great School Wars* the battles during which New York has alternately centralized and decentralized control.[2] In these monumental changes, control has passed back and forth between the central Chancellor's Office and the suboffices of the thirty-two local Community School Districts, each of which had its own elementary and junior highs and school board, and the ten high school and special districts that report directly to the chancellor through his subalterns. Never, though, has any of these changes ever passed control all the way down to the principals, as Edmonton, Seattle, and Houston have done. As a result, many New Yorkers are cynical about the idea of decentralization—but few realize that they've never actually tried it.

The recent schools chancellor, Harold Levy, wasn't in place long enough to change the organization or the management system. New chancellor Joel I. Klein reports to businessman-mayor Michael R. Bloomberg, who is taking strong steps to create an effective management system. For example, *New York Times* reporter Abby Goodnough wrote on March 27, 2003, that Klein and Bloomberg are asserting that they have the right to decide which school a principal will head. Now, the principals—protected by their union—get to pick their own schools! Klein inherits a system in which the veterans have never seen a chancellor who gave them any real autonomy to run their schools.

A high school principal in Brooklyn sees the present system this way: "The city has made its decision—to have a fraudulent system of decentralization." That assessment may be unfairly harsh, but the frustration that principals feel in this yo-yo of centralization and decentralization is understandable. At one of the city's high schools, the principal explains his staffing system this way: "The union contract says no more than 34 students to a classroom, so I get 250 units (one unit is one teacher). I cannot reallocate priorities across categories. As a result, I have discretion over about 2 units, or 1 percent of my budget."

One example of what the system means to this principal is that two years ago he and other principals were ordered to replace grade advisors, each costing 1 unit (the average pay of a teacher), with guidance counselors, each costing 1.38 units. The reason? Guidance counselors are specialists, and as licensed counselors, they might provide better protection for the district against litigation from angry parents. To make up the difference, a teaching position had to be dropped. It might have been the right decision for his students, but how could anyone at the central office possibly know?

At the famous Bronx High School of Science, one of the four test-in high schools, this system of central control means that an English teacher has 150 to 170 students during each semester. With that many papers to correct, the result is that a student typically writes only two two-page papers and one "major" paper of three to five pages each semester. Although these brilliant, highly selected students excel in mathematics and science, an English teacher at Bronx Science notes ruefully that "if they go to college and get a ten-page paper, they're in trouble . . . if they go to a high school like this, they've never had the experience." If Bronx Science had control over its budget and staffing, it would undoubtedly find ways to have more English teachers, assuming that is what the students and the parents want. Today, though, it does not have those freedoms.

A middle school principal in the North Bronx runs a typical school. The student achievement results are average for schools with similar proportions of recent immigrants and similar poverty rates. He hasn't a clue what his budget is, but that doesn't bother him. "Since everything is already mandated, what's the point?" That, unfortunately, is a typical response from a New York City principal. Another principal in Brooklyn sounds a similar note: "What we're doing now is not budgetary control, it's more like bookkeeping, just knowing where the money goes more than making real decisions about it."

Perhaps the local district that stands out most clearly for its very decentralized approach is District 2 in Manhattan, which had a long history under former superintendent Anthony Alvarado of having studied Edmonton Public. Principals in District 2 have nearly as much freedom as principals in Edmonton. Alvarado, meanwhile, moved on to San Diego as chancellor of instruction under Superintendent Alan D. Bersin. By all accounts the two struggled mightily to revolutionize the San Diego system, but it's not yet clear whether the forces of the status quo will win out or whether the winds of reform will prevail. Alvarado resigned from the San Diego position in late 2002, but Bersin is famously persistent and tough-minded, and the smart money has to be on him to win the day.

Most of the central office staff may not understand how District 2 is run, or why it succeeds, but they do respect success and they understand the power of parents who support their schools. Schools like East Side Middle School, the Manhattan New School, the Lower Lab, the Upper Lab, and several others are counted among the great schools of New York, the equal of the best independent schools. Jacqui Getz is principal at the Manhattan New School, K–5, 625 students, on the Upper East Side at Third Avenue and 82nd Street. Here is how she operates within the strictures of the New York City budget system:

> When I get my budget, I look at my numbers and this year, for instance, I felt that they gave me too few units. They underestimated the amount. So I just go ahead and do it off my own numbers. You know, ten kids, twenty kids more—it makes such a difference. I go on to my budget meeting and I say to them, I'm hiring more summer teachers and this is how much you owe me! And they'll do it because it is District 2.

Perhaps District 2 schools are good because they have parents who won't settle for less. At the Manhattan New School, for instance, 71.5 percent are white, 8.1 percent are Asian, and only

19.5 percent qualify for free lunch. If all parents would learn how to organize and be heard, all schools would be a good as Manhattan New School, where 90 percent of the students meet or exceed the state standards.

The New York City Department of Education is so vast that it contains some of the best as well as some of the worst schools and school districts in America. What's telling, though, is that most of the successes—such as Bronx Science, Peter Stuyvesant, Brooklyn Tech, Fiorello La Guardia, Edward R. Murrow High School, and the District 2 schools—all operate under systems that give them nearly as much autonomy and freedom as the schools in Edmonton, Seattle, or Houston.

Chicago—the city of "yes" and "no" in local empowerment

At least New Yorkers know what the score is. Unless you're in District 2, or in a similarly autonomous situation, you'd better remember to always follow the rules that emanate from the central office. Chicagoans can be forgiven if they can't figure out who's in charge.

Chicago is the third largest school district in the United States, with 435,470 students enrolled in 596 schools. The district is 52 percent African-American, 35 percent Hispanic, 9.6 percent white, and 3.2 percent Asian-Pacific Islanders. Eighty-six percent of the students qualify for free or reduced-price lunches. Houston and Los Angeles have similar percentages of students from poverty homes and similar total minority percentages, although Hispanic K–12 students are 55 percent of the total in Houston and 71 percent in Los Angeles. New York City schools are 40 percent Hispanic, 33 percent African-American, 15 percent white, and 13 percent Asian and other.

Shortly after Secretary of Education Bill Bennett declared in 1988 that Chicago had the worst schools in America, Chicago embarked on a major decentralization effort under a new Illinois state law. In essence, the law created local school councils made up of principals, parents, teachers, and community members. Each council gained control over the hiring and firing of the principal and over the portion of the budget that involved state funds for students from low-income families. Tenure for principals was ended. Teachers lost the right to choose their school assignment based on seniority, with the result that principals could hire the teachers they felt were best suited for their school. Although the changes involved only a few of our Seven Keys to Success, its backers made grand promises of improvement in the schools. However, what followed instead was near chaos. Professor Anthony S. Bryk of the University of Chicago led a team of researchers who thoroughly investigated those early reforms. In their book *Charting Chicago School Reform* (1998), they reached the conclusion that "the progress during the first four years certainly came up short. Some schools were unaffected, and others struggled."[3] In short, the public ended up being disappointed at the modest improvements in student performance and being upset by the cases of abuse of the local school councils, in contrast to the great promises that had been made. Several researchers would add emphasis to this advice, that school-based management alone—without an entire system of management—will not produce the desired result.[4]

The next stage was a 1995 state law that produced a takeover of the schools by Chicago mayor Richard Daley. Daley received the power to appoint the board of trustees of the school district, and through that body, to approve the school district budget. He appointed his former budget director, Paul Vallas, as CEO of the school system. The 1995 law left the local school councils in place but introduced an opposing, strong centralizing force in the mayor and his board of trustees. The Chicago Teachers' Union lost its power to bargain for virtually anything other than salary and benefits.

Under Mayor Daley and CEO Vallas, the Chicago schools made progress in several important areas. New CEO Arne Duncan, appointed in June 2001 to succeed Vallas, seems to be continuing the recent improvements. The district has ended its old practice of social promotion from eighth grade to high school. Students up to grade 9 who test below grade level must attend summer school, and test scores have rebounded somewhat from their previous lows. The school construction program is among the most effective in the nation, the anticorruption program is impressive in its thoroughness and toughness, and the administrative bureaucracy ranked high among our six cities. Several schools have been revived, often with direct attention from Vallas to the principal in question. However, the basic management system in Chicago has not yet fully developed, and it may be that when Vallas left in 2001, it was too soon to complete that task.

The situation today is confusing, because the local school councils are still in place and still have the powers granted under the 1988 law, but Vallas and Daley tightened central control over the schools. As a result, many principals feel that they are officially told to act independently while simultaneously being told not to lift a finger without approval from the central office. One of the high school principals put it this way: "There is a veneer or a facade of decentralization, and people use the rhetoric of decentralization at central office sometimes, but the reality is very tight central control over the budget and finances." At another elementary school, K–8, a very successful principal vented his feelings: "It's all controlled by central. It's very frustrating. We can't run the school." And we can all identify with a third principal, at a K–8 elementary school: "When you call central for help or with a question, you usually get an answering machine. The message will usually be: 'We're sorry, but the answering machine is full.'"

The lesson from the Chicago experience is that if your mayor, school board, or superintendent starts to talk about decentralization, encourage them, but remember that the devil is in the details. If you can see clearly how they will treat each of our Seven Keys to Success, their plan is thorough. If one or more of the elements are not addressed, though, look out.

The Chicago reforms entail heavy penalties for teachers and principals. As is often the case, the previous failure of the public schools was blamed on teachers—though the management should have been the main target of criticism. Much of the new system also provides harsh penalties for principals who fail, although they have little authority to make the changes that are needed at their schools. However, as long as parents and voters let politicians get away with this kind of finger-pointing, it will continue, and the underlying management problem will resurface every few years.

Los Angeles—Where top-down management hit bottom, but things are looking up

Roy Romer is a nontraditional superintendent—one of the new wave in school system chiefs. Like General John Stanford, banker Joseph Olchefske, university dean Rod Paige, budget analyst Paul Vallas, securities lawyer Harold Levy, and former assistant U.S. attorneys Alan Bersin in San Diego and Joel Klein in New York City, he had no previous experience as an educator. Romer was governor of Colorado and chairman of the Democratic National Committee. Now he is the superintendent of the Los Angeles Unified School District. Locals call the district headquarters 450 North Grand or Fort Moore—referring both to the former occupant of the buildings that house the headquarters and to the military command-and-control attitude of its former occupants.

Romer oversees perhaps the most troubled school district in America. His Los Angeles system is constantly attacked in the press and by watchdog groups, and the middle- and upper-class families of the area have long since fled the public schools. A series of audits has found that the system lacks workable information systems; the central office is bloated; and schools are too often left adrift, without oversight or help from the central office. The district's Inspector General wrote in a letter to school board members on January 22, 2002: "School district managers do not have a clear vision as to where the district is, where it is going, and how it is going to get there." In a June 2, 2002, editorial, the *Daily News* summarized the state of the district's schools thus: "They stink." Although Romer lacks experience in education, he has more than enough backbone to make up for it—and he needs it, and a tough hide, too.

According to a 2003 report by WestEd (San Francisco: WestEd), *Transforming Education in Los Angeles,* fewer than 20 percent of the students in any grade score at or above the "proficient" level on the California English / Language Arts Standards Test. Despite recent improvements made under new superintendent Romer, two out of three third graders are below national reading norms on the Stanford 9 (SAT9) test. In mathematics, only one in five are "proficient" or better on the California Mathematics Standards Test. Among high school students, on the SAT9 only 23 percent meet or exceed the national norm in reading and 34 percent do so in mathematics. Twenty-seven percent of LAUSD teachers are not fully credentialed. Of those who have taken the California High School Exit Exam, 45 percent passed English language arts, and 21 percent passed mathematics.

Since 1980, enrollment has grown by 180,000, but the district has added only fifteen schools with a total of 20,000 seats. As a result, 180,000 students must either be bused to a distant school or attend multi-track, year-round "Concept 6" schools, which have seventeen fewer school days. It must be added that Superintendent Romer has attacked the facilities problem vigorously, putting into place a bold new construction plan and successfully campaigning for the passage of state bond issues to fund that plan. It's beginning to look to people in Los Angeles as though things are getting better at last.

The Los Angeles Unified School District (LAUSD) is the second largest in the nation, with 733,000 students and 75,000 employees, of whom 36,000 are classroom teachers. This low ratio of teachers to bureaucrats means that Los Angeles spends only 35.4 percent of its budget on teachers' pay, while Houston spends 48.5 percent and Edmonton spends 55.8 percent. The LAUSD is beleaguered by problems: newspaper and television stories focus on toilets that don't work, schools without books, and the construction of the $170 million high school for 5,000 students that is on hold, bogged down in a fight over the safety of the site. The *Daily News* editorialized on June 8, 2001, that "it [the school board] must scale back the LAUSD's massive bureaucracy and impose a system of true accountability on teachers and administrators alike."

Within the next few years, almost all Los Angeles schools will be in Concept 6. Under this system, each school divides its students into three tracks, with two tracks in class at one time. One track is on vacation, while the school has enough classrooms and teachers for the remaining two-thirds of the students. This system limits each student to 163 days of instruction per year, compared to the 180 days in traditional schools. It also means that many families cannot vacation together, that athletic teams are broken up, that music and drama groups cannot maintain continuity or have access to their performance facilities.

As Romer arrived, a survey revealed that a majority of parents gave the district a mark of C or lower.[5] Ninety-three percent of parents expected their children to go to college, despite the fact that only 17 percent actually do.[6] Romer has made real progress in taking on these challenges, and he's raised student scores on the Stanford 9 standardized test. Like the other nontraditional superintendents in other cities, he's having a positive effect. Class size has been capped at a maximum of twenty students in kindergarten through grade 3 under a plan by former governor Pete Wilson.

Romer has produced steady gains in reading and math scores in the early grades. Fifth-grade scores have risen from the 24th to the 34th percentile nationally in reading and from the 28th to the 44th percentile in math over the last five years, for example. In the upper grades, though, things are not improved: tenth graders are in the 24th percentile on reading and the 37th percentile in math at the end of the 2001–02 school year, about where they were five years ago.

Although Romer has reorganized the Los Angeles district into eleven subdistricts, Los Angeles is finding, as both New York City and Chicago found, that simply forming subunits and appointing local district superintendents does not produce a district of entrepreneurial principals, since they still have little control over their schools. The *Daily News* criticized the reorganization in a July 20, 2001, article headlined "School Reform Bungled."

The mentality of central office control over virtually every decision is, to say the least, discouraging to principals in Los Angeles. At one inner city school, the highly regarded principal, weary of battling the central office, said: "There is no belief system in the district now that schools can make decisions for themselves—and it's only gotten worse."

At the other end of town, in upper-income Pacific Palisades, sits Palisades High School—one of the most troubled schools in Los Angeles. Every day, twenty-six buses bring children from eleven "sending areas" in the inner city an hour away, where the schools have no room for all of the neighborhood children. At 3:00 P.M. each day, those same buses take the students back to their home neighborhoods. Unfortunately, the bus schedule is set by the central office, and it takes the students away before seventh period, which is when tutoring is offered, when athletic teams and musical groups meet, when the life that makes a school into a community begins. Says another high school principal, "the habit of the LAUSD is top-down."

Many principals and teachers in Los Angeles are still bitter about the top-down, strong-arm methods that the staff at 450 North Grand used in 2000 to force all classrooms in the early grades to shift to Open Court as the one reading system and set of books. No one denies that the Open Court method can be successful, as can its competitors. However, experienced educators felt that they ought to be the ones to decide what's best for their students.

A typical story comes from a principal in the San Fernando Valley region: "Just as we had trained our staff for four years and they believed in our reading program, the Superintendent told us we had to do Open Court. It made no difference what we said—we had no choice."

Romer had a district in which 9,500 of his 36,000 teachers lacked full credentials and he was forced to put untrained teachers in many classrooms on opening day—surely a strong reason to require that all elementary classrooms use the highly structured Open Court system. On the other hand, he had another 26,500 experienced teachers, and those in the elementary schools had developed their own methods of teaching reading.

Experienced teachers in Los Angeles—the backbone of any district—are often very discouraged by the way they've been treated in the implementation of Open Court. One third-grade teacher who agreed to be interviewed without attribution described the situation in her school:

> You have to be teaching Open Court at the right time during the day, in the right chapter, when they come to inspect you, or you'll get in trouble. We call them "the Open Court Police"—our principal is one of them. . . . That's why so many of us veteran teachers want to retire. They don't respect us. You have to teach every child at the same level, on the same page. If you get a new child who is reading at the first- or second-grade level, it doesn't matter. They get the third-grade Open Court with everyone else. Now they're giving us so many practice tests for the districtwide tests—that's almost all we have time to teach, test preparation.

This teacher asserts that although it may appear that the reading ability of the children is rising, it isn't. The practice tests, she believes, are in effect giving the students the answers to the real test in advance. Other experienced teachers have had a more positive reaction to Open Court, but feelings still run high among many teachers.

Los Angeles is in a titanic battle for control over the school board. Under the leadership of prominent business and political leaders like former mayor Richard Riordan and businessman-philanthropist Eli Broad, the community rallied and threw out the old school board members who traditionally received their campaign funds from the teachers' union. In their place came a new majority with a feisty, reform-oriented president. In the 2003 school board elections, though, the teachers' union fought to gets its chosen candidates elected once again. The union spent a rumored two million dollars to elect two of its candidates, while the third candidate faces a runoff election. The *Los Angeles Times* headline on March 6, 2003: "Teachers Union Wins Back the Power in L.A. Schools." It's no surprise to find that public attention is turning to the school board. In Los Angeles, as in many cities, that's where the ultimate power lies for education decisions.

ENTREPRENEURS OR BUREAUCRATS— IT'S YOUR CHOICE

You can fight this fight on two fronts at once—and both are critical.

One: flock to your school's principal. Support him or her. Ask questions, demand answers, and be sure that your school's leader is on the job and on track. After that, defend the principal's positions by going to school board meetings to speak during the public comment, or "open mike" period. Organize a letter-writing campaign to the local superintendent and to the school board. Finally, get the parents together, seek advice from the principal, and call on these top school officials. Explain why your school needs its freedom, express your support for the direction that it's taking. The squeaky wheel gets the grease, so go and squeak in high places.

Two: agitate for change at the top. Again, write letters, respectfully but persistently visit the school board and the top school district officials, and ask what they are doing to give more local control to each school. Meet with parents from other schools, talk to city aldermen or council members, talk to state legislators (the state controls most of the school district's budget), to congressmen and congresswomen, to senators—all of them will listen, all of them are campaigning on promises to improve the public schools. Remember that asking for local neighborhood control should not be regarded as anti-American. Education is the most local of all democratic institutions, and no politician can afford to be against local control. You have to keep after them. When they realize that you're serious about it, they'll be serious about it, too.

You can also take some comfort from the fact that, troubled as they may be, these three big school districts are engaged in full-out reform. They are confronting their long-festering problems, and all seem determined to turn things around—but they have a long way to go. Chicago has made real progress in rebounding, yet many students there are still in inexcusably bad schools. New York City has some of the best schools anywhere in America, yet also some of the worst. Los Angeles has reversed its slide and has made real gains in the early grades, yet student scores there are still well below the national average and secondary schools have yet to show much progress. All three have strong, reform-oriented leaders who are under a public spotlight and who are determined to make more progress. You should notice that the reason for the new attention to schools in these cities is pressure from parents and other citizens. We'll examine some of their problems, and we'll show you how to keep them on their toes. While it's too early to say that these three have licked their problems, it's fair to say that cautious optimism is in order. If they can learn from Edmonton, Seattle, and Houston, and if they implement the Seven Keys to Success, one day they might be not only the biggest but the best.

4

Key #2: Every School Controls Its Own Budget

Weighted Student Formula came into place my second year here. My operating budget here was $25,000 a year. That was it. That was all we had to tinker with. Now, we have $2 million a year. We never got more money, by the way, out of Weighted Student Formula. We came out about even. There wasn't any more money, we were just able to think about redistributing it.

—Joanne Testa-Cross, Principal, John Hay Elementary, Seattle

*O*nce in a generation, a new idea appears that is so simple and powerful that it changes the way that an industry operates. The idea of franchising did that for fast food, and just-in-time ordering at Wal-Mart had a similar revolutionary effect. Edmonton's, and Mike Strembitsky's, invention of Weighted Student Formula may prove to be another such idea. Weighted Student Formula is a revolutionary new way to give budgetary control to each principal and local school. It was pioneered in Edmonton, Canada, over a period of twenty-five years, beginning in 1973. Since that time, it has migrated to Seattle and Houston, both of which we've studied, and more recently to Cincinnati. This system has just the right mixture of political, financial, and organizational elements to work in a wide variety of settings and to be enthusiastically accepted by school administrators, teachers, teachers' unions, and parents. It could be just the right solution for your school district. Let's see what it looks like in operation.

John Hay Elementary School, K–5, is located in a lovely

middle- to upper-middle-class section of Seattle known as Queen Anne Hill. Thirty percent of the children are minorities, and 24 percent qualify for free lunches. A few years ago, John Hay attracted the neighborhood children only until third grade, when they would leave for private schools. Not today. Fourth-grade math scores on the Washington Assessment of Student Learning (WASL) test have rocketed from 36 percent in 1998 to 61 percent in 2001. Perhaps the biggest result of local control of the money was the way that local autonomy brought everyone together to develop a common vision for the school. People who wouldn't ordinarily come out for parent meetings show up because they know that this time, they control the money and thus have the ability to implement their plans.

Not only that, but since 1996, Seattle parents have been free to choose any public school. Before, they were assigned to schools, sometimes with forced busing. The new system means that Principal Joanne Testa-Cross has to attract families—and that means both demonstrating student achievement and giving parents a voice:

> We worked on two things here. First of all, a very visible commitment that every child is going to be challenged academically—that public school can in fact keep up with private school in terms of its academic rigor. The second was . . . we are partners with parents. And we've found that if parents really feel they can make a difference and have a voice, they are much more inclined to want to be here.

Parents are involved in setting policy for the school, assisting in classrooms, serving on a number of school committees, and serving on the board of the umbrella organization, John Hay Partners. The school's academic plan is organized into five goals (Literacy, Math, Citizenship, Diversity, and Closing the Achievement Gap), with parents and teachers serving together on and chairing each of the five Goal Teams, which have tremendous leeway in deciding how to spend the money. They function almost like the board of trustees of an independent school. Final decisions still rest with the principal and her superiors in the district—unlike the ill-fated Chicago local school councils, which went awry without that supervision.

Dana Jackson is chair of John Hay Partners, a board made up of seven teachers and seven parents. The school has a whole second set of in-school committees appointed by the principal—and these, too, have joint parent-teacher membership. Many of the parents have bright children who might transfer to a specialized Spectrum program or a Spectrum school for gifted children, but they prefer to remain in the neighborhood at John Hay—so long as it can meet their needs. She says:

> We really would not be able to do things through the Partnership if it were not for the autonomy. We would still be subject to what the district would be putting forth.
>
> We were the first ones to put a reading specialist on site. We did not ask permission from the central office. We had the money and we went out and did it.

The reading program, clearly the pride and joy of the school, has exceeded all of the district's standards, according to one parent. She had one very high achieving child and two others who were slow readers. All three were provided for by John Hay Partners. Now, when people call this parent to ask how the school has done this or that, asking for advice, she tells them that school-site freedom and partnership with teachers are the keys.

Testa-Cross has also created a ten-teacher "building leadership" team. When she arrived six years ago, teachers told her that the first thing they wanted from her was to bring them all together into one team. Once the teachers in the building had developed some confidence in her leadership, they began to take bigger risks each year. They started to visit other schools, for example, to see what they could learn about teaching literacy in the early grades. Before, the teachers wouldn't start to worry about a student's reading until the child wasn't doing well in third grade. Now they asked themselves, should we wait till third grade? They visited schools, read the research, and made changes in their program.

At first, the teachers were concerned and cautious about making changes. As a group, and with parent involvement, they asked themselves how they could get the reading classes down to a maximum of fourteen students per teacher. They studied every aspect of their staffing and budget and decided that they could do without several activities that had been in place over the years. They took that money and hired a specialist reading instructor to work with the teachers and to take on one reading group of fourteen, thus enabling the other teachers to have just fourteen students for reading.

The team next put into place a data-based accountability system for tracking the performance of both students and teachers. Each kindergarten student now has a reading assessment as soon as she enters to establish her starting level. Twice each year, every student has another assessment to show how much progress she's made.

The principal keeps a data book. Turning to the section for her second graders, she points out that 75 percent of them are on track. The goal is for 100 percent of the class to be at reading level 24 (out of 44 levels) by May. With a glance, she can track every teacher and every student. In one class, for example, the teacher has nineteen out of twenty-three students on track. You owe it to your child to ask if your principal can do this. If not, shouldn't you be organizing your school's parents?

Teachers at John Hay receive extensive professional development training. Because the culture of the school now has high expectations of its teachers, those who don't have the necessary passion will move on. In six years, Testa-Cross has not had to put one teacher through the termination process. Instead, she observes, "When you experience success and you experience it both individually and as part of a wider group, there is a certain synergy that happens and you just feel revved."

Before Weighted Student Formula, Testa-Cross suffered the frustration of knowing that several students in each classroom were either way ahead or way behind and really needed to be pulled out of class for an hour or so of special attention several times each week. Because she was allocated positions rather than money, which she wasn't allowed to reallocate, she couldn't hire the reading coaches that she needed.

Today, though, every classroom has a tutoring station right next to the door. The school has hired a specially trained tutor and also has twelve certified teachers who want to work part time. Some of them are retired teachers who want to do something to keep busy, others are highly competent reading or math tutors who receive additional training at John Hay. Most are paid by the hour—again, not possible under the old system of budgeting that provided only for full-time teachers, and little cash. One tutor now works slightly more than half time and thus is eligible for benefits and can be paid out of grants. The total annual cost of the part-time tutors is a modest $35,000. Now those kindergarten children who are reading at the second- or even third- grade level are pulled out for a "turbo" reading session twice a week.

Please don't conclude from this example that every school needs this solution and that your superintendent must copy the John Hay way. That would make you a top-down, command-and-control bureaucrat. It's the management system that you need to fix. Once you do that, each school can identify and solve its own unique problems.

Now for a bit of the atmosphere at John Hay Elementary. Like Jasper Place in Edmonton, John Hay is a complex school whose detailed parts mesh together. The emphasis is on providing whatever will work for the children. For example, grades 4 and 5 are "looped"—meaning that the same class of students is together for two years with the same teacher—thus enabling the teacher to get to know each child at this critical stage when so much is changing in the life of the student. The grade 4 and 5 teachers are now discussing a plan to do some teaming, so that some can specialize in math and science while others focus on literacy and social studies.

Grades K–3 are not looped; they're in the traditional format. In Mrs. Carter's first grade, it's literacy time, so half the class has gone off to work with the reading specialist. The remaining eleven students are divided into a Red Group and a Blue Group. The Blues are working on a writing assignment while the Reds sit with Mrs. Carter to discuss *Amelia Bedelia Goes Camping*. The room has books everywhere. There are five little aquariums and five terrariums, each populated with a little ecosystem.

This school is hard work. The children's faces are contorted as they concentrate on their reading and writing. In a second-grade class, the twenty-two children have started a pen-pals program with a class from the Little Red Schoolhouse on Sixth Avenue at Bleecker Street in New York. One letter says (the names here are disguised):

> Dear Marla,
> I'm so sorry what happened on September 11, 2001. My favret collor is purple too. I am seven years old how old are you? My birthday is June 23. When is your birthday? I hope you are not hurt.
>
> From Petra

On the second floor, a wide section of the hallway has been converted into a "classroom." Here a part-time teacher is working with third, fourth, and fifth graders who are very high achievers in math and reading. Her students are working on projects on "altruism"—learning to integrate reading, writing, math, and technology skills in one large presentation. She also coaches the school's Math Olympiad team in the state competition.

How Weighted Student Formula works in Seattle

Weighted Student Formula, as we've said earlier, is a Canadian import. It came to Seattle in 1997–98 under General John Stanford and CFO Joseph Olchefske. In the Seattle system, students are assigned "weights" for supplementary funds for categories such as poverty, limited English proficiency, achievement scores in the bottom 30 percent, and special education designations such as autism, spina bifida, deafness, Down's syndrome, and so on.

The weighting scheme is easy to understand—a critical aspect of its success—and is described clearly on a single page in the annual districtwide budget book.[1] Weights range from 1 to 9.2. To arrive at the amount of money allocated to any specific child, a parent need only multiply the weight by the base funding factor, which for the 2001–02 school year was $2,616. A child with no additional weightings—for example, one from a middle-class home living with both parents, who is a native English speaker and has no learning disabilities—takes with him to the school a weighting of 1 and funds of only the base amount: $2,616. A child from a poor home with one parent and severe learning disabilities, who is not fluent in English, may receive the maximum weighting of 9.2 and will take to the school of her choice an allocation of $24,067. The Seattle budget book is a model that others would do well to emulate. It shows clearly how much money each school will have.

In addition to the funds distributed by Weighted Student Formula, each school receives a "foundation" or basic allocation per school. The amounts differ by level of school, with each high school receiving a foundation allocation of $529,000, middle schools receiving $418,000 each, and elementary schools $195,000. The foundation allocation adds roughly 20 percent to the amount of money per student at the school.

The school district as a whole actually spends a total of $9,173 per student, of which about half is allocated to the schools and the balance supports the district's central food preparation, busing, and specialized central office staffs. Seattle has a relatively large central office staff and lots of school buildings with relatively compact enrollments, perhaps because it is slowly resizing these costs as it recovers from the dramatic drop-off in enrollment that accompanied the onset of forced busing twenty years ago. One principal complained about these still-large central office staffs: "It just seems like there are more people working downtown than ever before." Over the coming years, it is likely that pressure from parents and principals will cause a steady decline in these central staffs, with more money going into the Weighted Student Formula.

Some scholars, such as Professor Paul Hill of the University of Washington, note another important subtlety of the budget system in Seattle. Schools are not billed for their actual teacher payroll. Instead, each school is charged for the number of teachers—multiplied by the *average* teacher pay in the district. Hill argues that because schools in wealthy neighborhoods, like John Hay Elementary, tend to attract more experienced, higher-paid teachers, they receive a "hidden" subsidy, while poor schools with mostly young, low-paid teachers pay a hidden cost.

Defenders of the system, which originated in Edmonton, argue that to use actual teacher pay as a criterion would cause principals to have a bias against hiring the more experienced teachers, which wouldn't be fair, either. Your district has a choice, though. In Houston, the Weighted Student Formula system charges each school for actual teacher pay—but schools have several years to get their teacher payroll in line, somewhat like the professional basketball NBA salary cap per team.

In a study entitled *It Takes a City*, published in 2000, Hill and his co-authors provided a thorough review of the early years of the Seattle reforms, along with instructive evaluations of reforms in five other cities.[2] Hill's analysis repeatedly found that districtwide success was not possible without a broad, multi-pronged approach such as the Seven Keys to Success. The partial and piecemeal reforms that so many districts have tried are destined to fail. Although Hill was correct to adopt a wait-and-see view of the reforms that had so recently been introduced in Seattle, the word is now out that Seattle is succeeding. For example, the principal of Nathan Hale High School, Eric Benson, now has so many visitors wanting to see the Seattle miracle that he can hardly get his work done: "So far this year [November 2002], we've had four or five groups come to visit. Every single high school in Portland, Oregon, came to visit us last year—about ten high schools!"

The introduction of Weighted Student Formula created lots of anxiety in the Seattle community. Parents in the wealthy areas complained that the system would penalize them with smaller per-pupil allocations, while they pay most of the taxes that support the system. Community activists argued that because all families, black and white alike, would want their children close to home in neighborhood schools, Weighted Student Formula would resegregate the Seattle schools. Some principals worried that their schools would be inundated with costly special education students with insufficient funds. In fact, some schools have become more racially homogeneous, although as a result of parent choice rather than district policy. Some schools in wealthy areas have lost money which has gone to schools in poor neighborhoods. Adjustments to the weights are made each year. The process of resetting weights is always one of tension, but as in Edmonton an open process produces broad acceptance.

In Edmonton, which was the first to introduce Weighted Student Formula in the 1976–77 school year, the annual debate over the weightings still takes place each year. Says Edmonton superintendent Angus McBeath:

You spend from now until doomsday arguing about the allocation system. The allocation system is a political instrument, because when we make it, we have said what value we place on X, Y, and Z.

At the end of the day, our principals believe the system is fair because their colleagues have wrestled this to the ground. And stayed in that room—weren't allowed to come out—until they believed that it was fair. When people believe it's fair, parents believe it is fair, teachers believe it is fair and there are no hidden pockets of money. So your budgeting process is very public.

The teachers' union has reviewed our book several times and believes that everything is on the table. So they have never meddled with, substantially, trying to get involved in the mechanics. Because they have confidence in the system.

Basically, though, you will find as Seattle found that the arguments are limited in scope, because the weightings already exist in each state. They are known as categorical funds.

WHY CATEGORICAL FUNDS ARE THE BUREAUCRAT'S DREAM COME TRUE

When a state legislator or a governor runs for office and talks about education, he or she will usually promise voters to allocate more money for whatever is the concern of the day. In the post-Sputnik era, the allocation was for science education in high school. When Nixon went to China, it was for foreign-language education. Today, the categorical funds are probably to reduce class size in the elementary grades, to buy new books, or to implement a new standardized test.

After the legislature allocates the new money, that cash doesn't go directly to individual schools—it goes to the district central office. There, the bureaucrats don't send dollars to the schools. Instead, they hire people to perform new tasks in the schools. The problem with doing it this way is that the decisions on exactly what kind of staff each school needs aren't made at the local school, they're made far away in the central office.

As one senior official in Los Angeles put it, one school might need only 0.6 of a specialist, while another school might need 1.3—but each school will get one whole person. Not only that, but the schools might have a better, more creative way of using that money to meet the goal—but they don't have the freedom to do so. And here is the topper: before the central office bureaucrats assign the new personnel out to schools, they'll create several new positions in headquarters—with several new executive positions to oversee the new offices—and to make matters worse, those newly created central office bureaucrats will proceed to tell the new teachers in the schools how to do their jobs!

Before the big change, Seattle was allocating staff rather than dollars to the schools. Odds are that your school district does it the same way. Seattle's formula provided for one principal, one secretary, half a librarian's time, and one teacher for every twenty-eight students. The big change came when money was connected to children so that the money went with the child to the school, and different amounts were attached to students with different needs. The reformers had two slogans:

Quality schools close to home.
Resources follow kids based on need.

In addition to the introduction of Weighted Student Formula, the change included ending the practice of allowing teachers to choose schools based on seniority, and introducing Open Enrollment—which allows a student to attend any school in the district and means the schools have to compete for students. All principals attended a newly designed management training program to prepare them to be the CEO of their school, with full responsibility for staffing, budget, scheduling, marketing, and just about everything else. The state establishes standards for curriculum and for student achievement and holds the districts accountable for performing up to those standards.

According to Joseph Olchefske, the reform gave each school four freedoms:

Freedom of enrollment
Freedom of money
Freedom of site-based hiring of staff
Freedom of program

You may find these four freedoms vaguely familiar. They're another version of the three tools of the entrepreneurial principal that we discussed in chapter 3.

The ultimate accountability, as in Edmonton and Houston, is that any school that cannot enroll at least 150 students is merged into another, successful school. As a result, several K–5 and grade 6–8 schools have been merged, so that Seattle now has K–8 schools that it did not have before.

Principals and teachers in Seattle have tenure, and both engage in collective bargaining with the school district. However, low-performing principals and teachers can be dismissed after a one-year probation. Strong unions have not proven to be a barrier to effective revolution in Seattle. In fact, most teachers' unions have become strong chiefly to protect teachers against the whimsy and caprice of thoughtless or even cruel bureaucrats. When the power moves down from the central office to the schools, and teachers are engaged in decision making, the union may remain vigilant, but it has no reason to object to this change and may well support it.

LOCAL SCHOOL AUTONOMY IN SIX CITIES—THE DIFFERENCES AREN'T BIG—THEY'RE *HUGE*!

Three of our cities are on Weighted Student Formula, and three of them are on the old-fashioned, top-down system. There are lots of ways to try to determine just how much freedom a school actually has, but our favorite method was to ask the principals.

We interviewed 5 percent or more of the principals in each of the districts, and we asked each of the 223 of them that question. The differences in their replies were dramatic. Keep in mind that Edmonton was the first to invent Weighted Student Formula, and thus the change there is the most complete. Seattle and Houston came later, and in those districts the shift is still becoming more pronounced each year. Chicago has a schizophrenic management system, with some of the money controlled by the local schools but most of it under the central control of the superintendent and the mayor. In New York City, most of the money is centralized, although some of the forty-two subdistricts (thirty-two community districts plus ten high school and special districts), such as District 2 in Manhattan, have given control of the money to their schools. In Los Angeles, which ranks second in central control of the money, there are no officially sanctioned units that give control to local schools.

Here is what our study found when we asked principals how much of the money is under their local school's control:

Percentage of the Money Controlled by the Local School

TRADITIONAL DISTRICTS

New York City	6.1
Los Angeles	6.7
Chicago	19.3

WEIGHTED STUDENT FORMULA DISTRICTS

Houston	58.6
Seattle	79.3
Edmonton	91.7

In the three old-fashioned districts, principals typically do not even know how much money their school has this year, and they don't care—because someone else controls it, not them. The central office will usually blame the teachers' union, and that will leave you wondering how it is that the union rather than the superintendent is running the district. Don't be fooled. Yes, many teachers' unions have become too strong, but that's because they're trying to protect teachers from a bureaucratic monster. My experience in Los Angeles is with a great union leader like the late Helen Bernstein, who was all too ready to show flexibility and a great willingness to lead her teachers to change their ways—if she could believe that the central office meant to change, too. The responsibility *does* lie with the school board and the superintendent; they get elected and paid to provide a great education for all students, and you should demand that they do their jobs.

If you've been reading the newspaper, you may be surprised at how much control the central bureaucracy has. Most previous studies of central office administrative bureaucracy report much smaller expenditures there than we found. The reason is that most researchers and reporters rely on the self-serving way that central offices report these figures. Odden and Busch, whom we quoted in chapter 1, for example, report that in New York City, only 2.5 percent of the money is consumed by central office administration, with a modest additional 3.6 percent used for administration at school sites. For Los Angeles, the numbers that they report are 4.5 percent consumed at the central office and 5.3 percent at the school sites.[3]

We were fed those same numbers by the central offices, but we went further in our analysis. We actually got the documents that enabled us to count the numbers of central office staff, most of whom the bureaucrats report as though they were under the control of the schools—which they are not. Also, for the first time we asked the principals in each district how much of the money that reaches their school they actually control. These analyses paint a very different picture from the one that you've been fed in the past. Big businesses can cook their books so thoroughly that they bear no relationship to the truth, and the same is true of school districts, so do your own analysis.

Weighted Student Formula in Houston

We've seen how Houston has undergone a revolutionary change that moved many decisions from the central office down to the schools. Tenure had been revoked for central office administrators and principals. According to former school board member Don McAdams, Superintendent Paige had moved 254 student evaluation specialists, psychologists, and other professional staff out of the central office and into one of the twelve local district offices. School choice for families and accountability for schools were in place. A great deal had been accomplished by the small band of revolutionaries. Still, McAdams tells of his worry that the Houston revolution wasn't firmly in place:

> District decentralization has significantly shifted power away from Central office, but real decentralization is still a dream . . . schools are still budgeted with staff positions, not dollars. The principal of a typical elementary school, with a total operating budget of nearly $2 million, usually controls less than $100,000.[4]

That was in 1999. Later that year, the Houston school board, led by Superintendent Paige, voted to implement Weighted Student Formula beginning in the 2001–02 school year. Now, Weighted Student Formula is a reality in Houston, as our study results show.

McAdams was right to worry about whether this revolution would stick. You can bet that unless the money moves to the schools, it won't stick. What McAdams knew is what you've learned, too, if you've been involved in trying to reform your schools. That lesson is, Show me the money! It's also known as the golden rule of power: He who has the gold makes the rules.

Most school districts know or suspect that local decision making works best—they just can't figure out how to do it. They've tried implementing school-based management, local school councils, site-based management, and whatever else they can think of. They've often found that the local councils were dominated by the teachers' union, and that the councils ended up becoming just another layer of bureaucracy. With all of these unnecessary layers of organizational fat, school districts have come to resemble Jabba the Hutt—the pirate leader in *Star Wars*.

Control goes with the money. If your superintendent smiles, invites your group into his office, and tells you that he agrees with you and that he's going to roll out a new school-based decision-making program that includes parent involvement—smile sweetly and ask him who will control the school's budget. Don't let him off the hook. Don't let him think that you can be so easily fooled.

If your superintendent tells you that Weighted Student Formula is for the big, urban districts, that something like that isn't needed in your small, intimate system, smile again. Then offer the opinion that actually, Weighted Student Formula should be much easier to implement in a small district that has fewer people to convince. Point out that even in a business as small as one hundred employees, decision making has to be moved down to the people close to the customers or on the factory floor. Tell him that in Santa Monica, California, the 13,000-student school district has given full budget autonomy to each local school. Your district can be next.

How to beat the experts in one easy lesson

There is one last major topic that has to do with school funds. Your school administrators will tell you that the amounts this book has described—$11,994 per pupil in New York City, $9,889 in Los Angeles, and $5,558 in Houston—are way more than they have. Don't believe them until you've done your own arithmetic.

To begin with, you need to be aware that most school boards and administrators have no idea how much money they have. You may find that hard to believe, and it is. But it's true. They simply don't know where the money is. The Los Angeles Unified School

District has been described by both state auditors and private independent accountants as dysfunctional. It has seven different accounting systems that don't mesh as a whole. They also don't have a complete list of the property that they own, and they can't tell you how many employees they have. And they're not alone.

The local reporters, just like the professional accountants, can't figure out how much money there is, so they ask the central office of the district. The number that the district gives out is not the total that they spend per student, it's usually the amount that reaches the schools, or the amount that reaches the classroom, or the basic allocation it receives, not including the categorical funds or the federal funds. The administrators hope to convince the public that they're doing a great job but just don't have enough money. Don't believe it for a moment.

In Los Angeles, for example, you might think that the school district is supposed to give each student at charter schools the same per-student allocation that it spends on its own students. The amount that charter schools receive is about $6,800 per student, about two thirds of what the district actually spends. But our study revealed that the Los Angeles Unified District spends only about $4,800 per student at the classroom level—because it wastes the rest on bureaucracy.

Here's a suggestion: do your own arithmetic, starting with two unshakeable numbers: one is the total operating budget (it does not include school construction or debt service expenses), and the other is the total number of students in K–12. You can find these numbers on your school district's Web site, or you can call the office and ask for a copy of this year's budget. Then do the arithmetic and calculate the total operating budget per student. Here is the example for Los Angeles in 2001–02:

Total district operating budget	$7,239,000
Total enrollment, K-12	733,000
Total operating budget per student	$9,876[5]

I have subtracted from the total district operating budget the amount spent on adult education, and from the total enrollment, I've subtracted the number of adult education students. The total includes salaries, benefits, cafeteria, books and supplies, and other services purchased by the district. It also includes a large sum that was left over from the previous year and thus is included in this year's budget. You can do the same in your school district.

If you really get into this, you might want to look at the total budget per student rather than the total *operating* budget per student. To do this, find the capital budget. For our Los Angeles Unified example, the total capital budget was $2.06 billion. If we divide this by the number of students, we get a capital budget of $2,810 per student (most of the cities in our study have annual capital budgets of about $1,300 per student, but New York City was at $1,812). Add this to the operating budget of $9,876 per student, and it comes out to a total budget per student of $12,686.

Now you're armed and ready. Ask the administration how much it spends per student. If you get the wrong answer, show them your arithmetic. Ask them politely what numbers they've used, and make them stick to the total budget and the capital budget. They won't want to do it your way—it's too embarrassing. They'll try to foist other, confusing numbers on you. You should also call the reporter at your local newspaper whose byline you see on stories about education. Ask her what she thinks the budget is per student, and share your arithmetic with her, too. Go to a school board meeting and ask the board members in public.

Your school district has a budget director who reports to the chief financial officer, who in turn reports to the superintendent and the school board. In Los Angeles, The Alliance, the school reform organization, for several years had regular meetings with the CFO to see to it that schools were not shortchanged at budget time, and to make sure that a school that manages itself well and produces a surplus was allowed to keep that surplus to use in the future. In a smaller school district, a parent group can call on the budget director or the CFO of the district and have this conversation at least once a year. They'll probably welcome you, and they'll expect you to put in the time to learn enough about the budget to make intelligent comments on it. Make sure that your group includes people who have budget experience. In the unlikely event that the financial staff won't meet with you, write a letter and then go to see the superintendent or a member of the school board, and he'll surely see that you have access to the financial people at headquarters. As long as you're open-minded and polite, your meetings will become regular and productive.

Once you understand where the money is being spent, you're prepared to start advocating for local school control of the budget. You can now point out how your own school's needs could be met more effectively if you had a system of budget decentralization, such as Weighted Student Formula.

The concerns that were raised in Seattle are legitimate concerns, and they'll arise in your community, too. Here's what actually happened there.

In the wealthy neighborhood schools, the budget per student did decline. As a result, class size rose slightly. However, the students who bring less money with them need less help. They're school-ready, and they're less costly to educate. As a result, the school is able to have larger enrollments in some classes and to free up money to spend on new activities, as at John Hay Elementary.

In the poor neighborhoods, the children bring with them more money per student than before. The result is that the schools have smaller class sizes and more of the specialists they need.

Special education students have more choices than before. Some schools will want to become special education schools— and with all of the additional money, they can offer an array of specialized services. Other families will prefer to have their children in a local neighborhood school—and they will accept the trade-off of having somewhat reduced specialized services in return.

As long as families have freedom of choice and schools have freedom of action, the results will be good. All children will be treated as individuals, and all can grow and develop as they should.

The emphasis is on having a variety of schools from which a family can choose. Weighted Student Formula is a tool—a powerful tool, but not the goal in itself. The goal is effective schools of many different types, so that each family can find the school that is right for their child. We turn next to that subject.

5

Key #3: Everyone Is Accountable for Student Performance and for Budgets

Last week I Xeroxed my checks that I've written and published them in the monthly bulletin that goes to all parents. We do that for everything—a lot of accountability.

If a kid causes trouble, I'll go to their house at eight at night. Teachers will do the same.

I give the standardized test results personally to each parent individually in my office.

—Sister Betty Smigla, Principal, St. Mark School, Chicago

*A*ccountability has become a much-overworked word, and in some cities, it's become anathema to teachers. That's because many parents, acting out of frustration, blame teachers for the failure of the schools. Their code term is that we should hold teachers "accountable." As we've already begun to see, though, if there's anyone who doesn't deserve to be blamed, it's the teachers. On the other hand, there is a need for a clear system of monitoring performance and behavior in every large organization, and school systems are no exception. Too often, the more centralized school systems are breeding grounds for poor performance and outright dishonesty. In this chapter, we'll see some examples of school districts that have found innovative ways to deal with the accountability issue. We'll explain the three forms of accountability that apply to a school system: (1) Performance

Accountability; (2) Compliance (anticorruption) Accountability; and (3) Political Accountability. We'll show you how you can become a more insightful observer of accountability in your district, and how you can help to strengthen these controls.

Accountability is as simple—and as difficult—as that. Sister Betty Smigla at St. Mark School in Chicago gets hugs every morning as her kids arrive at school. Her big smile and hearty energy are irresistible, but no one misses the fact that she's tough. St. Mark is in gang territory—many of the parents are in gangs, in jail, or on probation. This is a place where trust is a foreign concept, and Sister Betty knows that unless she builds trust, her parents won't support the school and her kids won't flourish. So Sister Betty lays everything bare—no fudging, no funny business of any kind.

Not only does she hold herself accountable for her spending, she gives student performance the same treatment. Sister Betty knows from experience that teachers will sometimes give a child a higher mark than they deserve, thinking that they're being kind, or wanting to avoid a confrontation with angry parents. Sister Betty can't tell the teachers what grades to give, but she can see to it that parents understand the often difficult-to-comprehend standardized test scores for their children. So she explains the scores, personally, to all parents. One parent describes her good feelings about the annual test score review with Sister Betty: "She is going to tell you exactly what the situation was and what do you think about this. It was really good."

Accountability at St. Mark has many facets. In this far southeast corner of the Humboldt Park neighborhood on Chicago's West Side, the most important aspect of accountability to families is the safety of their children. The corner of Campbell and Cortez Streets right outside the school used to be a favorite hangout for local drug dealers. The city put in a small circular planter to slow down the traffic, and that has helped to reduce the drive-by shootings at the intersection. The staff is ever vigilant, and the Chicago police go out of their way to help. Mrs.

Morrajo, a parent volunteer, describes it this way: "This school is like a safe haven for the kids and that is just the way it is."

St. Mark, like most urban Catholic elementary schools, is on its own financially, with no endowment, total parent donations of only $15,000 per year, and an annual subsidy from the archdiocese of $75,000 per year. The school runs one class in each grade, K–8, on a total budget of $480,000. It's on the edge of survival. Chicago's archbishop announced that he would have to close thirteen schools at the end of the 2000–01 school year for lack of funds.

Everyone makes a sacrifice to be at St. Mark. Teachers start at a salary of $21,500 that can rise after thirty-one years of service to a maximum of $37,510—less than half of what public school teachers earn. Most of the teachers have their teaching credential and a master's degree and have remained at St. Mark because they want to be there. Except for two nuns who run the library part time, all of the teaching staff are laypeople.

Perhaps because everyone is sacrificing, everyone expects total honesty and accountability. Accountability, though, does not mean a harsh, punitive atmosphere, according to Dennis Conley, who teaches the eighth-grade class: "We are held accountable for what we do. We are held accountable but at the same time [Sister Betty] is very supportive."

Ms. Fran Kinloch, the seventh-grade teacher, describes what teacher accountability means to her at St. Mark:

> Whenever we give a unit test, after we grade the test we have to give it to her [Sister Betty] and she'll go through it. She actually goes through it with us. Sometimes she'll stand there and say, "Well, what happened here?" That is how she can monitor what we are doing in the classroom.
>
> She also walks through the classroom—the kids are used to it—we just continue what we are doing and she walks around the room and she watches what is going

103

on, stuff like that. She does that at least once a day.

When I was interviewed for the job she said, "I hold everyone in this building accountable." And after being here—she does!

Accountability goes for the students, too, as Mr. Conley describes it: "You take the child out of the room, you talk to the child and you give the child the consequence, the child comes back into the room and it's over with. . . . In addition to holding us accountable, everybody in the community cares about each other."

What have been the academic results of all of this accountability in the eleven years that Sister Betty, a nun of the Sisters of Providence, has been at St. Mark School? Third graders' reading scores have declined slightly over that time on the Terra Nova standardized test from the 50th percentile to the 46th, perhaps a result of the deteriorating neighborhood. By seventh grade, however, the highest grade for which data are available ten years back, reading scores have risen from the 45th percentile to the 68th. It would seem that the school is producing very strong learning results for the children who stay throughout elementary school.

What role do parents have in accountability? They are the only ones to whom the school and the district *are* accountable. Parents need to know what questions to ask, what they can reasonably expect, and what not to tolerate. If they don't exercise their "shareholder" rights in an informed and interactive manner, they'll allow their educational system to become another Enron. Sister Betty knows that most of her families have to stretch to pay the annual tuition of $2,200—most of them pay by the month. Ninety-five percent of the students are minorities, and 92 percent qualify for the federal free lunch program. The principal estimates that 8 of the 211 students have special needs, and 25 percent are studying English as a second language. The number of special needs students may seem low, but that's because Catholic schools are not required to have students evaluated for special needs funding, and parents see no incentive to get their children classified as having special needs. In public schools, special needs students may have access to district-paid transportation and to other benefits, but that isn't so in Catholic schools. At a low-income school like St. Mark, parents aren't the sort who are aggressive with a principal, which means that if they aren't satisfied, they'll just drift away and take their children out of the school. Which rarely happens.

In your public school, though, the principal knows that the school can't or won't go out of business no matter how dissatisfied you may be. Which means that, unlike the parents at St. Mark, you do have to be more aggressive in holding your school accountable. Here are some examples of the most effective practices that we found and the most awful situations than can develop when accountability isn't expected.

THE THREE FORMS OF ACCOUNTABILITY

When businesspeople get interested in school reform—as many are today—they tend to focus first on accountability. They start with a preconceived notion that schools are lax on the subject because they know that any business that is soft on accountability will soon fail. Putting two and two together, they conclude that if you get tough on principals and teachers, the problems of education will be solved. Unfortunately, it isn't that easy. Marc Tucker and Judy Codding have described in their book *Standards for Our Schools* the important role that standards play in a workable system of accountability, and they point out that most school systems don't have standards for what students should know, say, by the end of middle school or high school.[1] Creating those standards is a big job. Most of these approaches have the same underlying idea: that accountability means knowing what students should learn and then testing them to find out if they know it. The basic idea is sound. The difficulty is that when applied in practice, the intense focus on accountability sometimes becomes instead a negative kind of teacher-bashing. We all know that if we want students to improve their performance, scaring or threatening their teachers is a poor way to get there.

We've put the forms of accountability into three separate "buckets." First is Performance Accountability, which refers to the variety of methods that we've observed, not in theory or in just one or two schools, but in 223 schools, 6 public school districts, and 3 Catholic school districts—for tracking student achievement. Second is Compliance Accountability—the methods to control waste, fraud, and corruption. The third we call Political Accountability, which refers to the new systems that governors, mayors, and legislatures are inventing each day, many of which do more harm than good. We'll go through a brief review of what we've learned about each of these three "buckets." As you read them, ask yourself which ones might improve your school district and which ones you ought to avoid.

1. PERFORMANCE ACCOUNTABILITY

The primary focus of this category should be student achievement—and it is. In addition, it includes the performance of principals, administrators, and central office staff—all of whom should be as accountable as the teachers. Just keep in mind Sister Betty, and you'll be on the right track. No one should escape accountability. Sister Betty, though, is not some hardhearted, iron-fisted person who enjoys beating up people. Accountability is often thought of in those terms, but that's shortsighted. Accountability should include a wide variety of mechanisms, some positive and others negative.

Teacher accountability is national topic #1

Although the great majority of teachers are effective and dedicated professionals, there are a few who shouldn't be in charge of your child's education. Too often, those low performers whose bad reputations damage the image of all teachers seem to escape discipline or removal. All across the country, teachers' unions have learned to be politically active. In many states and cities, they are among the largest donors to political campaigns, and they have used their political power to insulate teachers from true accountability. Their desire for protection against poorly chosen and undersupervised principals is understandable and perhaps defensible. Ultimately, though, children are not well served if incompetent teachers are not held accountable.

In Seattle, for example, the procedure for removing teachers, governed by state law and union contract, can take several years and is so complex that principals rarely try it. However, Superintendent Olchefske is trying to accelerate the process by giving administrative help to principals. He met with all principals and promised that his Office of Academic Discipline would help them through the due process procedures. Following the meeting, the head of the office reported that she was inundated with requests. During the following year, three times the previous number of teachers were on probation.

It is no surprise, then, that *The Seattle Times* reported on April 4, 2003, that 85 percent of the teachers' union members approved a resolution calling for the ouster of Olchefske. Olchefske, though, is a determined man, and he replied that he's staying put. Reform is not for the faint of heart.

In Edmonton, the Alberta Teachers' Association has a more protective contract than any that we encountered in the United States. A senior Edmonton official summed it up by saying, "We haven't successfully fired a teacher in thirty years." In one case, a teacher went on sick leave—remained on it for seven years, and then retired. Experienced principals and strong peer pressure, though, cause a few underperforming teachers to quit. It's a testimony to the power of positive leadership that Edmonton has perhaps the best school district in North America, despite its relatively weak ability to discipline a failing teacher.

In Houston, teachers are insulated from real accountability

for student performance by the Texas Education Code. That doesn't mean that real accountability doesn't exist in Houston. It does. At Jack Yates High School, home of the Mighty Lions, the new executive principal is Dr. Robert Worthy. In addition to running this comprehensive high school of 1,600, he has overall responsibility for the Yates Feeder Pattern, which includes two middle schools and twelve elementary schools.

Since 1926, Yates High had been the premier school for African-Americans in Houston. Upper- and middle-class blacks sent their children here. After school desegregation came to Texas, though, educated black families sent their children to the previously all-white top schools, such as Bellaire and Lamar. Jack Yates High fell on hard times. Soon, the walls were covered with graffiti and violence was commonplace. After fifteen years of failure, Yates was ready either to be closed or to be revolutionized.

Superintendent Rod Paige would rather fight than quit any day, so he imported a new principal from nearby Pasadena, Texas. Dr. Worthy moved fast. He shut down a program on Cleaning and Pressing, established new Advanced Placement (AP) courses, and with support from Paige, he moved out 50 percent of the teachers and most of the administrative staff in two years—nearly sixty teachers in all—in order to break up the existing negative culture of the school.

Today, the Mighty Lions are roaring once again. The hallways are clean enough to eat on, the students are in uniform, and the teachers stand by their classroom doors as the bell rings. Visitors can feel the pride that everyone has in their school. Every entering student is in the college preparatory program, and every student, including those in special education, takes the state test and thus counts toward the school's overall rating. No one, in other words, doesn't matter; every student "counts." In Houston as in Edmonton, an entrepreneurial superintendent combined with an entrepreneurial principal can move mountains.

In 1996, Chicago under former superintendent Paul Vallas developed the same approach as Seattle to remove truly incompetent teachers. There, as in Seattle and elsewhere, state laws and collective bargaining agreements had made it so complex to dismiss a teacher that most principals didn't try. Now, though, the Department of Teacher Accountability is proactive. If the teacher's contract says, for example, that the principal must visit the teacher's classroom on the fifteenth day, the department will call the principal the day before to remind him or her. In the first five years after the district central office started helping principals to fire bad teachers in 1996, four hundred teachers have been removed for incompetence, have resigned, or retired. Chicago has one of the strictest systems for teacher accountability, as it does for principals and other employees.

In New York City, the situation is similar. From 1998 to 2000, the Board of Education attempted to dismiss for incompetence only 3 teachers out of the 79,156 on the payroll, although others have been dismissed for misconduct—such as hitting a student.

In Los Angeles, the state education code makes dismissal of a teacher nearly impossible. The teachers' union has been particularly resistant to attempts to establish accountability measures. The irony is that while Los Angeles has perhaps the strongest teachers' union and the weakest teacher accountability, teachers there are the most unappreciated and the most unhappy of any of the cities that we studied. Here's my advice: focus on creating positive management throughout the district. Don't spend your time searching out and punishing the few bad apples. In those few cases where an entire school has developed a negative culture—as at Jack Yates High in Houston—then moving the teachers out to new jobs is the right thing to do. Over the entire district, though, if 90 percent of the teachers are well motivated and attentive to students, you won't notice the few bad ones. If, on the other hand, your district spends all of its time terrorizing the underperformers, the reign of terror will have a negative effect on *all* teachers.

Holding principals accountable

More and more, school districts are coming around to the view that a school cannot be successful unless it has a good principal. A good principal is one who motivates, trains, and leads the teachers—thus enabling them to succeed. As a result, New York City, Seattle, and Houston have all implemented new systems that have made more stringent principal accountability a reality. Before Joseph Olchefske took over in Seattle, failed principals were usually promoted into central office jobs or transferred to other schools as principal, thus joining the dance of the lemons. In 1999, though, four principals in Seattle were removed for poor performance, and were either fired outright or demoted to teacher positions (an idea of questionable merit, some say)—more than at any time in the previous thirty-five years. The result is that all Seattle principals now know that producing student gains is a real, no-fooling-around requirement. Meanwhile, Seattle has instituted new, more thorough methods for hiring new principals and for giving all principals management training.

Edmonton has tough procedures for hiring and training new principals. To become an assistant principal, applicants must go through a lengthy management training course—during which they are closely observed by current principals and by the superintendent. To get to principal, they go through another, even longer training program, which all principals regard as having been very helpful to them. Only some of the trainees are selected for principal positions. Principals are subjected to thorough grilling on their budgets and plans before, during, and after each school year. At the end of each school year, all principals undergo a "results review" by small committees of school board members. One result of the extensive reviews is that once principals are hired and given great freedom, rarely are any of them found to be dishonest or fired.

Chicago seems to rely more heavily on the stick than the carrot. Principals lost tenure under the 1988 law. Strong accountability measures implemented by Paul Vallas in 1995, in combination with the loss of tenure, brought the dance of the lemons to a halt. In addition, Chicago has several powerful options: if fewer than 20 percent of students in a school are reading at grade level, the school can be put on academic probation, which triggers a mass investigation and a slew of management changes. If the central office finds the principal to be incompetent, it can declare the school to be in crisis, which leads to a hearing, after which the principal can be fired. So far, three schools have gone through this procedure. In one of those cases, the principal spent $14,000 to build a luxurious bathroom in his office. He would also sit in the men's bathroom for hours, eavesdropping on conversations!

Since 1997, the Chicago system can reconstitute a school that is failing. The school is formally shut down and the entire staff is dismissed. Then the school is reopened and everyone from the principal to the custodian must reapply for his or her job. Starting in 1999, the Chicago system added the option of reengineering a troubled school, where the teachers are given the chance to recommend who should stay and who should go.

Houston's approach to principal accountability is almost the opposite of Chicago's. Houston motivates principals to succeed, where Chicago seems more interested in punishing the ones who don't. Like Edmonton and Seattle, Houston has a tough selection process and a highly developed management training program for principals. Each principal is on a one-year contract that specifies the goals for student achievement and for budget performance. In 2001, 110 principals got the maximum bonus of $5,000, 43 received partial awards, and 114 principals received no bonus. The bad ones don't have their contracts renewed and must leave the district. The Houston principals are by and large a motivated, well-trained, and capable group. Everyone that we met knew his goals, knew his progress on those goals, and was extremely focused on what he was doing.

Los Angeles might be the city that coined the term "dance

of the lemons." For nearly twenty years, this failing district did not dismiss a single principal. Weak principals would seek protection from their area school board member, who would often protect the principal in exchange for complete loyalty—almost a feudal arrangement. But no one was protecting the children! It was a terrible comedown from the excellent years under former superintendent Harry Handler from 1981 through 1987. Handler had set tough goals, measured every principal, and moved out those who couldn't perform. Handler demoted, early-retired, or put on probation fifty managers, from principals all the way up to an associate superintendent. In a June 9, 2000, *Los Angeles Times* article Superintendent Roy Romer said, "The dance of lemons, that just has to stop." Romer has been able to get three or four weak principals to retire early; but Los Angeles has 932 principals and center directors (yet only 677 school sites, many of which have schools-within-a-school), and it still tends to recycle its lemons, either as principals in other schools or by promoting them to jobs in the central office.

We were stupefied by the number of principals in Los Angeles who seem to be on remote control—with no idea why they are there or what they are trying to accomplish. Many principals, on the other hand, told us that they felt abandoned by the district—put into impossible situations with no help from anyone. The sense of abandonment is so great in Los Angeles that three of the principals we interviewed cried during the interview as they poured out their intense feelings of loneliness and frustration. We did not encounter that kind of hopelessness in any of the other districts we studied.

The sum and substance of our review of principals is that a great district gets that way by having a disciplined procedure for recruiting, selecting, training, and overseeing principals. In the good districts, there may be monetary rewards for high performance, but the key is that all principals know what is expected of them, and they are trained to be able to reach their goals.

Management review does not mean adding lots of bureaucracy

The core of a results-oriented system is the structure and the culture of management. Here, we found vast differences between the strong and the weak districts. Edmonton was alone in the clarity and effectiveness of its approach to top management review of the schools.

In Edmonton, Superintendent Angus McBeath has eliminated all of the layers that formerly existed between him and his principals, following the rule established by Mike Strembitsky that every principal should have only one boss. Before, a principal reported to one assistant superintendent for budget, to another for curriculum, yet another for special education, another for poverty programs, another for teacher training, another for standardized testing, and so on. Now, every principal has only one boss: the superintendent. The principals love this system.

We've pointed out that every principal goes through a rigorous budget-and-objectives review three times each year. In addition, the superintendent personally visits one third of the 209 schools each year. In preparing for each visit, he studies a report that includes all of the student performance, customer satisfaction, and budget data. He has the questionnaires that are filled out every year by every student, parent, teacher, and custodian in that school. Yes, *every student from grades 1 to 12.* Even first-grade students answer questions like these:

> Do you find your school work interesting?
> Does your teacher expect you to do your best?
> Do you like being in your school?

Teachers get to answer questions like these:

> Do you have confidence in the board of trustees?
> Does your principal provide effective leadership in your school?

Do you have an opportunity for input into school-level decisions that affect you and your job?

Here are a few selections from the questionnaire that parents answer each year:

How satisfied are you:
. . . with the overall quality of education that your child is receiving at school?
. . . with the school principal?
. . . that you receive enough information about your school's student achievement results (Alberta Learning achievement tests and and Highest Level of Achievement tests, etc.)?

Unlike most U.S. superintendents—who have a private car and chauffeur—Angus McBeath drives to the schools himself, armed with a good deal of information. He's so well informed that it's difficult for anyone—principals, parents, or teachers—to pull the wool over his eyes.

The management system in Edmonton is not all top-down, either. It's bottom-up, too. Once each year, all principals meet in executive session with the school board and the superintendent. They are quizzed by board members on what they think of the central office and the superintendent—Are they helpful to you as principal or do they inundate you with bureaucratic trivia? Are they responsive to your requests, and are they professional and knowledgeable? Ask your school board to give this a try. It will be an eye-opener to them, and it will send a clear message that will resound throughout the system. Here's how Angus McBeath puts it: "I tell my central office staff: if you want to be a star—apply for a job as a principal. The only stars in our district administration are the principals."

Other cities would do well to emulate Edmonton on this system, and so would your district. We've already pointed out that the Santa Monica schools use this accountability system, and the superintendent reports that about 80 percent of parents fill out the questionnaire each year, and nearly 100 percent of students and teachers do so. In most cities, principals have to report to many bosses, and much of their day is consumed by gathering data and reporting to one or another assistant superintendent on one or another useless task. If you are going to hold the principal accountable for creating successful students, shouldn't you let them do it and leave them alone unless the school shows signs of needing help?

Central office is a great place to hide—because no one cares

In the world of business, a large company is always divided into smaller subunits. Each subunit has to make a profit. However, each is also charged for the central office services that it uses—like legal services, insurance, or central purchasing. Each unit is also charged a fee for its share of the remaining central staffs, whether or not they use them. This is known as the general and administrative cost charge. In schools, though, it doesn't occur to most school administrators that they should first allocate the funds to the schools—and then make the schools pay for the central services that they use. Instead, the services of the central office are "free," and the schools can have all that they want. The result is high demand for the free services—and huge central staffs.

We've already pointed out that Edmonton has the ultimate solution: it gives 92 percent of the money to the schools and then lets them decide what, if any, services to buy from the central office—or from outside suppliers. In Edmonton, for example, Principal Scott Miller at the Ellerslie Campus, K–9, can have his parking lots plowed and sanded by central. But if he doesn't like their quality of service, he's free to get a local farmer to do the job instead. The same goes for hiring psychologists who evaluate or counsel his students.

In Chicago, unlike Los Angeles and New York City, none of

the employees at central is in civil service. Under the same 1988 law that ended principal tenure, the central office employees also lost tenure. Now, a manager needs only to notify a central office employee of his unsatisfactory performance, attempt to remedy the problem, and then—if improvement is not forthcoming—the employee can be dismissed.

Now, why should you care if there are a few too many people in central? Here's why: our study revealed that in New York City, only 53.4 percent of the school system's money actually makes it all the way to the classrooms—where the education takes place. In Houston, where the revolutionaries inherited a large central staff and still haven't worked it all the way down, only 52.6 percent gets to the classroom; and in Los Angeles, only 45 percent of every education dollar gets to the classroom. The best performances in our study were by Chicago and Seattle, with 58 percent of the money in the classroom, and Edmonton, where 65 percent of the money gets to the classroom. If Los Angeles were as good as Edmonton on this measure, it would mean an extra $1.4 *billion* per year in the classroom—an extra $1,975 per student of additional money each year.

Are you ready to say, "I'm mad as hell and I'm not going to take it anymore"? I hope that you are, but if not, read on. It gets worse.

2. COMPLIANCE ACCOUNTABILITY

If you read the newspapers or watch the news on television, you've already had a steady diet of scandalous examples of money being stolen from the children in your school system. What we call Compliance Accountability means ensuring that people follow the established rules and laws for spending a district's money. The big news is not that everyone is stealing. The big news is that they aren't! We found that our great school districts—Edmonton, Seattle, and Houston—have a very low incidence of theft.

Here's what we did. First, we ranked our six districts from top to bottom on the amount of school money (excluding what is spent at the central office) controlled by principals, from the 92 percent in Edmonton, to the 79 percent in Seattle, the 59 percent in Houston, and on down to the 19 percent in Chicago, and the unbelievable but true 7 percent in Los Angeles and 6 percent in New York City. These figures reflect the fact that even though money is allocated to the schools, it may be controlled by the central office or the union contract rather than by the principals. Next, we ranked the same six districts according to which ones have the highest or lowest incidence of cases of abuse of district standards by teachers and other employees, and by other measures of waste, fraud, or corruption. *We found an almost perfect match of the rankings.* The districts that have the most centralization and the largest central staffs also have the most, not the fewest, problems with incompetence and dishonesty.

To most school administrators, this is a paradox. When something goes wrong, the public demands that the superintendent get better control over things. The superintendent typically responds by tightening up on central control and builds up the central staff with more people to watch each other. The result, though, is not more control—it's less. Why? Because the bigger the central office, the more difficult it is to know who is responsible for anything. In addition, it's easy to steal a million dollars or hire a relative who does nothing at central, because hundreds of millions or even billions are flowing through the system there.

If the money is allocated to the schools, there are many pairs of eyes watching how every dollar is spent—parents, teachers, and students all care about every dollar, because they have a good use for the money. It's also less tempting to steal at the level of an individual school because there is less money in the till.

That's not to say that our outstanding districts are pristine. In Seattle, for example, a central office bookkeeper helped herself to $180,000 over a period of five years from 1990 through

1995. The director of Seattle's Office of Research, Evaluation, and Assessment told us that the district has a reputation with some reporters and outsiders as being reluctant to do investigations because it doesn't want to dig for dirt. More recently, accounting errors produced an unexpected budget deficit, followed by staff cuts and public criticism of the superintendent.

Edmonton, like Seattle, has a relatively small investigative capability. The province of Alberta audits Edmonton annually, and the district's Internal Audit Office pays close attention to the $30 million of cash that the 209 schools collect from families for field trips, and so on. We did an intensive search, going back through court cases for six years, reviewing old media files, and interviewing insiders and outsiders. We found that corruption is almost unheard of in Edmonton Public. From 1984 to 2001, there are only four documented cases of low-level theft, mostly people who received money for their school but did not deposit it. Even common kinds of school fraud like phony overtime seem rare.

New York City and Los Angeles are still mired in huge, complex centralized offices. Because they are so complex, misbehavior is difficult to detect. As a result, the stealing, padded overtime payrolls, and hiring of friends and relatives who don't work are rampant. It's all laid out in the book *Battling Corruption in America's Public Schools: New York City, Los Angeles, and Chicago,* by Lydia Segal, to be published in 2003 by Northeastern University Press. In Los Angeles, our investigation found, the only positive feature of the accountability system is the strong Office of the Inspector General. Unfortunately, the central office treats Inspector General Don Mullinax like the enemy rather than an ally in improving the district (see *Daily News* editorial, November 3, 2000). The superintendent has made several attempts to control Mullinax and to cut his budget. So far, the unified voices of reform groups and of the press have helped Mullinax maintain his office's independence.

No one likes to focus on the negative, but it's important to pay attention to this issue: what independent party is watching the school officials to keep them honest? If the answer is no one, because the auditors report to the superintendent, or if there is no inspector general and no Office of Internal Audit, you should worry. Prudence requires that your district have *someone* who is independent of the superintendent and his or her staff to perform regular audits of each and every part of the district as well as having the power to investigate any potential wrongdoing. This person should also be able to investigate waste and inefficiency, not just criminal wrongdoing. People, being imperfect despite their many good features, need to know that someone is keeping tabs on the money.

3. POLITICAL ACCOUNTABILITY

Perhaps the most dramatic case of reforming a corrupt system through political means has taken place in Chicago. The 1995 school reform law gave central control over the budget and school board to Mayor Richard Daley. Before then, control rested in part in the local school councils, each of which had an elected board of parents and teachers. Chicago had become a system that existed to create protected union jobs rather than to educate children—as Terrence Brunner details in his *Report* of May 17, 1995 (Chicago: The Better Government Association). For example, the district had retained 1,100 union employees to maintain the district's coal furnaces—which had been eliminated years earlier. During the period 1990 through 1995, the construction office built only one new school. The 1995 reform law gave the mayor of Chicago and his appointed schools chief broad powers to make changes—including the privatization of many school jobs. Superintendent Paul Vallas told us that he laid off 25 percent of the central staff, did away with the warehouses such as the one that held 24,000 pieces of school furniture that had been completely forgotten, and sent out auditors to uncover waste—such as removing dead people from benefits programs.

Vallas decentralized purchasing, giving the $1 million annual purchasing budget to the typical large high school to manage for itself, for example. He established a watchdog payroll unit after several cases of payroll fraud were uncovered by the district's inspector general. Created in 1993, the Inspector General's Office today has thirty staff and broad powers to get any information that it wants. Along with a small office of internal auditors, the I.G. sets the tone in Chicago, which today has no tolerance for waste, fraud, or corruption.

Unfortunately, Chicago has not duplicated its administrative victories with equal success in improving student achievement. Although Vallas proved himself a dedicated reformer in rooting out waste and corruption, he did not stay long enough to build a management approach of the sort that has emerged in the truly great districts. The transfer of power in Chicago from the old elected school board to the new system—in which the mayor appoints the school board and thus appoints the superintendent—has yet to demonstrate that it can improve education.

It almost seems as though reform through a change of Political Accountability is primarily an emotional reaction that wells up from a disgusted public eager to try something, anything, so long as it's different. That seems to have been the case in New York City as much as in Chicago.

In 1969, as Diane Ravitch describes it in *The Great School Wars*, the New York State legislature passed the School Reform Law in an atmosphere of desperation and frustration.[2] New York City's schools had suffered racial wars pitting black parents against the mostly white teachers' union and school bureaucracy. The conflicts escalated to a devastating teachers' strike that threatened to tear the city apart. State lawmakers agreed to give inner-city minorities greater influence over the education of their elementary schoolchildren by putting the city's thirty-two Community School Districts under the control of elected school boards. The goal of the legislation was simply to avoid a race war.

The result left all parents, black and white alike, dismayed. The local school board elections were at the root of the problem. Investigators on our study team have reported in earlier publications that only 5.2 percent of eligible voters turned out for school board elections.[3] Some board members needed as few as 238 votes to get elected, and a determined board member could guarantee reelection based on the votes of people to whom he or she had given jobs. More than two decades of exposés by grand juries, investigators, civic watchdog groups, and journalists revealed that many of the local community boards used their vast reservoirs of money and jobs to become centers of power and patronage. These boards carved their districts into fiefdoms where jobs were doled out to loyal campaign workers, lovers, and family—or sold for cash. Teachers and principals were reduced to errand boys and girls for school board members.

Finally, in 1996 the state legislature undid its previous work by passing the Governance Act, which stripped the local boards of their control over jobs and budgets, and gave all power to the chancellor of the system. As investigative activities have been increased it appears that the previously rampant corruption has been reduced to a more tolerable level. In addition, and more interesting perhaps, New York City is attempting to move to a decentralized system of budgeting, so that parents, teachers, and principals can see exactly how much money is going to each school. The system, known as Galaxy, was developed by senior district executive Beverly Donohue, who was inspired by a visit in 1995 to the Edmonton Public Schools. In a strong step to reduce administrative waste, New York City mayor Michael Bloomberg and schools chancellor Joel Klein announced a plan in late 2002 to eliminate 2,000 central office jobs.

It's difficult to escape the conclusion that changing the form of Political Accountability in your schools isn't automatically the answer. Perhaps the new mayoral takeovers will work, but it's too soon to know. In some states, such as California and

Hawaii, the governor and legislature have long held almost total control over the schools of the entire state. These are the two states that rank dead last in student achievement.

It seems much more likely that aspirants to the office of mayor will continue to take political advantage of parents' frustration by promising during election time to fix the schools—and gaining control once elected! Mayor Bloomberg in New York City campaigned on improving the schools, and after winning the election he followed through on persuading the state government to give him that control. He then picked his own new superintendent, and the two of them seem to be determined to get the job done. Stay tuned.

As a parent, you need to be an astute political observer. You already know that passing control back and forth between the city and the state, or between the superintendent and the subsuperintendents or local boards, means nothing. Unless and until control gets all the way down to the individual, local schools—and the money, too, goes to the schools—nothing will be different.

6

Key #4: Everyone Delegates Authority to Those Below

*P*assing authority down the line to those below isn't good only for central office bureaucrats, it goes for everyone in the school system. Just as the board of education should not micromanage the superintendent, the superintendents who succeed do so by empowering their principals, and principals who succeed are good delegators. This rule of delegating authority and responsibility downwards might seem to be in conflict with the rule of accountability, but it isn't. As we'll see in this chapter, in the schools and school districts that are high performers, superintendents and principals do delegate authority down, but each principal and each teacher who is on the receiving end of that increased autonomy is tightly bound into a network. These networks are both horizontal—with peers—and vertical—with superiors and subordinates. Thus, no teacher or principal is isolated or abandoned. They do have lots of independence and freedom to act, but at the same time, they're part of a network that both checks them and supports them. When it works well, it's like a supportive family in which each person's individuality is respected, but no one is left alone.

Tom Hudnut is an energetic and robust man, the sort who seems to be everywhere, always on duty. When he addresses a group, he projects the powerful voice that he developed as a young opera singer many years ago, which, combined with his considerable height, makes him an imposing figure. Hudnut is headmaster of the Harvard-Westlake School in Los Angeles, arguably the top independent school in the Los Angeles area and one of the best schools in America. The school is the product of the merger of the former Harvard School, an all-boys school, named by its founders for their alma mater, and the formerly all-girls Westlake School.

The lore of independent schools is full of headmasters who were either benevolent despots or out-and-out tyrants. In the distant past, many private schools were owned by their headmasters, and many of these people indeed did rule the roost—often without a care for the opinions of anyone else. Tom Hudnut, though, has the kind of strength that doesn't require bossing other people around.

Each of us can call to mind at least one person we know who is or was a strong leader. That person may have been a success or a disaster, but he brooked no interference, issued orders freely, and had his way on virtually every issue. Many of the corporate chiefs whose companies are in trouble today fit that profile. They ignored shareholders, subordinates, and even their own boards of directors as they ran their companies into the ground.

That seems like strong leadership gone awry. It's actually weak leadership. It is true that a strong leader has an internal compass that gives her direction even when things are confusing and ambiguous to others. Tyrants would seem to have an internal compass with the needle stuck in one position. A strong leader is one who also encourages the people around her to take the initiative and to become strong, too. It's really a sign of weakness to fear the development of strength all around you.

The strong leader is not afraid of an argument or a tough situation. The strong leader wants to hear all sides of an argument and has enough self-confidence to openly admit when she's wrong on an issue. In a school, that translates into leadership that doesn't hide from teachers or order them around but instead invites them to participate and delegates decision making to them.

AT HARVARD-WESTLAKE SCHOOL, TEACHERS MAKE THE DECISIONS

> We are radically decentralized here. If you ask what percent of the budget Tom Hudnut controls—approximately zero. The people who are doing the work are the ones who are best qualified to make the decisions. If not, you've got the wrong people!
>
> —*Rob Levin, Chief Financial Officer, Harvard-Westlake*
> *School*

Don't judge a book by its cover. Tom Hudnut, as imposing a figure as there is in the field of education, is the kind of truly strong leader who lets teachers make the important decisions. That doesn't mean that he's not informed. If he has an opinion on an issue, he'll discuss it with the deans and teachers. If it's a policy issue with broad implications across the school, he'll be deeply involved in the decisions. But for most of the decisions most of the time, Tom Hudnut—like the other great principals in our study—leaves it to those who know the students best, and that's the teachers. Perhaps Hudnut trusts them because, like most other independent school heads, he teaches every year, too.

In order to maintain a small-school atmosphere in this large school of 1,556 students, Harvard-Westlake has two separate units, the middle and upper schools. Each is guided by a school head who has considerable autonomy. Much the same kind of organization is becoming common in public schools today. For example, the Austin Community Academy in Chicago is internally divided into five small academies. The Madison Middle School in Seattle is organized into teams of 150 students each, and Junior High School 216 in District 26 in New York City is internally organized into three autonomous academies. In each case, the result is a more intimate, human-scale school.

Within each unit at Harvard-Westlake, teachers enjoy the freedom to design their own courses, yet all are required to cover the same range of material. It is this balance of giving teachers their freedom while getting them to cooperate that makes for a successful school. In order to achieve these dual goals, the school gathers teachers together in weekly team meetings. Many public school teachers consider this kind of planning time to be a fantasy. If school boards would give more budgetary freedom to the schools, though, schools would find a way to allow teachers to work together this way.

Constant interaction among the teachers also helps to build a consensus on the school culture—as at Goudy Elementary in Chicago. That is critical because despite what many people think, schools like Harvard-Westlake are not made up exclusively of young geniuses. The secret formula that gets them into first-rate colleges is a wall-to-wall commitment to hard work. Again, Tom Hudnut: "A school like this is not a school for geniuses, necessarily, but it is a school that will reward hard work and sustained effort."

It's very difficult for any school to maintain a hard work atmosphere, and it's impossible if grade inflation is rampant. Harvard-Westlake sees to it that teachers maintain the integrity of the grading system: in upper school English courses, for example, only 26 percent of grades are A or A-, while 64 percent of grades are B+, B, or B-, and the remaining 10 percent are a C or lower. Only with mutual support and consistency of standards is this possible, and that means strong teams of teachers.

The result of this attention to teamwork balanced against

individual teacher freedom is nothing short of awesome. Out of last year's graduating class of 253 seniors, 122 were National Merit commended or higher. Out of 1,413 AP examinations last year (taken by sophomores, juniors, and seniors), 95 percent received a score of 3 or higher.

IN GREAT SCHOOLS—LIKE BREARLEY IN NEW YORK CITY—NO TEACHER IS AN ISLAND

Another exemplary independent school is an all-girls school, K–12, on the Upper East Side of Manhattan. The Brearley School, established in 1884, received 467 applications for 50 openings in last year's kindergarten. It only had to offer fifty-six acceptances to fill the class. The student body is a diverse mixture of the rich, the middle class, and the working class. Twenty-three percent are students of color. More than half of the girls remain for the entire thirteen years. Under headmistress Dr. Patricia Winn Barlow (a zoologist by training), the school has a very comfortable and friendly, though high-energy feeling. Many families in New York City treat their Brearley interview as one of the most important meetings of their lives. Perhaps that's because the seniors in 2001 had average SAT scores of 750 Verbal and 710 Math.

The 130 teachers at Brearley provide very small classes for the 676 girls. By comparison, New York City Intermediate School 125 in Woodside, Queens, has 135 teachers for 1,867 students. An upper-grade English teacher at Brearley will have fifty-five students on the average, which means teaching four classes of thirteen or fourteen students each. Despite its reputation and desirability, though, Brearley doesn't have money to burn. The endowment, for example, yields a spendable $3 million per year, of which $2.5 million goes to scholarships. Although the abundance of the teaching resources is striking, the way Brearley is organized is really the most interesting feature of the school, and the one that your school can learn from.

Teachers at Brearley have a unique team approach. Their goal is to take advantage of the fact that the school goes from kindergarten to twelfth grade by producing a truly integrated curriculum. Clay Squire, for example, teaches ninth-grade biology at Brearley. He also teaches grades 8, 10, 11, and 12. In his five years at Brearley, he has taught biology to kindergarteners and fifth graders. As a result, he and the other biology teachers are able to lead their students through a multiyear learning experience of great depth that leaves them exceptionally well prepared for college courses, not to mention SAT tests. It's the biology teachers who do the planning, select the books, and take responsibility for the performance of their students, not a central office person who taught biology twenty years ago. The planning is so finely honed that it could only be done by the teachers who are on the line, doing the job.

The school is organized into three divisions: lower school is grades K–4; middle school is 5–8; and upper school is grades 9–12. Gail Marcus, who teaches seventh-grade history, says that everyone teaches in at least two of the three divisions, and some teach in all three. Ms. Marcus loves the variety of teaching that she has, and she feels that the students benefit greatly from this approach. When a student asks a question, she can refer to what they learned in an earlier grade to help them get the point.

First graders have language arts for forty minutes each day. They begin by being read to out loud by the teacher. The homeroom teacher and an assistant teacher (usually fresh out of college) are joined by three reading specialists, and they divide the twenty-four students into small groups for reading instruction. One reason for the small groups will surprise you: the school tries to prevent competition and social comparison between the young girls. In a class of twenty-five, it will be clear that some are already reading, while others aren't yet ready. The teachers know that every girl will read when she is ready, but they don't want some to get the incorrect idea that they are smarter, nor others to get the idea that they aren't smart.

All of the special courses at Brearley—art, science, PE, music, gymnastics, dance, and so on—are taught by teachers who teach their subject in all grades K–12. Again, the vertical teams, combined with the horizontal teams that meet each week at each grade level, create a densely knitted fabric. No teacher is an island. No student is a faceless number. Not only that, but the students are being taught by people who are true experts in their subjects and who know how to make the lessons both enjoyable and challenging.

The result of all this is a school that has an intensely intellectual flavor along with an informal, active style. The girls literally run up and down the staircases between classes, each with a shoulder bag or briefcase. Their hair tends to be in a ponytail and makeup is nowhere to be seen. Let's not miss the forest for the trees, either. Brearley is a school for girls only. While that choice is not for everyone, shouldn't there be at least some public schools in your city that are only for boys, and others only for girls? Why not give families a real choice when it comes to schools?

Brearley may cause some to feel admiration and others to feel envy. Whatever you might feel about the school, though, it does an outstanding job for its students. Brearley and Harvard-Westlake illustrate what is possible not only when resources are abundant but when teachers and principals know what to do with their resources. Their lesson is that the very best schools with the most money use their resources chiefly to enable teachers to plan and to integrate their efforts, both vertically and horizontally. What's visible to outsiders is the small class sizes, but what really matters on the inside is this integration. It's a lesson from which we all can learn.

DISTRICT 2 IN NEW YORK CITY MIGHT HAVE THE BEST TEACHERS IN AMERICA

District 2 is one of the thirty-two former local Community School Districts in the New York City Department of Education.

(In 2002, the districts were reorganized and the Board of Education became the Department of Education—a city agency that, like other agencies, reports to the mayor.) Under superintendent Dr. Shelley Harwayne, District 2 is made up of twenty-six elementary schools, ten middle schools, and four high schools. Because District 2 covers much of the island of Manhattan, including some very high income areas, the schools receive relatively few "categorical" funds and average only $8,775 per student, the lowest in the city except for District 26, which is in a middle- and upper-middle-class section of Queens.

Dr. Harwayne makes it clear that her number one priority is teaching. She says that she could step into any classroom in her district and be one of the better teachers in that school—and that most of her principals could step into her job and do it as well as she. When she hires a new principal, she first has the five finalists all gather at one school and has them observe each of five classes in session, along with the selection committee. She then takes them out one by one and asks them, "What did you see? What would you design by way of professional development if the entire school were like that class? How would you live your life as principal to improve those classes?" The responses will be very different and very revealing. She makes the sensible point that you can't be hired as a principal if you don't know instruction. All school districts say that their principals are instructional leaders, but it can't really be their expectation, because they don't even attempt to choose proven teachers as principals. Instead, most districts pick principals who are good at politics and bureaucracy.

On January 17, 2002, Shelley Harwayne gathered sixty-two principals and assistant principals in a borrowed meeting room at New York University in Greenwich Village. It is the monthly Principals' Conference, and it is unlike any other such conference in New York City or, most likely, the United States. Dr. Harwayne starts the morning by reading a poem in honor of two principals who have just gotten married. Eight other people take the microphone to read poems of congratulations, and a quartet of principals sings a Beatles song with customized lyrics. It becomes clear that these are not subordinates dutifully attending a dreaded monthly dressing-down, but a community of educators who enjoy being part of a winning team.

The remainder of the day is devoted to a discussion of the teaching of mathematics in grades K–12. The National Science Foundation has sponsored a big effort to bring the best minds together, and their advice on how to teach math has been reviewed by the District 2 math development staff and found to be valuable. All of the attendees read a brief article from the Center for the Development of Teaching in Massachusetts, and then discuss its implications. The central idea is that to teach math effectively, a teacher must first understand the worldview that the child brings to the study of mathematics, and then help the child to connect that view to mathematics and end up with an intuitive grasp of the subject. It's a demanding way to teach that asks a lot of the teacher.

Each principal and assistant principal works through a set of math problems, for example, using six different methods to subtract 38 from 53. During the discussion, the participants observe that subtraction can be taught through logic, by rote, or through a variety of algebraic routes. Each method has its merits, and each will get through to a different student effectively. A master teacher will have several of these arrows in her quiver.

The guts of the discussion is about how a teacher can handle this kind of instruction in class, and—more to the point— how each principal can help their teachers to learn several approaches. The big challenge will be with those teachers who are convinced that their old way of teaching math is best.

Even after this session is officially over, the participants remain seated in intense discussions. One assistant principal suggests that because every child in grades 3–8 is tested by the city or the state in math each year, you can sit down with each teacher, show her how much progress her students have made in a year, and make the point that how you teach them math is the key. Any parent of a child in a District 2 school would feel great knowing that these principals are so engrossed in the subject.

District 2 believes that the way to improve student achievement is to improve the quality of teaching. It's a lesson instilled by former superintendent Anthony Alvarado, who then attempted to instill those values in the teachers of the San Diego school district. (On February 5, 2003, the San Diego *Union-Tribune* reported that Alvarado would be leaving the district at the end of the school year.) And the district believes that the only tool that is available to improve teaching is continuing education, the professional development of teachers. As a result, District 2 uses its discretionary money on teacher development. It has twenty math developers, all successful, respected teachers, for example, who work with the teachers in the forty schools. The staff development specialists spend Monday through Thursday working in the schools, and they meet as a team every Friday to plan. A team of literacy specialists, many of whom are from Australia or New Zealand, has developed successful approaches to literacy. You get the feeling that District 2 would go to Mars to find experts on teacher development if they thought that the Martians had found a better way!

The principals go off for lunch in groups or four and five at their own expense. Most of the principals are women, and they table-hop at lunch, visiting with old friends. A principal will come by a table to chat and will compliment another by saying: "You look great. Look at your skin—you look like a teenager!" Believe me, you don't hear that kind of banter at a lunch at IBM or J.P. Morgan Chase.

After lunch, the small group discussions continue. One principal describes a teacher who is terrified that if she tries a new approach and fails, it may harm her students for a long time to come. The principals discuss different strategies that will allow her to relax and develop some confidence. One solution is to find a way to pull her out of her class and let her observe several teachers who have experience with different methods. The principals are expert diagnosticians, and all are focused on their ultimate objective—helping the students to master math.

The principals all worry that when a young child struggles with math, she won't think that the teacher isn't doing it correctly. Instead, she'll think that she can't do the math, that she isn't smart, that school isn't for her. This is a tragedy to be avoided at all costs.

District 2 offers choice and variety for its families. Fourteen years ago, then-Superintendent Alvarado started the program, which now includes four high schools as well as some middle and elementary schools. Ninety-five percent of the students who apply for admission get their first choice of schools, which have some leeway in selecting their students. The principals compare notes, and there's lots to compare, because each school has nearly total freedom and as a result, each is unique. The Upper Lab School, grades 6–12, is for students with very high test scores, while the Museum School, grades 9–12, has a close affiliation with several of the major art museums in Manhattan.

Anthony Alvarado was a collector of star talent, and he brought in a group of very bright and talented people as principals. When he ran out of those, he took very bright teachers and made *them* principals. He also chose only people who were totally absorbed by instruction. Since Alvarado arrived in the 1980s, District 2 has risen from the seventh ranked district in New York City in reading to second. (Number one is District 26, a relatively wealthy district that borders some upper-income suburbs of Long Island.)

Unlike the other community districts in New York City, District 2 is extremely decentralized, and principals have control over most of their budget money. Also unlike other districts almost anywhere, District 2 works hard to bring the principals together as a team. In turn, each principal sees to it that his or her teachers coalesce into a team. And finally, the staff developers from Dr. Harwayne's office reach out to all of the teachers by departmental specialty and thus knit all of the teachers in the district into another set of teams, each one districtwide. It's an overlapping matrix that provides strength, consistency, and integrity to the district. It's difficult for anyone to hide, and all understand expectations for their performance.

The final topic of the day is how to help at-risk students. There is consensus that getting parents involved helps a lot, and several principals describe their innovative ways of building parental involvement. One principal has specially trained her librarian, who runs a monthly Saturday session for parents that covers what is being taught in each grade and how it is being taught. Every other Friday, the parents are invited to sit in on their child's class. The school has found that when parents see their own child describing to the class how to solve a math problem, owning the knowledge and making it theirs, that has a fantastic effect; the support at home goes way up. The school had no money for a librarian, so the principal got a federal grant for half of it and then another grant to pay for half of an art teacher. She already had an art teacher, so she used the saved art teacher's salary to pay for the other half of the librarian. It's the small details in each school that add up to the big gains for children.

Another principal has developed a spreadsheet on which she has listed every teacher and under each teacher a list of the at-risk and special needs students in that class. Across the top of the spreadsheet are listed all of the special services that a student might receive, such as pullout math, pullout reading, resource room, reading recovery, occupational therapy, speech class, extended day, and so on. Once each month, each of these students is tested for their literacy level, and then the team of teachers meets as a group to determine which children need additional services. Good schools run on good data, not by the seat of their pants.

IN DISTRICT 2, THE VERTICAL AND HORIZONTAL TEAMS INCLUDE ALL FORTY SCHOOLS

District 2 teachers do things a certain way. For example, teachers here do not use textbooks. They are expected to put together their own materials and to share those materials with other teachers. The idea is to assemble whatever will work best for the specific group of students in each school, not to use a one-size-fits-all textbook.

One of the key things that is supposed to be done a certain way in District 2 is the teaching of literacy, about which teachers and principals have strong feelings. Take, for instance, Principal Daria Rigney at P.S./I.S. 126, on the edge of Chinatown. Ms. Rigney's office looks more like a library than an office. In fact, virtually every classroom in District 2 looks like a library. Every student is encouraged to read all of the time. At P.S./I.S. 126, though, where 68 percent of the students qualify for free lunch, reading does not come naturally to all of the students:

> For most kids (but not ours) reading is not an issue. Learning how to read happens fairly naturally. They've had five, six, or seven years of rich conversation—we call it "lap talk." They get marinated in book language, they've had books read to them, they pretended to read books, they memorized books, they've been immersed in literacy and storytelling.
>
> They come to our school and our teachers are under this incredible pressure to get them reading but unfortunately they don't have what kids need—which is 1,000 books read to them.

To continuously develop their skills at teaching literacy, the teachers in kindergarten through second grade at P.S./I.S. 126 work with a staff developer three days a week—one among the many who regularly come to the school, and with whom teachers work as a team and as individuals.

At P.S. 77, the Lower Laboratory School for the Gifted, K–5, Principal Elizabeth Kasowitz sounds a consistent note:

> Reading to children is the most important thing a parent can do. My husband read to our daughter every single night until she went to college. She calls from college and says, "Daddy, thank you." I tell that story to parents and I can't emphasize it enough.
>
> Our classrooms are libraries. Each classroom has a library with lots of books.

Principal Kasowitz learned from her teachers to let the children arrange the books in their classrooms—some do it by author, others by subject or by level of difficulty. They want the children to take responsibility for making the classroom their own. Everywhere in District 2, though, it's books, books, and more books. Every child and every parent gets the message.

District 2 classrooms also tend to have a similar look. Most of the furniture in the elementary and middle schools has been removed from the room. District 2 teachers feel that without furniture, the children can access the materials and other students more easily. Without desks, the children leave their little personal piles of books on the rug when they leave the room.

In the fifth grade, students in District 2 are expected to read at least twenty-five books each. By the end of the year they should be able to go into a library and pick a book that is appropriate for them. The teachers, working with their staff developers, have formed a strong consensus on that standard. Because all of the teachers share in the consensus, no teacher has to worry that what she asks of her students is unreachable or unrealistic, and thus students and parents accept the standard, too.

The East Side Middle School, grades 6–8, engages each student as a whole person through its program of advisories. Principal Elizabeth Saplin takes an advisory, which meets for half an hour once each week. Her goal is to create an opportunity for students to develop a trusting relationship with a teacher. If the children feel emotionally and physically safe, she believes, everything becomes possible for them.

East Side Middle School is considered by Manhattan residents to be one of the best. It gets the highest rating, five stars for both reading and math scores, in Clara Hemphill's book, *Public Middle Schools: New York City's Best.*[1] Located at 77th and York on the Upper East Side, only 10 percent of the students qualify for free or reduced-price lunch. East Side receives more than 400 applications each year for the 135 places in the sixth grade. To be considered, an applicant must have a score of at least 660 (out of approximately 800) on the standardized tests that all fifth graders take. The four hundred finalists visit the school in groups of forty-five, where they write answers to math and English questions and are interviewed by a team of teachers.

The classrooms have large rugs with little piles of books here and there. But that's not the key similarity between East Side and the other schools in District 2. The more fundamental similarity is threefold: first, everyone, from Superintendent Shelley Harwayne on down, delegates. Principals delegate responsibility to teachers, and teachers expect students to take responsibility for their own education. Second, District 2 is one big team. Third, there is an intense intellectualism to everything that happens—from the way that reading is taught, to the opposition to the use of textbooks, to the open-space classrooms. If you'd like to learn more about the history and the strategy of District 2, you can find it in *It Takes a City,* by Paul Hill and his co-authors.[2]

Even in top-down, command-and-control New York City, it's possible to create an educational oasis where local schools have budget autonomy, principals are expected to be entrepreneurs, and teachers have decision-making power. Perhaps that's because the parents in District 2 include high-powered executives and professional people who have clout. If it's that easy, then all you have to do is organize your fellow parents so that you'll have clout, too. You don't need money and power. To have clout you need to be organized. (People who are already on top don't need clout because they have raw power!)

What is especially impressive about District 2, Brearley, and Harvard-Westlake is that all of them treat students, teachers, and principals with respect. All have achieved their status by looking after the minute details of education that make all of the difference. They do that because they are willing to trust teachers to make these decisions, because the decisions are based on good data about students, and because no teacher is an island—all of them are part of one, big team.

One final surprise—although perhaps you've anticipated this quote from Superintendent Dr. Shelley Harwayne: "Everyone from District 2 has been to Edmonton." She doesn't mean that every teacher and principal has made the pilgrimage to this fountainhead of innovation, but the influence of the Edmonton approach is so widespread in District 2 that it seems that way.

7

Key #5: There Is a Burning Focus on Student Achievement

Some educators would say that this should be Key to Success #1. If your school implemented all of the other six keys to success but left this one out, you'd have a smoothly running school system, but you still wouldn't have successful students. How can you transform your school system so that everyone has the same burning drive for student achievement? In short, you have to have regular measurements of student progress—good data from standardized tests. Then, you must use that data so that teachers know just what kind of help each student needs, and principals know whether each teacher is delivering that help with good results. Superintendents need to know which principals are managing this process well, and which ones aren't. It all begins, though, with good data on students.

If there is one topic about education that gets people hot under the collar, it's testing.[1] For now, at least, the issue has been settled at least in one major respect. A new federal law, the No Child Left Behind Act, requires that each state must test children each year using any standardized test that meets certain broad criteria. There was a great deal of controversy over this requirement, but in the end, what carried the day was the idea that parents have a right to be informed about how their children are doing.

You may remember that the issue surfaced twenty years ago in Texas, when a citizen group headed by computer magnate H. Ross Perot managed to put in the requirement that high school athletes have a passing grade point average before they could participate in varsity athletics. There was widespread feeling that parents had become so enthusiastic about sports, especially high school football, that they had harassed high schools in Texas into caring more about sports than about academic subjects. Today, the Texas revolution has traveled with President George W. Bush all the way to White House, and it's now national policy that we should all focus on academic achievement.

The physical health and development of children is important—at least as important as their intellectual development. But it's not more important than other areas of development for children. Why, then, had we as a nation come to focus so on athletics and not on academics?

One answer—the one that I think is correct—is that we focused on sports because we could see the games with our own eyes, and we could very clearly see exactly how our team was performing. It's the same way with the long-running game shows on television like *Wheel of Fortune* and *Jeopardy!* Both the spectators and the players would lose interest pretty quickly if they couldn't see the score—and most of us have a very difficult time seeing the student achievement score in academics. Oh, we can see our child's report card, all right. But all of us know that the grades from a strict teacher aren't the same as the grades from an easy one. With grade inflation being rampant, we aren't even sure that grades mean much at all. For example, we know that an A student at a demanding school will get into the four-year college of his choice, but that an A student at a less demanding school might not.

One result of the unreliable grading is that schools across the nation have a ninth-grade buildup. Teachers give passing grades up through grade 8, but in the ninth grade, students run into high school teachers who are teaching courses instead of students. A lot of the children who received passing marks earlier really shouldn't have, and thus they are held back—with the result that the ninth grades have abnormally large numbers of students. That makes all of us skeptical about the meaning of grades, and leaves us feeling that we weren't knowledgeable about our children's academic performance. In fact, many people don't really find out how their child is doing in school until the child takes the SATs in eleventh grade—when it's too late to start working harder to get into college.

Not everyone is in favor of more standardized testing, though. One major criticism is that there isn't too little testing of students but too much. In Los Angeles, one principal calculated that there are so many different required tests that some students have only 119 days of actual education per year, rather than the official 163 days. Another criticism is that too much emphasis on a major test will put so much pressure on the teachers to produce high student scores that the teachers will "teach to the test" and produce children who really don't know anything but the narrow subjects that are tested.

Here's the key issue, though: we agree that good schools should have, and that all great schools already have, a burning, red-hot focus on student achievement. Does that mean that they use more tests or different tests than everyone else? What does it really mean, anyway, for a school to have a passionate focus on student achievement?

A good school does make use of several different kinds of tests, but it's what it does with the test scores that makes that school successful. A score on a standardized test is just one kind of information about the student, but there are others, some even more important. In addition to good information—data, as it's called in schools—a good school responds to high or low test scores. It's like the radar in an airplane—the pilot not only needs the information about where the stormy weather is, he or she has to use that information to alter course. Finally, a good school has a consistent approach to children across teachers, subjects, and grade levels. Good data on students; a method of responding to the information; and consistency of response—these are the three elements of a sound focus on student achievement.

WHAT IT MEANS TO HAVE GOOD DATA ON STUDENT ACHIEVEMENT

> Ninety-six percent of our grades 1–3 are reading at or above grade level, but only 76 percent of them had one year of growth last year. Why? We did an analysis and found that some second graders are coming into grade 3 already reading, and the programming by the teachers wasn't allowing them to soar.
>
> —*Scott Miller, Principal, Ellerslie Campus,*
> *Edmonton Public*

In New York City's District 2, some principals keep a spreadsheet that shows them the monthly reading test scores for every child who is considered at risk of falling behind and for every student who has been identified as having special needs. There is a regular, formal testing program and a method of using the information to see that all children get whatever help they need. At Baruch College Campus, the faculty advisor for each group of students is required to talk to all of the other teachers for their student advisees and be well informed of how the student is doing across the board. These are two different methods of gathering data on each student, and both of them work well. One of your duties as a parent is to ask what methods your child's school uses to gather data on the performance of each student. If the school can't give you a clear answer, the odds are that they don't have a clear method.

Neither Baruch nor District 2 relies on the standardized tests used by all schools in New York City. District 2 and Baruch students take those tests, too, but not to diagnose the progress and the needs of each student. Their real purpose is to hold the superintendent and the principal accountable for the performance of hundreds or thousands of students. That's very important to know, but you also want to know—and you want the school to know—how much progress your individual child is making.

If the Ellerslie Campus were to rely solely on the standardized tests, for example, it would know only that last year, 96 percent of the students in grades 1–3 were reading at or above grade level. The school would have a high rating compared to other schools in the district, the principal would trumpet the high scores widely to the parents, and everyone would be content. That would be a mistake, though, because if a school starts out with children who are already at or above grade level, some students can slip backwards a little bit and the school will still have great overall reading scores.

If your school is in a well-to-do suburban area, you probably take some satisfaction in reading each year that 90 percent or more of the children are at or above grade level and that the school has one of the top rankings in the district. That's nice, but it isn't the whole story. You also want to know whether your child, and the other children in the school, made a whole year's progress—or more—in one year's time. If they made *less,* then you need to worry about your child's study habits. If many of the children also failed to make good progress in a year, you need to worry about what the school is doing to all of its children. In your suburban school, most of the children probably came to kindergarten having had 1,000 books read to them. You've done your part, and now you want the school to take it from there and let your child soar.

THE CORNELIUS SCIENCE ACADEMY USES GOOD DATA OF ITS OWN TO GET GREAT RESULTS

They're soaring at the Cornelius Science Academy, pre-K through 5, a public school located in a blue-collar neighborhood of Houston. The building has a planned capacity of 650 students, but 1,070 have flocked to Cornelius, with another 250 on the waiting list. Sixty percent of the students at Cornelius are Hispanic, and 35 percent are African-American. Eighty percent of them qualify for free or reduced-price lunch; 470 of the children are classified as having limited English proficiency; many of the students are from single-parent homes.

As Mike Strembitsky says, parents don't keep their best kids at home, and these are clearly more than good enough. Student scores on the state achievement test are out of this world: in the fifth grade, for example, average scores on the state test are in the 99th percentile in both reading and math. Daily attendance is 96 percent, and only one half of 1 percent transfer out of the school at the end of a year.

Walking into the office of Principal Rhelda Ball, one immediately notices one thing. She's been the principal for fifteen years, and it is clear that Rhelda Ball is not afraid to be different. Her walls and easy chair are covered with a distinctive tartan plaid fabric, there are pictures and drawings of and by students everywhere, and a dish of wrapped hard candies sits on the corner of her desk.

It is October 8, 2001. At 7:45 A.M., a young student steps to the microphone in the office and reads an essay on Christopher Columbus over the public address system. Ms. Ball then steps to the mike and talks to the entire school in reassuring tones about U.S. airplanes that had started the attack in Afghanistan on the Taliban and Osama bin Laden. Her final closing message: "We're all safe here at school, and we have lots to do today. Okay, we just have one shot at October 8, 2001. Let's give it our personal best today!"

Although Cornelius is a magnet school, it does not test or select its students based on their past academic performance. It's a first-come, first-served school. "Why have we succeeded? We have an absolute, everyday focus on academics. That's what we do here." Principal Ball goes on to emphasize that focus means avoiding distractions: "My approach is not exactly orthodox in the district. I put a lot of requests in the trash. We don't do photo ops with politicians, nor cultural events—we have school."

The foundation of this focus on academics is the knowledge of where each student stands, gained by testing them frequently. The principal explains the system of testing, which is in addition to the eight days per year that are devoted to the required state tests, the TASS and the SAT 9:

> The teachers work in grade-level teams, and I meet with each team twice a month. We do an "inventory test" in math and reading at each grade level twice each month. We do these at grades 1 through 5, although the TASS is only 3–5. The inventory tests are about one hour, plus the fourth graders have one in writing. We make up the tests ourselves—we think the other tests are too easy.

One result is that both teachers and students know just where they stand, and they can see their scores. Having honest, reliable feedback is almost always motivating to people, and it works here. Another result is that the school exudes a sense of academic intensity, of focus, and of pride. Everyone adheres to the dress code: red, white, or blue polo shirt with khaki or navy blue pants, skirts, or shorts. In the hallways, the children are in orderly lines. Principal Ball, though, gets smiles, waves, and hugs from them as she passes by.

When visitors enter Ms. Reece's first-grade class, the twenty-one students stay on task. Not one looks up to see who the visitors might be. The same goes for Ms. Johnson-Page's twenty-three second graders. Although Cornelius has only 61 teachers for its 1,070 students, it doesn't seem to Principal Ball that she needs more. Starting this year, she has full freedom to allocate her budget, and next year, she looks forward to getting control over her budget for utilities such as electricity and telephone, where she expects to be able to make some real savings that can be used elsewhere. Here's her reaction to the new implementation of Weighted Student Formula in Houston: "I feel we have enough money to run a small country here. Sometimes we have to have meetings to think of things to spend it on."

Please don't tell Superintendent Dr. Kaye Stripling!

RIDEAU PARK SCHOOL RESPONDS TO STUDENTS AS INDIVIDUALS—BASED ON DATA

Rideau Park is a solidly middle-class neighborhood of Edmonton. On a large poster in the front hallway the test results on the Alberta Achievement Test are displayed for all to see. The poster shows that in the third-grade language test, for example, 98 percent of students scored "acceptable" and 32 percent were "excellent"—which means that they correctly answered 90 percent or more of the test questions. In math, 100 percent were acceptable and 57 percent were excellent. Results like these would make any parent happy. As we've learned, though, it's not only the averages that matter, it's knowing where each individual student stands that makes the difference.

Liz Warman, the principal, has been an educator for thirty-four years, and she knows the craft of teaching inside and out. She's a fan of standardized tests. Her reason is not just that she likes to keep score; she has found that standardized tests can get teachers to think about why other schools with similar students have better results: "It used to be that classroom practice was inconsistent. I think that standardized tests have changed that."

Every year in February, the teachers plan the curriculum changes that will take effect the following autumn. The first step is a close analysis of the student results on the Alberta Achievement Test. Principal Warman looks at each question at each grade level to identify the areas that need improvement. The Alberta Achievement Test provides detailed subscores that are meant to be used for just this kind of diagnostic work. The third-grade language arts test, for example, provides subscores for such topics as correct identification of ideas and details on both informational and narrative passages. The writing sample provides subscores for the organization of the written work as well as for sentence structure, vocabulary, and proper use of conventions. The math, science, and social studies tests provide similar detail.

Mrs. Warman prepares a detailed analysis by grade level and subject matter and identifies the areas of weakness. She then gathers the teachers together and asks them, "What are you going to do about it in your grade?" The teachers form a team to come up with an action plan. Every plan is summarized on one page, and each one has the same elements:

1. Their strategy for addressing the need
2. The resources necessary
3. The measurements they will use for assessment
4. Projected completion date

In the early years, Warman asked the teachers to perform the analysis of the test results themselves, but data analysis just wasn't their cup of tea. Now, she does the analysis, and the teachers come up with the plan. The plan is implemented the following year, supported by the budget allocations—all of it done locally, without the need for permission from anyone above.

Fine-tuning the curriculum turns out to be as much art as it is science, though, and there are always surprises: "One year we worked on sentence structure and content scores went down. Then we worked on content, and vocabulary went down!" Curriculum, teacher training, and budget are intimately connected at Rideau Park School. For example, the teachers decided on a balanced literacy approach that combines phonics training with whole language—much like they did in District 2—and the school spent $1,200 per teacher for training. Warman can't come up with this kind of money and paint or recarpet her whole school in one year, so she paints one classroom per year and changes one carpet per year. A central office planner might find that an awfully inefficient way to get a school painted, but Edmonton Public has such a small central office staff that there aren't any bureaucrats who have time to sit around and question things like that.

Now, here comes the really innovative and impressive part of Rideau Park School: *every student who tests below grade level has an individual program.* All Alberta students take a second standardized test, the Highest Level of Achievement Test (HLAT). The HLAT provides a different type of score than the Alberta test. It places each student's score on, above, or below where they should be for their grade level. If a fourth grader receives a math score of 4.2, for example, it means that the student is above grade level. A score of 4.0 would be exactly at grade level.

In all public schools in the United States and Canada, a student who is identified through evaluations as a special needs or special education student must have an Individualized Education Plan, or IEP. In Canada, it's called an IPP, or Individualized Program Plan. However, Rideau Park Elementary also prepares an IPP for every one of the fifty students who test below grade level on the HLAT. The school focuses on those children who have fallen slightly behind and gives them special attention so that they won't fall farther—and perhaps become dropouts one day. Parents must sign the plan, and each such student then goes to special classes, has tutoring, and gets whatever help he needs to get back on track.

You'll surely want to find out what your school is doing to identify weaknesses in its program and to remedy those weaknesses, including how it identifies and assists students who are in danger of falling behind. Once the principal and teachers in your school realize that you know what questions to ask—again, politely—they'll come up with answers for you. If you don't ask, though, they're likely to continue business as usual, with the same results as before. Children aren't able to look out for their own interests—that's what parents are for.

PERSHING MIDDLE SCHOOL—CONSISTENCY OF RESPONSE ON A LARGE SCALE

Pershing Middle School, located near the gigantic Houston Medical Center in the heart of the metropolitan area, is mammoth. With 1,903 students in grades 6 through 8, it's nearly six times the size of Rideau Park Elementary. Given the reputation of middle school as the most difficult setting of all—due to the raging hormones and strident independence of students at that age—a large middle school is a frightening prospect. But Pershing is anything but a chaotic warehouse for children—it's a school in which the adults know every child. It achieves an intimate scale by clustering students in groups of 150. Grade 6, for example, is made up of four clusters of 150 students each, and the same holds for grades 7 and 8. Each cluster has a team of teachers assigned to it who cover the core subjects and who get to know their 150 students and their families well. Each team meets every day to identify the students who need special attention for any reason, and each cluster leader has a telephone in her classroom so that parents can contact her easily. This pattern of smaller academies within the large school is becoming increasingly common in the United States. It gives students the best of two worlds: they can have the specialized programs like dance, jazz band, orchestra, football, swim team, and turbocharged classes in math, English, and other academic subjects, in the midst of small-scale intimacy.

The captain of this aircraft carrier–class school is Principal Joel Willen. Willen is an entrepreneur. According to him, "The culture of the school is—we all work hard, and we want the best for the kids. We will all do what is necessary to get the job done." He is also a man in a hurry, as entrepreneurs tend to be: "The real frustration for me, because I'm a doer, is when I can't get an answer from the bureaucracy. So I tend to just do it, and deal with the consequences later." In the revolutionized Houston Independent School District (HISD), though, principals count, and Willen has power: "The title 'Principal' carries a lot of power in the central office. One of the first things I was told was, when you call the central office—don't just identify yourself as Joel Willen. Identify yourself as Joel Willen, the principal of Pershing School. I think that where HISD is going is like Edmonton—giving the principals total control."

The results show that Principal Willen and his team are doing something right: Pershing's enrollment in this free-choice district has grown in five years from 1,610 to 1,903. The percentage of students passing the state test has gone up in seven years from 67 percent to 93 percent. Over that period, the percentage of African-American students passing all parts of the test has shot up from 47 percent to 84 percent. Hispanic students have made equally dramatic gains at Pershing, going from 37 percent to 79 percent passing. Many Pershing students move on to the two most elite public high schools in Houston, Bellaire and Lamar. How is Pershing doing it?

Out of the 1,903 students, 405 are part of the fine arts magnet program. This year, 1,100 students applied for the 140 openings. The applicants come to the school to audition for a panel of teachers, which makes the admissions decisions. The fine arts students are not segregated but are mixed in with the other children, although they may take some fine arts classes that are out of their cluster. That's the pattern in this school. A very diverse set of students is mixed together in a cluster, while a highly organized and complex web of adults keeps track of each student.

Another source of diversity at Pershing Middle School is the mix of races: 38 percent are white, 28 percent African-American, 24 percent Hispanic, and 10 percent Asian, and each cluster mirrors the racial mix of the school as a whole. Thirty-three percent of the students qualify for the free lunch program, and 18 percent are identified as gifted-and-talented. These students, too, are part of the rich mix within each cluster.

Given its dual goals of honoring diversity and meeting the educational needs of each student, Pershing has a complex planning issue to solve. It must preserve the diversity of race, level of educational attainment, and area of interest in each cluster while offering courses for each of the specialized groups of students—for example, for fine arts or gifted-and-talented. The gifted-and-talented students participate with their fellow cluster students in some courses and join the gifted-and-talented students from other clusters in courses such as advanced math. Students in the fine arts magnet program receive similar scheduling, so that each specialty program maintains its sense of identity without being so separate that the clusters lose their ability to integrate all students into one community. To manage this task, Pershing makes unusually good use of the Houston district's information technology.

In years past, teachers would spend the first few weeks of the year analyzing test scores, identifying each student's strengths and weakness, and attempting to put all of this into one schedule of courses. The alternative, of course, would have been to give all students the same coursework, as though they were so many gingerbread men. In Houston, where families have a choice, that would have resulted in an empty school building with no students.

Today, teaching teams at Pershing go online to access the district-created intranet database known as PASS (Profiler for the Academic Success of Students), which contains all of the test score, attendance, and demographic data for each student. Administrators use it to determine how many sections to offer of regular, pre-AP, or pre–AP/GT (gifted-and-talented) courses—the highest level. Teachers use it to design the pace and content of their courses, based on the profile of their specific students. The district central office system uses a combination of grades, test scores, and teacher recommendations to place each student at Pershing. After they've enrolled, though, teachers and counselors work with the students and their parents to fine-tune their placement.

One of the inputs to the database in PASS is the STAR program, a computerized diagnostic reading test that determines each student's reading level. According to information in the school's application for the 2001–02 Blue Ribbon Schools program, each student selects his or her own books from a specially designed series and undertakes a self-paced reading program for course credit throughout the year. Students regularly visit any of the school's network computers after completing a book, take a multiple-choice test, and the computer system scores the test and records their progress.

Teachers may also assign students to make use of two additional computer-based instructional systems, Skills Bank and Scholastic Network. These two instructional packages give students additional support in the core academic subjects. Both are available in the three computer labs on campus.

One of the activities that unifies the school and reminds everyone of the importance of academics is DEAR: Drop Everything And Read. Every other day, all students and teachers drop everything and read for forty-five minutes. DEAR is followed by forty-five minutes of enrichment or tutorials, depending on the academic needs of the individual student. DEAR is the academic equivalent of watching the Super Bowl on television—there's a special feeling of community that comes from knowing that everyone is doing the same thing at the same time.

Teachers are not only members of a cluster team, they are members of an academic department in which the entire planning and coordinating process goes on. For example, the math and science teachers at Pershing participate in a teacher training initiative of the National Science Foundation, which aims to improve the level of instruction in K–12 schools. The goals of the program are to motivate more children to study math and science, to engage parents in this process in a meaningful way, and to improve the content knowledge as well as the classroom skill of math and science teachers. The entire math department of Pershing meets for an hour and a half each week to share "best practices" and to plan together.

Grades are given at Pershing every six weeks. Throughout the Houston district, parents must be notified after three weeks if a student is in danger of failing. There are two additional sources of feedback to parents at Pershing. If a student is achieving at high levels, that notice goes home after three weeks, too; and the student's progress on the self-paced, computerized STAR reading tests is also sent to parents.

All of these systems and all of the student test data can be confusing, so Pershing provides parent sessions on topics like "The State Achievement Test and What It Means." The school provides food and child care and draws 150 parents to a typical session. Parents are constantly reminded through both talks and newsletters how important the standardized tests are.

It's hard to imagine a school that makes better, more consistent use of good data about its students in order to give them what they need. It happens in all subjects, in all grade levels, and it touches students, parents, teachers, and administrators. Pershing Middle School could not possibly develop the information technology on its own—that credit goes to the central office. The central office should also be credited for having the self-discipline to leave the principals alone to run their schools. Perhaps the best summary of it all comes from Principal Joel Willen:

> The focus on the tests is one of the things that really drives the district. Our tests really give us good data that pinpoint what the students know and what they don't know, so that we can focus our efforts on the areas where we need improvement.

The results suggest that the focus on student achievement in Houston is paying off. Houston and Los Angeles can be compared in several ways. Both are large, urban districts, both are predominantly minority and poor, and both use the same standardized test, the Stanford 9. In Houston, the average score in 2001 was the 42nd percentile in reading, compared to the 33rd percentile in Los Angeles. For math scores, Houston students averaged in the 49th percentile, while Los Angeles students averaged in the 42nd percentile. In Los Angeles, the greatest gains have been among first graders in reading. This is likely due to a combination of smaller state-mandated class size and Superintendent Roy Romer's introduction of the Open Court phonics-based, direct instruction reading program in all elementary schools. In Houston, though, the gains are at every grade level and in virtually every subject. That kind of broad-based gain isn't due to a new program being imposed by the central office—it's due to every teacher and every principal in every school having the freedom and the responsibility to focus on student achievement.

Joel Willen fits the model of the new era of principals in Houston. He's a doer, an entrepreneur, a marketer of his school. Margaret Stroud, who oversees school administration in the central office, captures the dynamics of the new situation: "The principals are ecstatic that they have control over all these things at their schools—things that have been talked about for years. But they're also worried—there's so much to deal with, so much to do. The concept that 'The principal is the CEO of their school' has meaning to them for the first time."

She's right. It is a big challenge for Joel Willen, but he is meeting that challenge. Try to imagine, if you can, what Pershing Middle School would be like today if instead of having one CEO, Joel Willen, it had to answer to each of seven or eight different bureaucrats in the central office. One assistant superintendent would be overseeing the gifted-and-talented programs in the school, another would be making up the rules for the fine arts magnet students. The free lunch children would come under yet another assistant superintendent, and all mathematics programs would have to use books approved by a central office math guru. It would be a nightmare—and that, unfortunately, is exactly what it is in too many schools in America.

The Seven Keys to Success enable each school to focus its staff and its energies on one goal: the academic achievement of children. A burning focus on achievement means using good data to provide an individualized response to each child, with a consistent schoolwide approach. When it's done right, as we've seen in these examples, it works.

8

Key #6: Every School Is a
Community of Learners

We just had our evaluation and the team that came—it was like twenty-two people—said, "Your school is poetry in motion, it's like everybody is in sync and they are all moving."
—*Lucinda Lee Katz, Director, University of Chicago Laboratory Schools*

*P*oetry in motion? Does your school fit that description? Or, perhaps, do you hear the grinding of gears that won't quite mesh when you talk to teachers and to the principal? It was John Dewey who first made the case that a student learns best in a community of learners. What he meant was that the school must begin with a shared understanding of where each child and each family stands both intellectually and emotionally, and then the educational program grows up from those strong roots like a tree whose roots give it life and strength. In this chapter, we'll see what a school looks like when *everyone*—teachers, students, and parents—is in harmony on what they're trying to achieve. We'll unearth some of the basic steps that you can take to give your school that lovely image of poetry in motion. And we'll see how teachers flourish in such an environment.

Dewey founded the University of Chicago Laboratory Schools in 1896 in partnership with the celebrated progressive educator Francis W. Parker. Unlike many other successful schools that we've seen, at the Lab Schools there is no pro-grammed teaching of reading in the lower grades. Instead, each teacher has the skill to diagnose the situation of each child and the experience to guide them to make their own learning discoveries. Students do not go through reading instruction as a class, but instead work one-on-one with their teacher. One requirement is that each teacher must know how to bring a classroom of individual students into an effective community, so that each child both learns from and teaches the others. The students and teachers must together take on questions that are challenging to all of them. They do this, in part, by asking the biggest questions of the youngest children—those in kindergarten. Says the school's director, Lucinda Lee Katz:

> Nursery–Kindergarten is the place where we want to explode the child's world with ideas and stimulation. So that's where we are asking the kids the biggest questions: Why, when the *Titanic* went down, did the women and children go first to be saved? You have to get the kids, at that point, to push the boundaries of what is enlightened thinking. If you don't do that, then you have trouble the rest of their school life.

To achieve that ambitious goal, the 1,689 students are divided into four small units: pre-K and K, grades 1–4, grades 5–8, and the upper school, grades 9–12. Each unit has its own principal and considerable independence. Each has a different staffing plan in the classrooms, different schedules and sets of educational goals. Teachers place a great premium on their ability to ask students in all grades the "elegant question." That means the teacher has thoroughly researched the issue, has anticipated the questions that the children will ask, and has put all of that preparation into the question that will get the child and the teacher to think deeply about it.

Parents are very much a part of this learning community, too. Says Director Katz:

> When I first came to the Laboratory School, they had notes on the doors saying, "No Parents Allowed"! I said—what is this? I said—you will not ever tell parents they can't be in the school.
>
> You want that parent to say, "Man, that school is so hard—I'm going to go in and talk to your teacher about how much homework you have." That's a parent saying, "I care about you, I care about your education."

Almost every expert who has studied successful schools says that they are learning communities where everyone is on the same page. The adults involved in the school—meaning the parents and the teachers—must share the same vision of what the school should be. Otherwise, there is no chance that the children will be integrated into a powerful, motivating flow that will help them to become outstanding students.

A community is a group of individuals who have come together around a common goal, the unique definition of what kind of school they want to have. It will be different for each school, as it should be, but it will always focus on the welfare of the children.

How is a school transformed into a learning community? Our study found that it isn't a mystery, it's plain, old-fashioned hard work. Step One is for the school to identify what the families of its community want and need. Step Two is for the school to organize itself, if necessary, into subunits that permit a face-to-face community to develop. Step Three is for the teachers to agree on what they want to teach and how they want to teach it, and then to develop ways to bring about a consistent approach that touches all teachers yet gives each the freedom to design his or her own classes. We'll take each of these steps in turn, and then we will look at the very special case of the inner-city Catholic schools, which serve the poor as well as they do because they create strong learning communities.

STEP ONE: IDENTIFY THE NEEDS AND DESIRES OF THE COMMUNITY OF FAMILIES

We've made the point that just as every child is unique, so each collection of families within the school is unique. A successful school is one that finds the goals that *all* of the families support. That underlying goal may not be readily visible. If you stick with it, though, not settling for the easy answer, you'll find it. It will be the guiding light from which each teacher can gauge the content of her course, allowing individual flexibility while bringing coherence and unity to the whole.

The Brentano Math and Science Academy, located in the Logan Square neighborhood of Chicago, is a good example of how this process can work. Brentano has nine hundred children in grades K–8. Ninety-five percent are Hispanic, 3 percent are African-American, and 2 percent are white; 95 percent qualify for free or reduced-price lunch. Reynes Reyes has been principal for eleven years, during which time reading scores have risen from the 11th percentile to the 32nd percentile, and math scores have gone up from the 11th percentile to the 40th percentile. Eighty percent of the students score above the national norms in science. The school is a success by any measure.

When Principal Reyes arrived, he hoped to establish an arts magnet school. The community, though, surprised him, and he was persuaded by the data to change course:

> First thing I did was to analyze the situation both inside the school and outside—who's who, what's what, what makes things move. I surveyed the community—a parent team wrote the questions—to find out what the community wanted the school to become.

I hoped for an arts school, but it came back that they wanted it to be a math and science school. They asked everyone in the community—people without children and people with children. This started a change of culture in the school—we were caring about people in the community and what they think.

The direction was set: Brentano Academy, an ordinary school rather than a magnet school, would nonetheless adopt a focus on math and science. Brentano became affiliated with a math-science cluster of schools, and it accepts about thirty students who are not admitted at the math-science magnet school. The other children, though, are from the neighborhood.

Nice work, you might be thinking—but he's created a monster! What does he do with his thirty-five teachers, almost none of whom are math or science teachers? You can't simply ask what the community wants, because you're stuck with the teachers that you have. That kind of thinking is bureaucratic thinking, not entrepreneurial thinking. If you want a successful school, you have to first analyze the situation and find out what people want, and then you have to have the courage and the persistence to move all of the obstacles out of the way. The key, though, is that the parents stuck to their guns, and the principal and the teachers took them seriously. What resulted was not a conflict but a creative struggle that produced an entirely new path for all.

Mr. Reyes, an entrepreneur of the first order, faced up to the problem of the misfit between the focus of his new school and the training of his teachers, very few of whom had a teaching certificate in either math or science. His first reaction was to change teachers. He asked his local school council and the Chicago Board of Education to certify Brentano as a Specialty School, which meant that he could hire new teachers. Meanwhile, he and a team of about ten parents, teachers, and administrators signed up for a course on school management at the Kellogg School of Management at Northwestern University.

At Northwestern, Principal Reyes learned the principles of W. Edwards Deming, the father of the Total Quality Management approach in both Japan and the United States.[1] The experience was another eye-opener for Reyes and his team, and they changed implementation strategy 180 degrees: "After that, I felt, I can't fire all these teachers—that's against Deming's principles! So I said to my teachers, if you'll work with me, if you'll go back and get your certificate, we'll work together."

The next challenge was to find the right university to train the teachers. He left that up to the teachers, who chose the nearby Illinois Institute of Technology. Because Reyes had control over the portion of his budget that came from the state for low-income students (State Chapter I), he was able to put aside $35,000 in the first year for teacher training. So that all teachers would feel they were getting their fair chance at the training, training began with science teachers from the eighth grade down and math teachers from the first grade up. The school's budget flexibility also enabled Reyes to hire substitutes so that teachers could go to school during the week, and to provide a stipend for those who went to class on Saturday or during the summer. Because the school had no science labs, it also set aside $40,000 (again out of its flexible budget) for laboratories to be completed over a period of years.

Brentano Academy had been seriously overcrowded for years, with 1,300 students, because the previous principal brought in about 350 students from other overcrowded schools. The result was a loss of a community atmosphere, and with it, problems of student behavior and of poor attendance. Reyes stopped that practice.

In 2001, the school joined with four other schools and won a grant from the U.S. Department of Education for parent training. The money has enabled the school to create a Community Center within the school that offers education services and health services to families. Parents are brought into regular contact with their child's education through another program, Parents as Teachers First. Under this program, a parent is employed half-time to work with other parents, showing them how to encourage and assist their child's schoolwork.

The feeling of community responsibility for each child also extends to special education classes. Brentano attempts to provide for special needs children who live in the community and works to get them into regular classes as soon as they are ready (known as "mainstreaming"). The school has only one "self-contained" special education class, for fourteen children in grades 3–6. It includes children who have been classified by licensed psychologists as emotionally/behaviorally disabled, trainable-mentally handicapped, or autistic, as well as those with IQ levels below 60, although some have had levels as low as 40. By grade 5, almost all will be back in regular classrooms unless their behavior is disruptive to other students. Social workers and other specialists visit the school every week to provide students with continuing support.

Brentano Math and Science Academy is succeeding because it has thoroughly integrated itself into the surrounding community, the Logan Square neighborhood. For other schools, the relevant community might extend to other nearby neighborhoods or even to an entire city. It took engagement by the principal, teachers, and parents—the adults of the school community—to make it happen. All parents, rich and poor, care about the education of their children, though, and learning communities can be created everywhere.

STEP TWO: ORGANIZE INTO SUBUNITS THAT PERMIT INTIMACY AND COMMUNITY

At Jasper Place School in Edmonton, each student has a home, whether it be special needs, information technology, welding, or college preparatory courses. At John Hay Elementary in Seattle, students in grades 4–5 are looped into subunits that create an intimate setting in which each student is known. These examples demonstrate how small-scale education gives students the attention they need to flourish. Even more dramatic is the turnaround that is underway at Corliss High School on the gang-infested far South Side of Chicago, in the Pullman community.

What is happening at Corliss is very much a work-in-progress. Although the outcome won't be known for a few years, the strategy is clear: to save an inner-city school that is plagued with problems by dividing it into small learning communities.

The George Henry Corliss High School, grades 9–12, is at 821 East 103rd Street; 99.8 percent of the students are black, and 82 percent are from low-income families. Daily attendance is only 82 percent, which is low compared to the citywide average of 92 percent. The school does not have the kind of parent involvement that has developed at the Brentano Math and Science Academy. Only 79 percent of parents had personal contact with the school last year, compared to 99.9 percent for the school district. In 2000, reading and math scores were in the cellar. Worst of all, 20 percent of the students dropped out. At one time, the school had 2,000 students, but that dropped over time to 1,000.

The problem wasn't money or class size. Corliss had $7,361 per student, well above the average, and the typical class had only 14.6 students, below the district average of 18.3. The problem was that the school was an uninviting bureaucratic chaos that treated students like so many widgets. That was the case until Anthony Spivey arrived as principal in 2000.

Anthony Spivey is a big man. He stands head and shoulders above most people, and he commands respect. Before he came to Corliss High, he was at a Transition Center, a school for the students nobody could teach, a school for those who could not pass the required Test of Achievement and Proficiency, the TAP. Spivey is a take-charge manager, but at the same time, he's delegated authority to the heads of the three academies that he's created within the school.

When Principal Spivey arrived at Corliss, he found hundreds of students sitting out in front of the school in the morning, eating hamburgers and smoking marijuana. The bell rang at 8:00 A.M. but not one of them made a move to enter the school. Spivey directed his head of security to lock the doors (they could still open from the inside in the event of fire). The loiterers ambled up the front steps in their good time, but found that they were locked out. Alarmed, they tried the side doors and found those locked, too.

The principal opened the doors to the gymnasium and had the latecomers assemble there:

> I suspended all three hundred of them. Told them I wouldn't let them in unless they came to see me with their parents. The next day, when they got off the bus they hit the ground running to get in the door before 8:00. The television cameras were here and the phone was ringing. Superintendent Paul Vallas was on the line. I didn't know if he'd fire me or what, but he said, "Kick some more ass, I'm supporting you!"

Spivey's goal was not to kick his students out of school—he wanted them *in* school.

He and his staff—with the help of the Chicago police—made regular rounds through the neighborhood, picking up children and bringing them to school. They still walk the nearby streets and tell the local businesses that they are contributing to the delinquency of minors if they let kids play video games during school hours. When school opened on August 22, 2000, only 650 of the 1,000 students were present. Within two months, all but sixteen had been accounted for.

The next job was to organize the school into small academies where each student would know that he or she mattered: the Payton Academy is for freshmen, the Douglas Academy is for sophomores, and the Howard Academy is for juniors and seniors. Each academy is self-contained, with its own classrooms and cafeteria. Each has its own dean, assistant dean, counselors, and social workers, plus at least two of its own security staff and its own core group of teachers.

The Roland Howard Senior Academy, for juniors and seniors, is immaculate. The hallways sparkle and the classrooms are attractive. It is a place for students and teachers to be proud of. In eleventh-grade chemistry classes, the students are attentive and all are on task, with no daydreaming or hijinks visible. In the commercial art class, the students work with seventeen of the latest MacIntosh G4 computers on large layout tables. They also have a new color printer that produces full-sized posters, which the school bought with a grant. Over twenty seniors made the honor roll in the first semester this year, and Howard Academy has arranged for free college tours for all juniors and seniors. Still, the dean—Mrs. LaTanza Boarden—reminds students that red, blue, or gold shirts indicate gang affiliation and students wearing those colors are suspended IMMEDIATELY.

In the Payton Academy for freshmen, banners hung everywhere remind students and teachers alike that their goal is to "Conquer the TAP." Freshmen start the year with an orientation program that sets their expectations for good behavior and high achievement. Acting Dean Dr. Frank Lacey oversees a new after-school program, tutorial programs, and a new ninth-period reading program. All students are tested for their reading progress every two weeks.

The Corliss High School Marching Band, 150 strong, opened and closed the Mardi Gras Parade in New Orleans in 2001–02. Another grant has allowed the school to purchase $20,000 in new band instruments. The school has a new 700-seat auditorium and a radio and television studio, both state-of-the-art. This is clearly a school that is on its way up.

Today, Corliss High School looks like the organized, purposeful school that it is. The classrooms and hallways are immaculate and there is no graffiti anywhere. Principal Spivey picks up gum wrappers as he walks the hall. He remarks that

"When I got here, gangs were running the school. It was dirty, and gang-bangers were hanging outside on Cottage Grove." Today, the truancy staff visits families when necessary, and if a student receives two such visits, the principal pays a call on the family. Students are in uniform—white shirt and black pants or skirt—and "If a student comes in out of uniform, we put a uniform on them." Spivey has used his flexible budget to hire a security staff of thirteen, successfully meeting the first requirement of a school—providing a safe environment.

Spivey moved equally quickly to establish a new expectation level for the teachers. Understandably, many of them decided that the new approach was not for them. "After I arrived, I laid out what we were going to do, and people left. I didn't have to fire anyone, they just left. Most of the teachers who were here when I arrived have either retired or have left. After-school programs, tutorial programs—teachers get paid extra for all of those. A lot of times if you take that away, they'll just leave."

The teachers are now held accountable for assigning homework at the district standard—180 minutes of homework per week per class. Lesson plans and assessments are now done in a uniform manner. Every teacher teaches reading the same way, using an approach developed at the University of Chicago. Uniform lesson plans, uniform homework, uniform student assessment, uniform reading method, and uniforms on students! This approach might not appeal to every teacher, but Corliss is not in a situation comparable to most schools. How about the results?

Students know that advancement to the next higher academy is a privilege, and that to earn that privilege, they must conquer the TAP and pass the required courses. Corliss has been taken off probation. And here's the best news of all: in just one year, the reading scores have jumped from an average of the 17.5th percentile to the 24.7th percentile. We'll all have to wait to see how this story unfolds, but we'll be rooting for the students at Corliss High School. It already looks as though they'll succeed.

STEP THREE: FOSTER A STRONG COMMUNITY OF TEACHERS—AS AT BRONX SCIENCE

The Bronx High School of Science may be the most famous high school in America. It counts among its alumni five Nobel Laureates, and it is the leading school in total winners in the annual Westinghouse/Intel Science Talent Search. In addition to being famous, it's huge: 2,704 students in grades 9–12. If that weren't enough, Bronx Science both benefits and suffers from its status as one of the much-desired "test" schools in the New York City system. Each year, approximately 24,000 students take the admissions examination to one of the three elite public high schools: Brooklyn Technical High School, Bronx Science, and Stuyvesant. Of these 24,000 applicants, only about 3,500 are admitted each year to one of the three schools.

Today, Bronx Science is as much an academic powerhouse as ever. Students in New York State must pass a tough set of Regents examinations in several subjects to receive a Regents diploma rather than a local diploma only. In New York City, plans call for requiring *all* students to pass these examinations in order to receive any diploma at all. That won't be an issue for the students at Bronx Science. After three years of high school, 99 percent of the students already pass the Regents exam in English, and 100 percent pass the exam in math. For New York City as a whole, the comparable figures are 42 percent for the English exam and 47 percent for math.

The student body is 46 percent Asian, 36 percent white, 9 percent African-American, and 9 percent Hispanic. A relatively low 19 percent of students qualify for free or reduced-price lunch, but that figure is probably an underestimate as it is at all high schools, because high school students tend to be sensitive and don't apply for the poverty program funds.

If you had the opportunity to sit through classes at Bronx Science for two full days, you'd notice several things. For one, you'd notice that the classes tend to be large, with twenty-eight in an Honors biology class and thirty-six in a Regents biology class. The class on electronics and circuit design has thirty-four students, and eleventh-grade Regents physics has thirty-three students. Second, you'd notice that the facilities are old and much in need of repair and updating. Third, you might notice that the students are a bit different from those in most high schools. That's not to say that they're not still teenagers—there is some of the usual hugging and kissing in the stairways in between classes. However, at Bronx Science, a physics teacher can tell a joke like this one and draw a laugh from the class:

In 1798 Lord Cavendish developed the Universal Gravitation Constant, and thus when someone says they are attracted to you, you can add their mass to your mass and calculate the total gravitational attraction!

But an attentive observer will see what is perhaps the most important thing of all—how the teachers teach. Over the years, they have adapted their teaching to their uniquely bright and highly motivated students, and the result is a culture of teaching that may exist at few other schools. The teachers at Bronx Science are pedagogical athletes—they work so hard at their teaching that they break a sweat—and they are exhilarated by the exercise. One other thing you'd notice is that teaching this way is so much more difficult that the veteran teachers have to inculcate their work ethic and their methods in the novice teachers.

The teachers have developed a way of doing things that works in this setting, with these particular students, in this unique school. Undeniably, these highly selected students would excel at any school. Here, though, it is common to see entire classes run through interaction that is largely driven by the students. The school succeeds primarily, perhaps entirely, because the teachers nurture and maintain their very strong learning community. In a less obvious way, the teachers are the key to an effective learning community at every school, including yours.

Valerie Reidy is the new principal of Bronx Science. It's a bit like being put in charge of Yellowstone National Park or *The New York Times*. You've got to prove yourself before the natives will allow you to lead them. Principal Reidy, though, has lots of ideas and lots of backbone, and her initial moves stirred up some of the teachers. Of the culture of Bronx Science, she says: "You have to understand that we're very serious about what we do in the classroom here. I just extended the daily announcements by two minutes. It took me three meetings with groups of twelve teachers each to settle it—that's two minutes less that they've got to teach." Did you get the point? These teachers want more, not less class time, because they have a burning passion about what their students learn.

Alfred DiNapoli is in front of his class, eleventh-grade Honors physics. The entire class stands and repeats the Pledge of Allegiance, then Principal Reidy's announcements come over the public address system. The class reviews the homework from last night, and then Mr. DiNapoli asks if anyone knows what a "pile" is. No one does, so he asks why it is that Manhattan has a whole bunch of very tall buildings down on the tip of the island and up to 14th Street, and then there are no tall buildings until the Chrysler Building and the Empire State Building in midtown. He explains that the bedrock in between 14th and 34th Streets lies so deep that you cannot drive piles to reach it. Below 14th and above 34th Streets, though, the bedrock is close to the surface.

A pile is something like a telephone pole, and a pile driver is a crane that lifts a weight and then drops it, driving the pile into the ground. He discusses how much work it must take to lift that weight and points out that in the old contest between students and teachers running up two flights of stairs, the typical student was able to generate 0.75 horsepower, with the best ever being 2 horsepower. He asks what happens to energy when you work. After someone gets the right answer (energy is transferred when work is done), he asks, what kind of quantity is energy?

This goes on for a double class session, two periods of forty-two minutes each. It is obvious that Mr. DiNapoli is teaching through the Socratic method of asking well-formulated questions that will lead the students to come up with their own answers. Through this process, each student will arrive at the central ideas, including the laws of physics, in this case Newton's second law of thermodynamics. But Mr. DiNapoli doesn't tell them that until the end of class. In fact, at Bronx Science, students in the math and science courses are not supposed to read the textbook before class, because the teaching method is to have them discover what's in the textbook for themselves through a well-taught class. After they've reasoned their way to the general rules, they will read about these general principles in their books.

Principal Reidy describes what Mr. DiNapoli is doing as "the inductive-discovery approach" to teaching. She goes on: "We approach science the way a scientist would—you observe phenomena, you observe data, and then you arrive at conclusions. We give students the facts; they have to come up with the concepts. It's hard to teach these kids—it's physically draining."

A successful teacher using this method has to prepare thoroughly each day. The process is described by Kerry Garfinkel, an English teacher.

> You start the class with a Motivation, which is some provocative question, something that relates to current events, something that the kids will have something to say about and chew on.
>
> This method was designed for a teacher-led discussion where the teacher asks what are called the pivotal questions. It is not simply that the teacher is the hub of the wheel, just asking questions one after the other and putting kids on the spot—you want them to engage each other. The teacher has to be prepared, not just with the first line of questions, but with the second and the third—where are you going to take them?

Susan Bowerman is a fourth-year veteran biology teacher at Bronx Science. Before this, she taught biology at New York Medical College. She has a doctorate in immunology, and she loves the challenge of teaching here, although she, too, says: "It is very hard and it takes a lot of work. My first year—I spent maybe four hours writing up the lesson plan and scripting it, so that I knew exactly what I was going to ask and I predicted what they were going to answer. I had directions written down. So it's a very, very hard way—it's a very demanding way." Biology teacher Richard Lee describes his impression of teaching at Bronx Science: "This style of teaching does take a lot longer to deliver. If the questions are off, if the sequence is not there, if the logic of the question isn't there—there is no discovery learning."

The system that creates this approach is on display every day. New teachers are typically hired for one year with the knowledge that their positions are not guaranteed beyond that. If they make that cut, they are on probation for three years. During this time, a new teacher is observed in class at least six times during the year. Tenured teachers are observed at least twice a year until their sixth year, and once a year after that. Forever. The most senior math teacher, who has been at Bronx Science since 1965, says that he is still observed and evaluated every year. The principal, assistant principals, and the departmental coordinators all regularly visit classrooms.

The socialization system that maintains the learning community is not all top-down control, though. In the math department, for example, the teachers share lesson plans, help each other, and appear to enjoy their friendly relationship. In the faculty lunchroom, teachers from each department tend to sit together. In many schools, the lunchroom is a quiet place where a few teachers sit exhausted, reading magazines and decompressing. Not here. Here, the conversations are lively, the energy is high, the teachers are engaged.

There can be too much consistency, at least for some teachers. To a young teacher who is under pressure to earn tenure, the consistency may seem oppressive and deindividualizing. The bottom line, though, is that teachers don't leave Bronx Science voluntarily. Yes, it's hard work. At times, it can be overly restrictive. Yet in the end, everyone understands that good education flows from a learning community, and that Bronx Science is one of the best.

CATHOLIC SCHOOLS SUCCEED THROUGH COMMUNITY—BUT IT'S NOT WHAT YOU THINK IT IS

The Catholic schools in our study operate on one half to one fourth the budget per student that public schools have. Yet they consistently outperform public schools. Why is that? Many people think that it's because they select only students who come from families that are devoted to the school and who become active volunteers in the school. That isn't so. Perhaps the most compelling answers came from University of Chicago professor Anthony Bryk in a series of studies of Catholic schools.

Bryk began by believing that Catholic schools outperform public schools on smaller budgets for one of two reasons: either they are able to select better students or they have better teachers. He tested his theory by gathering data on many Catholic and public schools. Bryk couldn't prove his theory, but he did find that Catholic schools consistently have higher student achievement scores—and we found that, too.[2]

In Los Angeles, where the Catholic schools and the Los Angeles Unified District both use the same Stanford 9 standardized test, the 269 Catholic schools outperform the public schools by a wide margin—by 53 to 33 in reading percentiles, and by 49 to 42 in math. In New York City, researcher Raymond Domanico found in a 2001 study that on the New York State exams in English Language Arts and in mathematics, students in 286 Catholic schools outperform students in the public schools by substantial margins.[3] In 2000, for example, eighth graders outscored their public school counterparts 703 to 686 in English and 706 to 686 in math. Domanico also found, as other researchers have, that the longer students remain in Catholic school, the larger is their margin over public school students. *New York Times* reporter Patrick J. McCloskey reported on April 29, 2001, that more than 95 percent of minority students attending Catholic high schools in New York City graduate, compared to 42 percent of their public school peers.

In Chicago, the Catholic schools use the Terra Nova test, and average student scores were in the 71st percentile in reading and the 53rd in math. The public schools, which use the Iowa Test of Basic Skills, scored in the 38th percentile in reading and the 43rd in math. Although the two different tests cannot be compared to each other, the results show that Catholic school students are in the top half of their test group, while public school students are in the bottom half of theirs. The Catholic schools have larger classes and lower teacher pay. So why are they doing so well?

Bryk concluded that they outperform because they have a commitment to the idea of a school as a community. For him, this means three things: shared values; shared activities; and a cohesive team of teachers who relate to the students as whole people.[4] That means that the teachers pay attention to all aspects of each child, not only to her math performance or reading ability. It does not mean, however, that the families are always involved in the everyday life of the school.

Many people have the incorrect impression that parent volunteer time is a requirement in all Catholic schools, and that it is parent "free" help that provides them with an edge. That might be the case in suburban Catholic schools, but most Catholic schools are in the inner city, where they carry out their educational ministry to the poor. Most of their students are from single-parent homes, and often the parents are not U.S. citizens or documented aliens. Many fear coming to the school as they fear any official institution other than the Church itself. That means that many Catholic schools have to carry out their mission without the daily engagement of parents. It also means that the story of Catholic schools today is twofold: the schools succeed because they create remarkable learning communities, and they constitute an entire class of schools that is endangered because it serves the poor of the inner cities—with no government funding.

At the all-girls Josephinum School on North Oakley Boulevard in a tough Chicago neighborhood, Sister Donna Collins is principal. She describes the mission of her school of two hundred girls in grades 9–12:

> They come because things are chaotic in their home or in their neighborhood.
>
> They can't safely go out—they don't go to museums, to libraries, to plays. They come here because it's orderly— it gives them order in their lives.
>
> That's why we need this school. We don't have more than twenty-five kids who haven't had a close relative or friend who's been shot or killed. Their lives have too much chaos. If this school weren't here, these kids would be lost.

A typical new student is two years below grade level in reading and in math. Sixty percent of the students are Hispanic, primarily of Puerto Rican descent, and 30 percent are African-American. Those who can pay tuition fees of $3,500 per year, but the school must raise another $800,000 in donations each year in order to break even.

It's clear from Sister Donna's remarks that she knows her students as whole people, not just as math or social studies students. It's equally clear that she defines her job as caring for them. In a real sense, a school like Josephinum is the only stable community in the lives of its students.

Josephinum is doing a remarkable job. The school is clean and orderly, and the classes are rigorous. In last year's graduating class, 100 percent were accepted to college and 96 percent enrolled. Still, with a capacity to take 240 students, the school has only 200 signed up.

Regis High School, on East 84th Street in New York City, is a unique school. Regis was established by a wealthy donor to educate Catholic boys who could not afford the tuition at the other Catholic high schools in the city. Today, the endowment has grown and alumni have become loyal donors as well. Regis is tuition-free to all of its students, and it has the pick of a very large applicant pool. Judged by academics and college admissions, Regis may well be the best Catholic boys' high school in America.

Regis, though, is not only a top-flight school, it's also a learning community. One key aspect of community is a diffuse relationship between the teachers and their students. That means teachers who play multiple roles, so that they and the students come to experience one another from more than one angle, and are humanized in the process.

Eric Dimichele, for example, is the admissions director at Regis. He also teaches freshman social studies. This year, the aim of his course is to achieve a deep study of the Middle East. He wants his boys to learn about that critically important part of the world, and he wants them to find out what it means to achieve mastery of a complex subject area. He also teaches another course, a senior seminar in Contemporary Social and Political Issues, and coaches the school's Speech and Debate Team.

Jill Johansen is teaching her tenth-grade chemistry class. At Regis, there are no Advanced Placement courses because the teachers feel that their courses should cover what the students should know, not what a standardized test designer thinks they should know. She's given them the following problem to work through in class: If you mix 50 grams of aluminum metal at 125 degrees Celsius with 70 grams of H_2O that is at 30 degrees Celsius, what is the final temperature at which this mix will achieve equilibrium? She asks them questions that allow them to work through the logic of the problem, and by the end of class, they've solved it. Ms. Johansen worked as a chemist at the drug company Merck for two years before being hired at Regis, though she has no teaching credential. Like most other faculty, she advises about twenty-eight boys, sophomores, in her group. She meets with her advisee groups every morning and afternoon to take attendance and make sure that she can account for every boy. She counsels them on their progress in all of their classes and tutors those who need it. She plans regular activities with her advisees—perhaps a class night when all of the sophomores and their advisors will stay late after school to watch a movie and, as she puts it, "You know, do bonding kinds of things." In the spring, Johansen took her advisees to a three-day retreat at a Jesuit facility on Staten Island. By the end of the year, she'll know her students as whole people, and they'll know her.

Both Regis and Josephinum achieve some sense of community, although in quite different settings. In other Catholic schools the idea of community may be more a dream than a reality, though. It's hard to develop those broad relationships without some additional staff. Unlike Edmonton, where both Catholic and public schools receive the same per-student funding from the government, U.S. Catholic schools are operating dangerously close to the margin. Some public money does flow to religious schools in the United States, but it's a drop in the bucket. Catholic schools once served both the middle-class and the low-income Catholics in urban areas, but most of their middle-class constituency has moved to the suburbs. Over the period from 1965 to 2000, enrollment in Catholic schools dropped by 55 percent, from 5.5 million to 2.5 million. The number of Catholic schools in the United States declined over that period from 13,292 to 8,102, according to a recent study by Bruce Cooper and Mark Kramer.[5]

A general turning away from religious schools does not seem to be the issue. Jewish day schools, according to Cooper and Kramer, increased from 345 schools to 691 between 1965 and 2000, while enrollment surged from 73,112 to 169,751.[6] Among the Jewish day schools, enrollment is by far the largest in

Orthodox schools, at 127,067 students; there are 15,682 students in Conservative schools, 5,781 in Reform schools, and 21,221 in Jewish community schools. Jewish, Catholic, and other independent religious schools place a heavy emphasis on developing a strong sense of community, but it is the Catholic schools that face the most serious threat to their survival.

They are not the only schools that understand the importance of establishing a learning community. Their success highlights the beneficial effect that a total, caring relationship has on the development of the young. We've seen that there are many facets to a school as a learning community. We've seen that a strong learning community can overcome all kinds of obstacles, including large class sizes, terribly disadvantaged neighborhoods, and even a group of teachers who at first don't fit the mission of the school. If your school pulls together in order to overcome its obstacles, you'll find that it will become a strong learning community, too.

A SCHOOL DISTRICT CAN BECOME A LEARNING COMMUNITY, TOO

Do you remember the monthly Principals' Conference led by Superintendent Shelley Harwayne at District 2 in New York City? The principals in the district are each involved in the learning community at their schools, but they are also part of a wider community of other principals, reading and math specialists, and district administrators. Becoming a manager in a school district doesn't have to mean becoming a bureaucrat. These school managers—for that's what principals are—sustain their own vitality in part by engaging other principals in a constant process of study, learning, and teaching one another.

In Edmonton, most principals are moved to a different school about every five years. One result is that they are eager to help one another's schools succeed—because someday they might be heading that school. It also means that every principal understands the need to maintain a consistent set of student performance records and budgetary records so that a new principal can step into the cockpit and be familiar with all of the dials and controls right away.

A learning community recognizes that each person needs to be constantly challenged mentally and emotionally, because by exercising those "muscles" the community is strengthened. It also recognizes the need of each person to be acknowledged, to be known and cared about by others. As the members of a community engage in many different kinds of activities with one another over time, they discover and reinforce the central values that underpin their school, and they broaden their knowledge of one another as whole people. Nothing could be better for nourishing the human spirit, whether of little children or the adults who care about them.

If you have the privilege of seeing a classroom that looks like poetry in motion, keep in mind that what you're seeing is the result of lots of hard work by a teacher who just happens to be able to make it look effortless. But it isn't. Not only that, the teacher has to start all over again next year, assembling a new group of energetic, unique individuals into a new community of learners. Don't be afraid to thank her for what she's achieving.

9

Key #7: Families Have Real Choices Among a Variety of Unique Schools

There ought to be a law against rotten schools.

Wait! There is a law against rotten schools, if they receive federal money to educate poor children.

—*Editorial,* Los Angeles Times, *July 13, 2002*

On July 2, 2002, the U.S. Education Department announced that 8,652 public schools—9 percent of the total—failed to meet required learning standards. Under the No Child Left Behind Act established that year, students at the failing schools were entitled to transfer to other public schools of their choice, with the district paying for their transportation. Many school districts were scrambling to comply and place all the students who wished to transfer. The *San Diego Union-Tribune* reported on July 3 that year that 64 schools in San Diego County would be among the 1,009 California schools that would be forced to comply with the new law when school opened in the fall. Maria Newman of *The New York Times* reported on July 4 that in New Jersey, 274 of the state's 2,300 public schools were on the failing list and would be required to allow students to choose a new public school. David Herszenhorn of *The New York Times* reported on March 27, 2003, that "more than 16,000 New York City children have demanded transfers out of failing public schools" under the law for the next school year, up from 6,400 the year before.

No one knew whether these families would actually have a choice—the other public schools might not have room for them. In Baltimore, for example, the *Baltimore Sun* reported on July 10 that the school district said that it would offer only 194 places for the 30,000 students who were eligible to transfer to a better school. The *Los Angeles Times*, in a July 13 editorial, applauded the stricter federal standards but lamented that the students in the 122 Los Angeles Unified School District schools that were below par would probably have nowhere to transfer, because there was little space in other schools. More than 220,000 students were eligible for transfers, but no places were available in good schools in this overcrowded district. A new national direction had been clearly defined, though: families had a right to a good school, and if their neighborhood school was failing, they had a right to a choice.

On August 28, 2002, *New York Times* reporter Diana Jean Schemo recounted that nationwide about 3.5 million students had a legal right to choose a better school, but few places were available in good schools, and few families wanted to send their children to school far from home each day. In Chicago, for example, she reported that although 145,000 students could legally transfer from their struggling schools, only 2,245 had applied for the 1,170 slots that were available. Nonetheless, the new law seemed to be achieving one of its goals—to let parents know that they have a right to a good school for their children, and preferably one near home. In other words, every school should be a good school.

Choice is now part of our national education policy—but only if your child's school is scraping the bottom and failing to improve. For these schools, the new federal policy acknowledges that giving families a choice may be the best way to overcome an unresponsive school district bureaucracy that won't or can't fix the schools. Now, though, the national debate is turning to the question: why can't *all* families have a choice of schools?

The skeptics argue that choice could lead to a segregated

school system and ultimately to a two-tiered system in which the rich will find a way to send more money to their schools than to the schools of the working class and the poor. School district administrators observe that they'd be happy to offer choice, but who will pay for the increased costs of busing? And besides, they point out, we could offer freedom of choice tomorrow, and how would that improve the schools? The schools that are already strong will be inundated with applications that they won't be able to satisfy, and the weak schools will still be weak.

The debate over choice can be confusing. Perhaps you're thinking that all you want is a good neighborhood school for your children—you don't *want* to have to choose another school. If they would fix the schools, you'd be happy to have your children go to the school to which they are assigned by the district.

On the other hand, you might have a son or daughter who started speaking at nine months, had a vocabulary of more than one hundred words at twelve months, and was speaking in sentences at two years of age. You'd like to find a school that will challenge this bright child. Another family might be firmly committed to the belief that its child will grow up in a global world, and that family would like to be in a school that teaches a second language beginning in first grade. You might have an autistic child and feel that he would do best in a specialized school that has teachers trained to help him. Or, you might feel that being included with nonautistic children is a better preparation for life, and you'd like a school that can provide that option. In any of those situations, you want a choice, and not just among identical schools.

The point to be stressed here is that there are two important aspects to school choice: one is the simple *freedom to choose*—to vote with your feet, so to speak—and the other is having a choice from among a wide *variety* of different schools.

School choice, by itself, won't do you much good if all of your choices are bad ones. If a district were to neglect the other Six Keys to Success and implement choice alone, it wouldn't solve its problems. Imagine having a traditional, top-down bureaucratic school district subjected to the pressure of a voucher system. Principals would be faced with mounting public demands, their schools would see conflict and turmoil, yet they would be handcuffed—denied the freedom to make the hundreds of small changes that have enabled schools like Jasper Place and John Hay to be successful. The anger and the pain that would develop are difficult to imagine.

There is increasing movement across the country to establish new kinds of schools that give all families the power of choice. The result is that our old image of a single, monolithic public school system is rapidly being replaced by a garden in which many different choices are blooming. Among the most often talked about are vouchers, which in their current form are like education food stamps; and charter schools, which require authorization by state law and have the autonomy to bypass the school district bureaucracy. We'll review each of these emerging new forms of school choice. We'll also look at the possible options that can exist within a public school district, such as magnet schools, option schools, and alternative schools. Finally, we'll see that in Edmonton, Houston, and Seattle, choice is a reality for almost all families—and it could be so in your district, too.

VOUCHERS AS A WAY TO ACHIEVE CHOICE

On June 27, 2002, the U.S. Supreme Court in a 5–4 decision upheld the legality of a Cleveland, Ohio, voucher program. The program had been challenged because 96 percent of the approximately 4,200 vouchers were used at the city's Catholic schools. The Wisconsin state supreme court had earlier upheld a 1990 voucher program for low-income families in Milwaukee. In 1999, Florida introduced a voucher program for students who attend failing schools, with fifty-seven students using the $4,000 vouchers to attend private schools beginning in the 1999–2000 school year, according to a RAND study released in 2001.[1] The

RAND study also reported that in 2001, Pennsylvania followed the 1997 lead of Arizona and established tax credits for businesses that contribute to private voucher programs.[2] It seems clear that more voucher programs will be coming, although the numbers of students on vouchers will be very small for years to come.

The Cleveland voucher program grew out of public outrage over the failure of that city's public schools. In 1995, a federal court declared the 76,000-student Cleveland school system to be in a "state of crisis" and ordered that the state take over the district, according to an analysis by Amy Stuart Wells of Columbia Teachers College in New York City.[3] The Ohio solution, in part, was to create vouchers of up to $2,250 per student for students in grades K–8 to transfer either to another public school or to a private school of their choice. Ohio, meanwhile, was spending more than $7,000 per student in its public schools. As we've seen, though, even $2,250 is within the tuition of most urban Catholic schools, whose mission includes serving the poor.

The court found that because families have a choice of charter schools, magnet schools, alternative schools, and other public schools as well as religious and nonreligious independent schools, the vouchers are allowable.[4] The dissenting justices argued in part that because the vouchers were so small, families really had no choice of where to use them; they could be used only at Catholic schools.[5]

As the education landscape changes, it's likely that vouchers will grow and become a permanent part of our system. Vouchers might cause the now stable independent school sector to grow slowly from its present 10 percent of school-age children to perhaps 11 percent or even as much as 12 percent. Some observers believe that when the combined market share of independent schools and charter schools rises above 20 percent, the public system will be roused into a state of competitive improvement—and everyone will win. That could happen if independent schools grew to, say, 12 percent of all students in school and charter schools took another 8 percent to 10 percent.

Perhaps one day vouchers will be based on Weighted Student Formula. If that were to occur, the maximum voucher in Ohio might be as much as $10,000. If school districts could dismantle their huge central office bureaucracies, even more money would be available for the schools, whether through vouchers or not. In that case, the average Ohio voucher could be worth as much as $5,000, and the maximum voucher for a special education child might be several times that amount. Then, public education as we know it would be transformed.

Vouchers are a very recent arrival on the school choice scene, and at present they are available to only a few thousand of the 47.4 million public school students in the United States. Another recent option is public charter schools, and they are growing rapidly.

CHARTER SCHOOLS AS A METHOD OF IMPLEMENTING SCHOOL CHOICE

Charter schools can exist only if a state passes a law to permit them. Minnesota passed the first such law in 1991. Today, thirty-six states and the District of Columbia have these laws, and about 2,500 charter schools are now in existence. Although charter schools today enroll only 1 percent of the schoolchildren in the United States, the movement is growing rapidly. Charter schools are an anomaly—they are public schools, but they do not report to the school district. Each is chartered by the state, although the charter is awarded either by the local public school district or by another state-certified authority. The advantage of charter schools is that in most cases they are free of the district and state bureaucracy. The disadvantage is that they receive at most only two thirds as much money per child as the public schools. That might sound like a nonstarter: giving up one-third of the money in exchange for freedom from the central office bureaucrats? How could that possibly be a good trade? Read on and see.

A study published by the Center for Education Reform in Washington, D.C., in 2001 rated the charter laws of thirty-four states according to eleven criteria.[6] The Alaska charter law allows a maximum of sixty charter schools, while Delaware allows an unlimited number. Massachusetts grants new start-up charter schools an automatic waiver from local district laws only but not from state education laws (e.g., uniform salary schedules, no authority to issue bonds) and permits no automatic waivers to existing schools that convert to charters, while Minnesota grants all charter schools automatic waivers from most state and local district laws. Mississippi allows only six charters in the entire state and requires that a charter be approved both by the local school board and by the state Board of Education, while Michigan permits unlimited charters and allows them to be granted by local school boards, intermediate school boards, community colleges, and state public universities.

According to the study, the seven state charters that earn a grade of A are Arizona, Delaware, Minnesota, the District of Columbia, Michigan, Indiana, and Massachusetts. The six states that get a D are Alaska, Hawaii, Arkansas, Rhode Island, Virginia, and Kansas. Mississippi gets an F for its charter law. In the states whose districts we studied, New York, California, and Texas receive a B, Illinois a C, and the state of Washington had no charter law at the time.

Two of the schools that we've described so far—View Park Prep in Los Angeles and Mabel Wesley in Houston—are charter schools. Both have taken advantage of their freedom to carve out a new agreement with their school districts and custom-design their programs to meet the needs of their students. There still isn't a clear-cut and well-established set of rules and procedures for charter schools in each state. Those who start a charter school have to work their way through a new system of laws whose meaning isn't yet fully understood, and they often have to do it by working through a central office bureaucracy that is hostile to the idea of charter schools. As a result, the principals who lead these schools tend to be very strong entrepreneurs.

Jacqueline Elliot is a human dynamo, in constant motion. Elliot established the Community Charter Middle School, grades 6 through 8, in the far reaches of the San Fernando Valley area of Los Angeles. The school opened in the 1999–2000 school year in a small facility, and two years later expanded to a second campus. The "campus" is a very modest group of buildings and temporary bungalows with a dirt field that is on the list of improvement projects to be undertaken when funds are available. The 350 students come from the neighborhood: Eighty-four percent of them are Latino, 14 percent are African-American, and 2 percent are Anglo. Eighty-four percent qualify for free or reduced-price lunches. The typical entering sixth grader comes from a Los Angeles Unified School District elementary school and reads at fourth-grade level.

There is no teachers' union and no one has tenure. Every teacher is evaluated twice a year. The teachers are paid with the state funds for charter schools, but they are employees of the school, which has great independence. For example, Jackie Elliot pays her teachers at or above the scale at the Los Angeles Unified School District (LAUSD), and her nine-person board of directors decides on her compensation. More important is that she shares power with her teachers and treats them with respect. Everyone shares the same vision, which Elliot states very simply: "My vision is that every student will graduate from college."

As she was making plans for her school, Elliott went wherever she could find a good model or thoughtful advice. She traveled to Minnesota and to Houston, where she found the Success for All reading system and the idea of making college a real option for her students. She got advice and help from neighboring charter school pioneer Dr. Yvonne Chan at the Vaughn 21st Century Learning Center and from the nearby California State University at Northridge. Today, the students at Community Charter Middle School begin each school year with a visit to the university campus, where they hold classes, eat in the university dining hall, and get accustomed to the idea of being college students themselves one day.

Community Charter School has its own unique schedule: Period 1, language arts and community circle, is two hours long, followed by a break and then by Period 2, which has three ninety-minute segments devoted to other content. Period 3 follows lunch and lasts for three hours, with breaks in the middle. Its reading program is unique, too: all teachers use the Success for All system, which is not used in the LAUSD. New students are tested for their reading level when they first arrive. Every eight weeks after that, the students are retested and then reassigned, so that all are in homogenous reading groups. Both teachers and principal have at the ready their lists of every student in every class and the progress they've made. The focus on student achievement is intense and the progress that the students make is so rapid that it's nearly unbelievable—but it's very real. Every teacher can tell you exactly how much progress each student has made this year and what problems each one is working to overcome.

It's not all work, though. Today, for example, Robert Tilles is teaching his eighth-grade class in U.S. history dressed in full Continental Army regalia—complete with three-cornered hat and cutaway jacket with brass buttons. He is explaining that the colonists believed that King George III sent troops not to protect them during the French and Indian War, but rather to enforce the payment of the unpopular taxes he had imposed. Principal Elliot, who is visiting the class, chimes in that she was a British citizen until four years ago—when she joined the Revolution!

The classrooms at Community Charter School are plain, and the supply of books is scanty. Community Charter receives only $6,800 per student from the state (plus federal funds and state categorical funds), about two thirds of what a public school gets. Charter schools are accustomed to this—some say it's because the teachers' unions have successfully put pressure on their state legislators to keep charter schools on a starvation budget. Elliot, though, applies for grants, and as she says,

> The philosophy in this school is you don't waste any-thing. I pay $4,000 a month to lease the property, I pay $6,000 to lease the other site, and I paid $30,000 to install the modular classrooms. I pay $600 per month for the open field next door as a playground. I got a loan of $250,000 from the state, and I pay it back over four years.

Jackie Elliot is not a complainer; she's a doer. "I don't want to say that money isn't everything, but look at our scores! Look at these kids—they feel they're part of an elite school, but we oper-ate on a shoestring." This year, the school has a waiting list of over three hundred families, and it's only in its third year of exis-tence. Word spreads fast when a school can consistently produce what families are looking for—a safe school, students who learn respect for one another, and academic success. On the Stanford 9, Community Charter already outscores all of its neighboring public middle schools, and the students who have been there for two years have scored a marked increase in both math and English language arts. In 2001, Community Charter seventh graders scored over 660 in language, while among its four neigh-boring schools, the seventh graders of two scored below 630 and the other two were at approximately 640. Those seventh graders who remained at Community Charter School for the second year increased their language scores from an average of 630 to 663. Overall, the state set an improvement target for the school last year of 14 points on its Academic Performance Index. Commu-nity Charter beat that, too, going up by 59 points, from 528 to 587 on the state's 1,000-point scale.

Not all charter schools have succeeded, though. As the 2001–02 school year drew to a close in New York City, then-Chancellor Harold Levy announced that he was closing the Reach Charter School in Harlem, grades 2–8, after only two years. According to a news story in the *New York Post* on July 3, 2002, only three of the school's twenty-six fourth-graders passed the state's standardized English exam.

In Texas, where the first 20 charter schools opened for business in 1996, there are now 270 campuses (some operate more than one campus under a single charter) serving approximately 47,000 students. Many of them are struggling, which prompted the state legislature to open a review of all charter schools. According to the *Houston Chronicle,* the principal of one such school in Houston allegedly pays himself an annual salary of $210,000 and pays his wife $50,000 to work as a secretary. At another charter school, also in Houston, only 22 percent of the students passed the state tests this year, compared to 85 percent of public school students. The Houston school district has lost 12,000 students to charter schools, although it vows to win them all back.

The 2001 report by the RAND Corporation in Santa Monica, California, evaluated research done by a variety of scholars on charter schools. The authors summarized their findings as follows:

> Achievement results in charter schools are mixed, but they suggest that charter-school performance improves after the first year of operation. None of the studies suggests that charter-school achievement outcomes are dramatically better or worse on average than those of conventional public schools.[7]

The RAND researchers noted that parent satisfaction is high in charter schools, but added that their results should be viewed with a grain of salt, since charter schools are still very new and small in numbers.[8] Nonetheless, it is well established that a charter school is not automatically a good school. They succeed only to the degree that parents exert pressure on them to be good. If you are thinking of opting for a charter school for your child, ask for an explanation of the school's spending, get a copy of the budget, and above all, make sure that you get the results on at least two years' worth of standardized tests. Are the scores rising or not?

Proponents of charter schools agree that state laws need to be amended to toughen both financial and student achievement accountability, and they believe that as these start-up problems are solved, charter schools will come into their own as a major alternative to traditional public schools. One of the more interesting new developments was aired at the New Schools Summit held in Silicon Valley in March 2002. At this meeting, panelists discussed the idea of *branded* charter schools. Parents, they argued, need to know that they can have confidence in a charter school's management.

Just as the brand names Oxford University, Tiffany, or Sony represent consistent high quality, the panelists thought that charter school brands, both for-profit and not-for-profit, will be the wave of the future. One of the nonprofit brands that is establishing a national presence is KIPP (the Knowledge Is Power Program). The first KIPP academy started in Houston in 1994, and one opened in the South Bronx a year later. There are currently five KIPP academies in four states, with ten more about to open. Students spend long hours at school, in a program inspired by famed Los Angeles teacher Rafe Esquith of Hobart Elementary School.[9] A typical KIPP academy shows 100 percent passing rates for all students who have been enrolled for at least one year.

Another interesting new wrinkle has been the recent development of "cyber" charter schools. Companies like K12 Corporation and Einstein Academy provide books, computers, and Internet access to families who choose home schooling. Because these virtual charter schools receive the same allocation per student as bricks-and-mortar charter schools but don't have to provide the bricks and mortar or a full staff of teachers, they can provide a better alternative for home schoolers within the small charter school budget while still making a profit. Particularly in rural areas, these cyberschools may prove to be a success. At the moment, though, they are coming under heavy criticism from teachers' unions and politicians.

According to the Bucks County, Pennsylvania, *Courier Times*, the Einstein Charter Academy was to go before a hearing to decide whether the Morrisville school board would revoke its charter on July 16, 2002. Only eight of the school's forty-six graduating high school seniors within the Morrisville district had completed the required 990 hours of online learning. Supporters of the cyberschool had, of course, opened a Web site, and a fierce battle was underway. *The Philadelphia Inquirer* reported on December 11, 2002, that the Morrisville district had revoked the school's charter and that enrollment had dropped from 3,000 students to 600. Although it's far too early to predict the future of these cyber charters, it's already clear that the future will be one of more innovation, not less.

Charter schools will probably continue to be a source of controversy for several years. In the end, though, the charter school movement is likely to grow because its underlying logic is unassailable: Parents don't have to send their child to a charter school unless they want to, and if a charter school is truly bad, it will go out of business. It sounds a lot like what they already have in the regular public schools of Edmonton, Seattle, and Houston—and it is.

STARTING A CHARTER SCHOOL

If your state allows charter schools, you should know that it's usually parents who are responsible for getting one up and running. You can either start a new school from scratch, or you can convert an existing school to a charter. Each method has pluses and minuses.

If you start a new charter school, it's up to you to find and pay for a building. That usually means raising private donations.

In many cities, the major foundations have taken an interest in charter schools and will provide some of the money with which to lease a building or begin construction on a new one. In some states, the per-student allocation that you receive will include a few hundred dollars per student to cover these facility costs, which means that you'll have to borrow the money and then repay it out of those student fees. You'll then be free to recruit your own principal, decide on how to measure his or her performance, and decide whether to offer a performance-based bonus or not. You'll also be free to decide on almost everything else about the school, from how many days of instruction to have beyond the state minimum to how many teachers, paraprofessionals, and teachers aides your school will employ.

In order to convert an existing school into a charter school, you'll have to get a majority, sometimes a supermajority of two thirds or more, of the school's teachers. That usually means finding a school that is already successful—where the teachers respect and like their principal—and one that feels it could do even better if it could get out from under the central office bureaucracy. That can be tough to do, particularly in states like California, where the charter law says that after five years, the teachers have to either go back to teach in the public system or resign from the public system. If a teacher elects to stay at the charter school, she loses seniority in the public school district, which could be important if at some later point she decides to leave the charter school. In Los Angeles, a few charter schools have now passed that five-year point, and virtually all of the teachers have elected to stay because they're happier than they ever were in the public school district. By comparison, the *Houston Chronicle* story cited earlier says that 77 percent of charter school teachers did not return to their charter schools last year. It all depends on how good the charter school management is compared to that of the public school district.

In either case, start-up or conversion, you'll want to gather a group of parents who are willing to serve on the board of the charter school. Next, you'll want to contact the charter school liaison in your school district, who will lay out for you the steps that you are required to go through. Then, go on the Internet and find other parent organizations and consultants who have chartered schools and ask them for advice.

You'll find that charter schools are still so new that you'll be able to negotiate on most of the critical points. For example, in some cases either you can agree to accept a flat per-student allocation based on the average categorical funding for each student in the district, or you can calculate the actual categorical funds that are due each year based on the students who enroll—what you'd get if your district used Weighted Student Formula. In order to negotiate effectively, you need to be well armed with careful analysis and plenty of advice from others who have been down this road before you.

Be prepared to discover that the district may only let you have about 40 to 60 percent of its per-student budget—unless you live in a place like Houston, where charter schools get 90 percent of the money that public schools receive and the district encourages charters, or Michigan, where charter and traditional public schools receive the same $6,700 per student. The good news is that you can actually run a school on a small fraction of what the public schools have because they are paying thousands of central office bureaucrats whom you won't have to pay. The bad news is that you won't be able to afford any extras, so your school will find that applying for federal, state, and private grants will be a part of everyday life. As the charter school movement grows, the pressure will mount for school districts to dismantle their huge central offices and allocate more money to all schools, both charter and district schools.

If you are going to start a charter school, be aware that many school districts will throw barriers in your way, hoping that you'll become discouraged and give up. First comes the consumer warning, like the one on every pack of cigarettes—Warning: Trying to change your school or your school district could be harmful to your mental health! It is only for the stout of heart. Do not try this at home unless you really care about your children.

You think I'm exaggerating? Here's a small sample of what Jacqueline Elliot went through to open her Community Charter Middle School in Los Angeles. She needed permission from the LAUSD to cut free of them. It's roughly like asking someone to cut off one of his fingers for you.

> There were about twenty-five people on the committee. I remember this man leaned forward and he said, "You know, we just don't understand." I remember I said, "You don't understand? I don't understand what you don't understand! You keep telling me what to do and I keep doing it and then you tell me you don't understand, but you just don't want to approve this petition. You just don't and I'm not quitting and I'm NOT going away! I will keep coming back and you are not getting rid of me and I don't understand what you don't understand, but you are playing some game where you keep changing the rules but not telling me!"

Don't lose heart. Jackie Elliot did get her independent charter, and after only three years the test scores are strong and rising and the families are lined up begging to get their kids in. You can do it, too, but you've got to be tough.

CHOICE IN PUBLIC SCHOOL DISTRICTS

Public school districts offer a range of choices. In a big district like New York City, there's one of almost anything you can think of. In a homogeneous district like the Los Angeles Unified, though, the range can be very small. Nationally, the trend seems to be toward more choice for families and more variety. In Washington, D.C., for example, *The Washington Post* reported on a successful new design that separates the students into single-gender classes at Moten Elementary School. After just one year in this new format, scores on the Stanford 9 leapt in math from 49 percent scoring either "advanced" or "proficient" to an amazing 88 percent. In reading, the rise was equally dramatic, from 50 percent to 91 percent. In Long Beach, California, the *Los Angeles Times* reported on the success of the Jefferson Leadership Academy, where 1,200 boys and girls in grades 6 through 8 are also separated by gender in all classes except for band. According to the *L.A. Times*, some ten public schools across the nation now have complete separation of classes by gender.

Another element of choice is the small-schools movement. The Bill and Melinda Gates Foundation, for example, is giving $40 million to school districts around the country that create or redesign small high schools of no more than four hundred students each. Some education experts, such as Harvard professor Tony Wagner, argue that small schools outperform large schools so consistently that there is no excuse to have any large schools at all.[10] Other education experts disagree, though. We've seen that a large school can achieve small-school intimacy by creating subunits such as academies.

In many school districts, though, parents have no small high schools from which to choose. In some cities, even elementary schools have as many as 1,500 students or more. It is difficult to establish any sense of intimacy and teamwork among the scores of teachers that it takes to staff a very large school. Without that close working relationship, a school is in danger of becoming a faceless factory where teachers close their classroom door and spend days, weeks, and even years in near isolation.

If your district is building new schools, insist on small, human-scale schools. If you are stuck with an existing large building, you can urge the district to subdivide it into several small, independent academies. If you go the academy route, keep in mind that the key factor is having a truly empowered principal in charge of each academy, not an assistant principal or a program director. The academy will be a coherent small school only if the principal pulls the teachers together into a team. Teachers know that an assistant principal often doesn't really have much power, and they won't listen seriously to anyone but a true principal.

Diane Ravitch in her influential book about school reform, *Left Back,* identified the way a bad idea like big schools can catch on when it has an influential promoter. Back in 1959, in the aftermath of the Soviet Sputnik satellite, which beat the United States into space, James Bryant Conant, former president of Harvard University, published *The American High School Today.*[11] In it, he argued strongly that small high schools should be closed and replaced by large schools, which could offer the array of challenging courses that would be necessary for the Space Age. Ravitch points out that "This meant reducing the number of high schools in the United States from 21,000 to 9,000."[12] According to John Chubb, Chief Education Officer of Edison Schools, the *average* school size from K to 12 has increased from 227 students in 1930 to 515 students today.[13] If only all schools had more autonomy, they wouldn't be subject to the seemingly endless waves of fads and reforms that are imposed on them. If you will set your feet firmly and refuse to go along with these central office–initiated ideas, your school will benefit.

MAGNET SCHOOLS

Among the most common forms of school choices are magnet schools. A magnet is meant to draw to it those families who are seeking a particular focus for their child's education. Fine arts and math-science magnet schools are common in most districts today, as are magnets for the gifted-and-talented. If a magnet school is free to select only those teachers who have both the specialized knowledge and the desire to be there, it's likely to deliver what it advertises. If teachers are allowed to choose their schools, though, a magnet may be specialized in name only. You should find out what the policy is in your school district, and then you'll know what to expect of a magnet school or program.

Chicago, for example, has seventy-two magnets. Some, such as the Chicago Military—Bronzeville High School—are true magnet schools. Located in the renovated Eighth Infantry Armory Building, the three-year-old school is home to 270 students. All are enrolled in the Junior Reserve Officers Training Corps (JROTC). Other Chicago magnets are schools-within-a-school, including the fifteen International Baccalaureate programs for the college-bound, twelve international language and career academies, and four law and public safety academies.

In Chicago, though, school autonomy is a sometime thing. At one magnet elementary school, grades pre-K through 8, the principal notes with a sigh that "I think that there's more decentralization than there used to be, but in the end, they [the central office] have the final decision." The school does have some extra money for arts education, but it's more like a regular neighborhood school than a true fine arts magnet.

In Houston, where every school enjoys a high level of local autonomy, magnet schools and programs tend to be very distinctive. In Los Angeles, which is still a top-down system, a magnet has to struggle to maintain a unique personality. In many cases, magnet schools were introduced in districts which didn't generally allow freedom of choice to families but which responded to middle-class families that demanded better schools and could afford to opt out of the public schools.

Because public school administrators felt that politically they could not openly offer specialized college preparatory schools for these families, they did so under the guise of magnet schools. Thus, many so-called magnet schools are really just schools for middle-class families. Our research reveals, for example, that although in the Los Angeles Unified 82 percent of elementary children qualify for subsidized school lunches, along with 74 percent of middle school and 66 percent of high school students, at magnet schools only 16 percent qualify for the low-income subsidized lunches. All magnet schools are required to admit all children and to admit students by lottery if there are not enough places for all applicants. Families with more education and more money, though, always find a way to get around any bureaucratic system, while the low-income families are left with the scraps.

Despite these criticisms, magnet schools are a step in the right direction. They introduce the concept of choice into otherwise monopolistic public school districts, and in many cases, they've gathered together dedicated teachers who produce a terrific education. As a matter of principle, one could argue that all public schools should be magnet schools. If each school had a crisp educational goal, a clear focus for its curriculum, and the freedom to choose its own teachers, it would in effect be a specialized magnet. Why shouldn't this be true of all public schools?

ALTERNATIVE SCHOOLS AND OPTIONS SCHOOLS

Every district has alternative schools. In New York City, the Park East High School in East Harlem is one of them. Park East has students up to the age of twenty-one, some of whom have repeated the ninth grade two or three times. According to the new principal, Nicholas Mazzarella, "This is the last stop. After this, it's drop out or a GED." Park East offers many options in its attempt to get its students to complete high school, including an evening program from 3:30 to 9:00 P.M. for students who have day jobs. It's a struggle, though. Attendance was a dismal 64 percent when Mazzarella arrived, and student morale was so low that the school had not had a yearbook since 1964. Many of the female students are pregnant, and most students come from homes so dysfunctional that school just doesn't matter to them. Still, the new principal has ambitious goals, and the students are getting another chance at a high school diploma.

At the top of New York's system of choice schools stand four test-in schools. We've mentioned or described three: Brooklyn Tech, Bronx Science, and Stuyvesant. The fourth, Fiorello H. La Guardia High School, specializes in the performing arts, and many of its graduates pursue music, opera, and dance in conservatory studies after high school.

A few other cities also have test-in schools, although they are far from being universal. Chicago expanded its set of test-in schools to eight under Superintendent Paul Vallas. Northside College Prep in Chicago, for example, opened in September 1999 and today a score on the admissions test of at least the 95th percentile is usually necessary for admission. In Houston, schools like Michael DeBakey High School for the health professions also admit by test. Los Angeles as yet has no test-in schools, nor does Seattle.

At the next tier, New York has created several options schools. An options school is one that has elected to institute an application process. One of these is the Edward R. Murrow High School, located in a residential neighborhood in Brooklyn. Edward R. Murrow represents a compromise—it's a school that focuses on college-bound students with a high-powered academic program, but it avoids being labeled elite by allocating half of its places by lottery. Students apply during their eighth-grade year, based solely on their seventh-grade transcript, including scores on standardized tests and grades. The school is not permitted to interview applicants or to give them any admissions test. Half of the class is selected based on those criteria and the other half is admitted by lottery. In addition, no more than 12 percent of an entering class may be from the top group by reading score, and at least 12 percent must be from the lowest reading group of applicants.

The school appeals to families who have a desire both for a diverse student body and for a rigorous, college preparatory setting. Of the approximately 3,600 students, 49 percent are white, 23 percent are black, 16 percent are Asian, and 12 percent are Hispanic. It seems that the formula works: 60 percent of the graduates go to four-year colleges and 28 percent to two-year colleges. According to veteran principal Saul Bruckner—who opened the school in 1974—it's common to have more than a thousand parents attend open school evenings and afternoons. Although there is some economic diversity, Edward R. Murrow is essentially a middle-class school, with only 19 percent of the students qualifying for subsidized school lunches. The formula is immensely popular with parents, so much so that the school is a favorite with the district's central office staff, many of whose children are enrolled here.

As a side note, Principal Bruckner mentions that he has long regarded "the famous Edmonton" as a model for how to run a school district. Although he says that "compared to Los Angeles, we have a lot of freedom in New York City," he can only imagine what it would be like if he had as much freedom as do the schools in Edmonton. Still, he manages to offer instruction in seven foreign languages, along with a large variety of other academic courses. Edward R. Murrow was listed as one of "Ten Hot Schools" by *New York* magazine in its April 13, 1998, issue, and was described by *The New York Times* as an academically rigorous school "with an almost collegiate atmosphere" in an October 19, 1995, story.

Among the sixty-six public schools that we visited in New York City, we saw many that were simply ordinary and some that were terrible. However, we also found several brilliant schools, and we found more variety there than in any other city. The test-in schools and the options schools are among the most encouraging. They offer an attractive choice to the middle class, which has felt forced out of many urban public school districts. There's no good reason why your school district can't emulate these examples. It takes a willingness on the part of the school board and the superintendent to experiment with new ideas, and it takes pressure from parents who care. Many school boards and superintendents lament the flight of the middle class from public schools, but few offer those families an attractive option. It's time to quit the hand-wringing and start to do something about this.

CHOICES AMONG REGULAR PUBLIC SCHOOLS

As public scrutiny of public education increases, even traditional school districts are offering more varied choices. Most of the attention has gone to private companies like Edison Schools, Inc., which manages public schools and attempts to make a profit doing so. A guide to private businesses that operate public schools was published by the Center for Education Reform in Washington, D.C.[14] It lists 19 companies that among them run a total of 350 schools, although both of those numbers are increasing almost daily. A few, like the Aspire Public Schools in Redwood City, California, are not-for-profit. Most, though, such as Beacon Education Management in Westborough, Massachusetts, are for-profit businesses. Beacon operates twenty-five public charter schools in five states, including Massachusetts, Michigan, and Missouri, as well as in the District of Columbia.

Best known among these for-profit companies is the Edison Schools company, which by 2003 was operating 150 schools in 53 cities and 23 states, with a total of 80,000 students. Edison includes a mixture of charter and noncharter public schools. Edison schools, according to the Center for Education Reform's report, use the Success for All reading program and the University of Chicago math program. Edison has recently been selected to operate twenty of the Philadelphia public schools. However, companies like Edison face the same problem that confronts all charter schools—school districts will give them only a fraction of the per-student budget that they have, because they need to continue to feed their huge central office staffs. In addition, Edison and other for-profit operators bump up against a fundamental public skepticism about anyone who wants to make money from the education of children. After all, no one wants to see an Enron happen to education.

As a result of these and other difficulties, Edison's future has been questioned. An article in the May 19, 2002, edition of Time.com reports that Edison Schools lost one of its flagship accounts, the Boston Renaissance Charter School, after 69 percent of Renaissance eighth graders failed the statewide math test and 22 percent failed the English test—in both cases a lower performance than the public schools. The story added that a Securities and Exchange Commission inquiry found that Edison Schools had omitted crucial information from its filings, "allowing it to report revenues from 1999 to 2002 that were 41 percent to 48 percent higher than it actually generated." By early 2003, Edison's stock had dropped to less than $2 a share, far below its peak of $35 in January 2001.

WHAT CHOICE IS LIKE WHEN THE SEVEN KEYS ARE ALL IN PLACE

Although Edison may be getting the headlines, the real story is what's happening in districts with the Seven Keys to Success in place. There, it's as though every school was a charter school and every student had a voucher based on Weighted Student Formula. What happens when every school is set free and parents are empowered with choice? The answer is that great variety develops among schools—as is happening now in Seattle. Two regular Seattle public schools illustrate the variety that can develop under the Seven Keys to Success.

The John Stanford International School in Seattle, K–5, has found its own way. Principal Karen Kodama and her staff were determined to take their upper-middle-class neighborhood back from the private schools. They did some market research and found that their location next to the University of Washington had produced an international community of professors, graduate students, and others. They designed a school for 380 students in which each class is taught from a global perspective. In addition, each first grader must choose a second language and receive half of her instruction in that second language for all of grades 1 through 5. John Stanford School has allied itself with a wide array of resources, including a three-year federal magnet grant, another grant from Seattle Central Community College, and a designation by the University of Washington as a Partnership/Lab School. The school receives curriculum development help, student interns, tutors, and advice on internationalization from the university. Inaugurated in the 2000–01 school year, the school already has a waiting list of 170.

On the south side of Seattle, where the population is heavily immigrant, poverty rates are high, and many children live in single-parent homes, lies the Bailey Gatzert Elementary School. It was founded more than one hundred years ago as the Main Street School and later was named the Spring Street School; in 1922, it was given its present name in honor of the first Jewish mayor of Seattle. Had he known what this school would become, he'd have been proud indeed. Principal Jean Anthony and her teachers have created a school that targets the most difficult groups of children to reach—the poor and the homeless. Of the 416 students in grades K–5, about one hundred are homeless, 50 percent have limited English proficiency, and virtually all are from families that live below the poverty line.

Because of Weighted Student Formula, Bailey Gatzert has more money per student than most Seattle public schools, and as a result the classes are small: most have seventeen or fewer students. The school selects only teachers who share its sense of mission, and it has a team of specialists that includes a parent liaison, a family support worker, an intervention specialist, and a school psychologist. This team assists each teacher to plan how to help a family to help its own children. The school building looks good—in fact, it's the best-looking building in the immediate vicinity. The students, many of whom are living either in homeless shelters or on the streets, come each day to a place that tells them that someone cares enough about them to give them a handsome place to go to school. Some children are gone after a month, and others stay in the school for only a year or two, but 60 percent return from one year to the next—a good rate even for a school with a less difficult population.

Jean Anthony is a serious, tough-minded person—simple in her dress and in her manner, economical in her expressions. She is not the kind of principal who would be at ease raising money at social events with the upper classes of Seattle. She is expert at special education, and knows what it takes to build the self-confidence of children who come from the streets. She is enough of an entrepreneur, though, to have brought in volunteers from Starbucks Corporation and from Big Brothers and Big Sisters. Nearby Bishop O'Shea High School provides five volunteer tutors. Another local organization, Team Read, pays forty-six high school students to work at Bailey Gatzert as reading coaches. Stockbrokers come after work (the New York Stock Exchange closes at 1:00 P.M. Seattle time) to help the children with their homework.

Children who are homeless often display very defensive behavior—they don't want to connect, don't want to establish relationships, and they are angry. In some cases, the school is able to help them. Principal Anthony describes one such child, whom we will call Albert:

> Albert came to us in third grade. He was an extremely angry child. Homeless, father had died, mom not mentally well—not able to help the kids and not able to keep a home. [Albert] would throw a chair, run away, break things then run out of the building—somewhat of a dangerous kid.
>
> He is . . . extremely bright. So through the work of Randy [parent liaison], the classroom teacher, and the intervention specialist really working—really focused on the parents [the mother had presumably remarried], meetings and plans and pushing, we were pushing the parents to do the right things . . . he began to experience success.
>
> He is in fourth grade now. Yesterday he got an award for the most improvement, but, of course, he would not

come up and get the award, which would have been too much. We are not miracle workers but she [the mother] is at least allowing this child to experience some success and she is not sabotaging everything that he does. But it was a huge team effort . . . I think we did save a life.

Anthony explains that it's the budget control that enables her school to marshal its resources in a way that makes sense for these children: "I will tell you that it made a huge difference—coming from a school district where the district's business manager tells me how many teachers I can have."

Anthony has used her flexibility to divide the school into three groups: K–1, 2–3, and 4–5. Each of the three teams has an additional certified teacher and an instructional aide who provide direct assistance to the children. Each team also has a different schedule. The instructional assistants are fluent either in Vietnamese, Spanish, Oromo (Ethiopian), Somali, or Tagalog (Filipino).

Mrs. Morrison runs a kindergarten class at Bailey Gatzert, and thirteen students are present today. There is also a big, friendly black dog, and stacks of books everywhere. Supplies are plentiful, from crayons and markers to little plastic boxes of letters and mathematical symbols. Each child's picture and name is posted on the wall—another daily reminder that they belong here.

When you first enter the classroom, it's difficult to see Mrs. Morrison, because she's on her knees, moving from child to child measuring each one's height with a tape measure so they can write it down next to the self-portrait that each is drawing. She speaks in a warm, respectful manner, not a patronizing or stern tone. Even her posture—on her knees—conveys respect rather than superiority.

The front office of Bailey Gatzert sees a constant flow of volunteers. The local Rotary Club is here today to run its Giraffe program—it teaches the children to stick their necks out for the common good. The Seattle Chess Foundation Program comes every Wednesday to teach the children to play chess.

The school has a strong focus on literacy. The teachers are schooled in Reading Mastery, in the balanced literacy approach, and in Read Well. Each teacher can use whichever approach she favors, but all students are expected to be reading by the end of first grade.

Jeff Fording, a new fifth-grade teacher, came from a school in Athens, Georgia, because he'd heard of Bailey Gatzert and wanted to be a part of it. Jeff tries not to miss a day of school, because he's learned that for his students, who move from shelter to shelter every few weeks, "this is the one consistency in their lives. This is why you see our teacher attendance so high as well—because we know that we are the only consistent thing. And when you are out for any reason, they freak out. When we come back, they ask you, 'is everything okay? Are you going to be here today? You're not going home, are you?'" A second-grade teacher adds, "I think that what is so special is that we teach so many difficult children, children that have been kicked out of other schools. The philosophy here is that we don't throw kids away, we don't pass the buck, we don't give them to someone else . . . we care enough to deal with family issues, deal with the student issues, and make it work and teach them."

Can it really be true that you don't have to pay teachers extra to get them to come to a place like Bailey Gatzert, that all it takes is giving them the freedom to do what they trained to do, what they love doing, and what they do best? Again, Jeff Fording:

> We are okay. We know that we got into this business not for money. We didn't get into it for wealth, for glory—we got into it because we want to help children. . . . Here you matter, you matter to these kids, what you say matters to these kids. And you really see a change when they walk out.

That, in a nutshell, is what the Seven Keys to Success are all about. When the teachers know that they matter, then the students and their families will know that they matter, too. Given a difficult task but with adequate resources and lots of local autonomy, these teachers have found a way to succeed.

The weekly staff meeting is underway, and thirty-nine people are present, which must be just about everyone, since there are only twenty classroom teachers plus the many specialists. The discussion is a serious one about lengthening the school year and going to a year-round schedule next year. Principal Anthony wants everyone to participate because they will have to take part in focus groups with parents if the decision is to go ahead. The rest of the district won't be making this change, so the school will have to figure out how to compensate teachers and Anthony will have to negotiate for the money with the central office.

One of the senior teachers points out that everyone should make the decision based only on what is best for the students, because a year-round schedule is not going to work for some of the teachers. She says that she and some other teachers may have to move on, much as they love this school. There is general agreement that this is the correct attitude for all to take.

School is out, and nine yellow school buses stand out front. One of the children pops out of her bus to wave good-bye to a visitor. They have the curiosity of all children and the toughness of street kids. They're not afraid to walk up to a stranger in a hallway and ask, who are you and what are you doing here? For a lot of them, this is the best part of their day—the only place that they have that is nice and clean, and where they are respected and even loved. A school like this is a pretty special place.

Part Three:
A Parent's Guide to School Improvement ✔

10

How Good Is Your School?

*I*f you are going to improve your child's school—and you *are* going to—one of your first steps will be to diagnose what is going on right now. In order to carry out that analysis, you'll want a detailed profile of what the school is really like. In this chapter, we'll review eleven key indicators that you can inspect at any school. These range from what you see as you approach the school building to what the classrooms look like to what you see when you observe a teacher at work. We'll then move on to the more subtle aspects that involve listening to and watching the interaction in the classroom more closely, and finally how to understand the underlying organization of the school. There's an old saying in business: "If you can't measure it, you can't control it." For parents, the appropriate maxim might be: "If you can't see it, you can't influence it." This section is for those of you who spend time in schools and would like to know what the experts notice when they visit a school.

Many parents visit their children's schools regularly. Sometimes, the visit is just to pick up a child or bring something that they've forgotten that morning. Other times, it's for a parent conference, an open house, or perhaps a stint as a volunteer for a few hours. What did you notice the last time you visited your child's school? Treat this like a detective movie: You were in the room—what was the teacher doing? Were the children working in separate centers? Were the walls covered with professionally printed posters or with the children's work?

There's no reason to be afraid of the idea that you can become an astute observer of your child's school. Former secretary of education William J. Bennett and his colleagues put it well in *The Educated Child:* "It takes no expertise to recognize whether a school is doing right by its students. You can begin to get a good sense of it just by spending a little time in its classrooms and corridors."[1] Soon, you'll be able to go beyond simply getting a good sense of the school—you'll be able to make out the major details, too.

When you discuss your observations with your principal, you'll most likely have an engaged response once the principal understands that you know what to look for. In other cases, though, it's sad to say but true that some principals don't know what to look for. In fact, we've found that one of the most telling signs is whether a principal offers to take you on a tour of classrooms or prefers just to walk you down the hallways. In most good schools where the atmosphere is open, teachers don't suspect or fear visits from the principal, and a principal who is proud of her school will want you to see every classroom for yourself.

This chapter brings you lessons from some of the most experienced educators anywhere, so read on and learn how to be a more effective observer.

1. APPROACHING THE SCHOOL

Vincent Grippo has been an educator for thirty-four years. He's been through the chairs—teacher, dean of discipline, assistant principal, assistant superintendent. For the past seven years, he's been superintendent of New York City's District 20 in Brooklyn, which covers the Bensonhurst, Bay Ridge, and Dyker Heights neighborhoods. His staff is lean and mean, because Vinnie, as he's called, is a hands-on superintendent. He tries to visit one of his twenty elementary or eight middle schools every day. How do you tell a good school? Vinnie leans back in his chair and smiles, relishing the memories of his years in the trenches. "From the moment I approach the outside of a school, I begin to notice things":

- Is the school clean? Did the custodian clean the hallways?
- The security guard at the front door—does he or she greet you warmly? Does he or she know their procedures?
- There are usually parents in the school—how happy do they look?
- Are the kids smiling? What's the tenor of the building?
- Do the secretaries have "the disease" where they look down, not at you?

Ethel Tucker, who is superintendent at the nearby District 21, sounds a similar note: "One of the things I would hope would happen is you'd be stopped at the gate and asked for identification so that you know this is a safe school. Then I would look to see if it is inviting, whether the people that you first met were welcoming."

A third New York City superintendent, John Comer of District 22, also in Brooklyn, has served in his current post for sixteen years. Ever since the new law in 1996 that gave more autonomy to principals, he has left it up to each school to decide how to spend its money, as they also do in District 2. What he expects of them is improvement in student achievement. Comer tries to visit one of his schools every day, and each school receives three unannounced visits from him each year. Here's a sample of his approach to the overall quality of a school:

> I can tell usually after thirty seconds in the front door by listening to the tone of the school. If I hear kids running through the halls yelling, that's a problem. I'm not against noise, but I know that order precedes learning.
>
> Principals have to spend their money in a way that advances student achievement. I don't want them hiring teaching aides just so they don't have to be in the lunchroom and on the playground. That's a bad principal, and things will start to fall apart. A principal should be out of their office, active around the school.

Superintendent Comer also has a pet peeve that is common among experienced educators: "A phony bulletin board has a lot of commercially produced art work. A good one displays lots of student work."

Kathy Wiedeman is the magnet coordinator at Mabel Wesley Elementary School in Houston. She, too, agrees that the attitude that greets you in front of the school is an important indicator: "Once you come in, how are you treated by the office staff or by the people who receive you? Do they want you to be there, or are they letting you know that you are not wanted? You get a feel for it and—I hate to say this—your first impression is very important." Ms. Wiedeman also shares Superintendent Comer's pet peeve: "As a parent, I have a child right now who is getting ready to go to high school. I did go to the high school, and I walked into the classrooms. I wanted to see what was on the wall: was it instruction or was it camouflage?"

As you can see, some of these are universally held observations, and others are more particular. It's instructive, though, to learn that experienced educators begin to evaluate a school even before they walk in the front door. What's more important, of course, is what you notice when you walk into a classroom.

2. What to notice when you first enter an elementary school classroom

Vinnie Grippo has spent a lifetime in classrooms, and he knows how to get the feel of one very quickly. "You can tell a good classroom from a bad classroom in five minutes," he says. For one thing, he wants every elementary and middle school classroom to look like a library, with books everywhere. For another, he doesn't want to see rows of desks facing the teacher—not in the elementary and middle schools. As he says, "I've never seen a company that wants its employees treated like that." He also likes to see the students engaged with one another, talking seriously, helping one another. Grippo believes that young children learn best by touching, by doing, by learning to do their own research on a topic. They can't do that if they're sitting in straight rows with the teacher at the front of the room. Ethel Tucker of District 21 agrees and adds that often it's difficult to spot the teacher in an effective classroom, because the children are at work in several separate small centers at once, with the teacher down at eye-level with the students. The teacher's desk, she observes, is often hard to pick out at first—and that's a good sign.

Many experienced educators would agree with John Comer of District 22 that an elementary classroom should begin each day with reading and writing, when the students are alert. If the class is not settled down and at work thirty minutes after the start of school, he believes, there's a problem. He seconds Ethel Tucker in believing that a good classroom is one in which different things are going on in several centers or clusters of four to six students, all at once.

Veteran educators place great importance on a school setting that communicates safety, warmth, and acceptance. Especially for the little ones, feeling emotionally and physically safe is a necessary precondition for learning. You'll see these elements in bold relief at the Abraham Joshua Heschel School (nursery through eighth grade) on the Upper West Side of Manhattan.

Under Director Roanna Sherofsky, this independent school has prospered by accommodating families from all of the major denominations of the Jewish faith. There are two guards at the front door, and the entry protocol is strictly enforced.

Inside, the first-grade classrooms are a bazaar of visual stimulation. Four children are working at a table with the teacher, while six others are cutting and pasting with colored construction paper. There are two separate reading corners, each with rugs and oversized pillows. The walls are covered with the children's work, and more of it hangs overhead from clotheslines strung from the ceiling. Each child has a plastic bin for her work, and books are everywhere. In a connecting room, a group of children is baking the Jewish bread, Challah—to be eaten tomorrow, on the Sabbath. There is no obvious place for a teacher to stand in front of the class, because most of the teaching is done by allowing the children to experiment and learn on their own, guided by their teachers. According to the teachers, there is very little "frontal" teaching at Heschel School. The words that come to mind to describe the way it looks are "cozy," "warm," and "secure."

3. GET A FEEL FOR WHAT THE STUDENTS ARE DOING

You remember having met Joanne Testa-Cross, the principal at the John Hay Elementary School in Seattle? She's a data-based leader, and to know a school, she likes to see data on student achievement and spend some time there. But she, too, has some rough-and-ready indicators when she visits a school. They have to do with how the people—both children and adults—interact with each other, and what they do when they're in school.

> What are they doing when you walk in? Is there a sense of warmth, friendliness, and belonging? Do you feel welcome when you walk through that door? In other words, do you see relationships? Second, do I see people

engaged in tasks along with those relationships? Is what they are doing related to learning?

Listen to the conversations in the halls, the cafeteria, and in the classrooms, she counsels. For example, one day Testa-Cross came to school in the morning on election day. Two six-year-olds were having an argument over who was the better presidential candidate! A lot of their political awareness probably came from their parents, but for these children, school is a place where you discuss the important things that are going on in the world around you. Another time, Testa-Cross was taking parents through her school when they came across a second-grade class sitting in the hallway with their teacher. The class had completed an important project, and the teacher had posted their work on the hallway bulletin board. The class was going through the work and offering comments on what was important about it. If you look in some schools, you can see the learning literally spilling out of the classroom into the hallways and everywhere else.

Like many other educators, Testa-Cross says that when she enters a classroom, she looks at the students before she looks at the teacher. The teacher can put on a temporary show to impress visitors, but the students will show you in their expressions how they really feel about school. Like so many others, she also places great stock in what you see (or don't see) posted on the walls of the school: "I can almost sell this school just based on taking people through the hallways because they will see the work of the students everywhere and they are so jazzed by what they see that they know when they go into that classroom it's going to be exciting."

4. IS THE TEACHER AMONG THE CHILDREN OR IN FRONT OF THE CLASS?

Alice Young is the principal of Middle School 131 in District 2, Manhattan. Here are her observations:

Well, the first thing when I walk into the classroom, I look around on the walls, I look to see what is there and is everything inviting—appealing to the eye. If there are books. If there is children's work that the teachers have put up. And then I look to see where the teacher is.

   . . . I like to be able to walk into the classroom and not be able to find the teacher—that means she or he is among the children. Sometimes [if] I walk into the classroom and I [can't] find the teacher, then I get a little nervous—is she here? And I look around and ask the children: "Where is your teacher?" And they say, "Oh, she's over there."

A lot of times the teacher does stand up and teach. But then every eye should be on the teacher. And everyone should be engaged and everyone should be on the edge of their seats listening.

I usually then walk in and sit down and say to a child, "Tell me what you are doing, show me what you are doing." I would point to something hanging up and I would say, "Can you tell me about it?" Can they tell me how what is hanging up is relevant to what they are doing? Because a lot of times people just hang up things and it is not work, the teacher just does it because it looks good.

5. DOES THE CLASSROOM LOOK AS IF IT BELONGS TO THE STUDENTS OR THE TEACHER?

To say that an elementary classroom should look like a library does not mean one of those closed-stacks libraries where you have to fill out a form and wait for someone to bring your book to the front desk. Young children should be encouraged to explore for themselves, and that means giving them the run of the place. If a five-year-old child in a room of twenty children has to ask the teacher each time he wants a book, a crayon, or some glue, he is not likely to do it very often. Ideally, the books and materials should be down at child height, and in open shelves, not behind closet doors.

The office of Principal Daria Rigney at P.S./I.S. 126 in Manhattan is full of children's books—it looks like a child-friendly library, and it is. It's also full of work by the children, such as this letter on the wall:

Dear Mrs. Rigney,
We are glad you liked the dumplings. Class 100 will send
you the recipe. Can you share a recipe with us?

Each student has signed the letter, and it looks as though each took turns writing one of the words in the letter. It's a good guess that "recipe" was their word of the day, because it's specially highlighted.

Mrs. Rigney believes that reading comes naturally to children when they are ready, even for the predominantly low-income population she serves. Same thing goes for writing. Children have to practice both of these skills, but the real teaching, she says, has to do with learning to acquire the meaning of a text, not just to decode each word. "Reading is making ideas," she says.

For example, Rigney encourages kindergarten children to work on their drawing. A drawing is a story, and as a child learns to put more details into a drawing, she or he is learning to develop a more complex story line and thus a more complex logic. A drawing may have several characters, a major plot, subplots, and will likely communicate feelings as well as action. The story that is told in the drawing is likely to have a beginning, a middle, and a conclusion. The children at P.S./I.S. 126 are encouraged to draw and then explain their drawings. For this reason: children who have not been read to much at home should be told stories and read stories at school. Hearing stories not only helps with letter recognition and word sounds, it develops one of the important comprehension skills—the art of understanding the structure of a story.

When Principal Rigney walks into a classroom—which she does several times every day—"I can tell by the environment—I can tell if it is an environment that is clean, colorful, filled with books and blocks, with discrete places for the kids to work and play. I can tell looking at the way kids are in the room whether they understand that the room belongs to them—that they have access to blocks, to lots of math materials. I probably could tell just by the way the library is set up—that it is arranged in familiar authors and familiar books that the kids have read aloud." She emphasizes that it's obvious to anyone who knows what to look for who the classroom is really for—the teacher or the students: "You can tell whose classroom it is by the way materials are organized. Do the kids feel that this is their laboratory, their workshop, that there are rules, but I can use this if I need to . . . ? I can pull out music sheets or I can pull out blocks or I can show you how I figure out $2 + 3 = 5$."

Rigney also listens to each teacher's tone of voice. Some teachers use a conversational tone that invites a response from the child, while others will use an instructional tone that is telling the children what to do. Most experienced teachers, of course, will use both voices at different times.

> What does a teacher do when a kid talks to her? Does she listen carefully? Does she try to push the child's thinking? Does she ask a question back?

She notices whether there are opportunities for the children to have conversation with each other, even in kindergarten. Some classrooms are set up so that students are basically trapped at their desks, while other rooms invite the children to access each other, to borrow crayons, share paints, or build a bakery together.

Every teacher at P.S./I.S. 126 organizes her classroom a little bit differently from the others and each teaches in an individual way, but all try hard to make the children feel at home and in charge in their classrooms.

6. Master teachers are multi-taskers

Vinnie Grippo, District 20 superintendent, said it best: "Watching a really good teacher perform is watching an artist creating a masterpiece!" Joanne Walsh, who is principal at the Sacred Heart School in the Bronx, would define an experienced teacher this way: "The kids are not all doing the same thing. They are all doing very different things." A group of four children is in one corner of the room assembling a jigsaw puzzle together. Another group of five is at a kidney-shaped table with the teacher, working on identifying shapes, colors, and the letters of the alphabet. Other children are working independently, writing letters or words. Still others are drawing pictures at their tables. Are you old enough to have been to a three-ring circus? Well, an experienced teacher resembles nothing so much as a ringmaster.

We've heard that when everything moves together, a school is poetry in motion. There are some educational poets at St. John's School, K–12, an independent school in the well-to-do section of Houston. Of the students who enter St. John's in kindergarten, about 60 percent will be there all the way through twelfth grade. The emphasis is on teaching a consistent set of practices in the lower grades that continues all the way through. Perhaps the most remarkable aspect of this school is the extent to which the students learn to take responsibility for their own conduct and, eventually, for their own learning. In Olga McLarron's first-grade class, the results are clearly visible to a first-time visitor.

Ms. McLarron is covering a particularly difficult math lesson today, so she's moving between two small tables, each with four or five children, helping them to complete their assignment. Meanwhile, the other children are not just playing or sitting idly by. In the far corner of the room, another group of children is doing shared reading. Those who wish to read today have signed up on a list. One by one, each takes his or her turn—they give a book talk, read a few passages, and then take comments and questions from the little audience of their classmates.

The striking feature is that these six-year-old children are running shared reading all by themselves. Ms. McLarron has sixteen children sitting quietly and respectfully, listening to the book report, while she works with the other ten children on their math. Ms. McLarron is just across the room, but there is no adult sitting with the reading group. Still there is no fidgeting, no getting up and walking around, no troublemaking. It sure doesn't fit the stereotype of a bunch of self-centered brats who are impossible to deal with. Ms. McLarron is a teacher with forty years of classroom experience, and she knows that to be a successful multitasker means teaching self-discipline to the children.

Twelve years from now, Dr. Ruth Bellows might have these children in her AP English class. Today, she has fourteen seniors. It is a cold winter day at the end of February, which means that college applications have long since been sent off, and in fact most of the students have already received early decisions and know which college they'll be attending next fall. Normally, it's difficult for a teacher to hold the attention of her class at this final stage of high school. If that weren't enough of a challenge, the discussion today is of a very tough book by the Algerian existential philosopher Albert Camus, *The Fall*.

Dr. Bellows begins by drawing the students into a dialogue with one another through a few well-chosen questions. After a few minutes, the students are carrying the thoughtful, serious discussion with no intervention at all from their teacher. Dr. Bellows is not an idle spectator, though. Her body language says that she's in this discussion, too, even though she's exercising the self-discipline not to say a word. If you hear it once, you'll hear it a hundred times: the teacher today should be the guide on the side, not the sage on the stage. Well, when you've seen it in action, you'll never forget it. What you're seeing at one time is two effects: one, a very skilled teacher, and the other, a consistent learning community, in this case from kindergarten through twelfth grade.

In both the kindergarten and twelfth-grade examples, though, you're seeing how education looks when the teacher has the skill to develop self-discipline in each student as well as to develop a culture of self-discipline in the classroom. That culture enables Ms. McLarron and Dr. Bellows to multi-task. Ms. McLarron obviously has several things going on in her classroom at once, but Dr. Bellows is multi-tasking, too—she's focusing on each student one by one, understanding what progress each has made and what each needs next, while they are teaching and learning from one another. In a sense, while the students attend to the subject, the teacher attends to their learning process.

7. DOES THE TEACHER GIVE EACH STUDENT WHAT SHE NEEDS?

If you know what to look for, and if you're patient, what looks like a class full of little children will be almost magically transformed into an educational process with levels of detail that you didn't realize were there. It's like being back in your eighth-grade science class, when the teacher passed around a test tube full of pond water and asked you what you saw? "Nothing. It's just water," you replied. Your teacher next put a drop of that water on a glass slide, placed the slide under a microscope, and invited you to take another look. "My gosh," you might have exclaimed, "it's full of life that I couldn't see before!" Well, put on these analytical lenses, and take another look at your child's classroom. Here's an example of what might appear before your empowered eyes.

Ms. Carter has twenty-two children in her first-grade class at John Hay Elementary School in Seattle. Half of the class has been pulled out by a reading specialist, and Ms. Carter will take the remaining eleven students for their reading instruction. She's assigned six of them as the Blue Group and the remaining five as the Red Group. The students in the Blue Group have been paired off, with each pair assigned to read a story and write sentences about it. Meanwhile, the Red Group students go to the library-like bookshelves and get copies of *Amelia Bedelia Goes Camping*.

Soon, everyone is reading and writing, but in two separate groups—for ease of classroom management, right? Not quite. Look again, more closely. While the Blue Group students work in pairs, the five Red Group students have gathered on the rug with Ms. Carter, who has pulled down a projection screen and is showing some slides.

Closer inspection reveals that the Blue Group pairs are taking turns reading a page in their book. As they read, they follow along with their finger, using the gestures that they have learned in direct instruction to indicate each syllable of each word.

Meanwhile, the Red Group is sitting in a semicircle around their teacher. She is asking them questions: "What is the setting of the story? What is the problem in the story?" Next, they are going to write a structured analysis of *Amelia Bedelia Goes Camping*, in which they will identify the setting, the characters, the problem, and the key events.

Ms. Carter has divided her students into two reading groups, each working on what will be right for them at this point in their development. The Blue Group readers are working on decoding words like "could" and "should" and are reinforcing their ability to comprehend words like "me," "my," "home," and "map." They are writing simple sentences made up of the words that they have practiced. The Red Group is working at a very different level, developing comprehension and analysis of an entire book and writing more complex sentences about it. Ms. Carter is working with them on their punctuation, emphasizing the correct use of periods, question marks, and exclamation points.

Ms. Carter's approach is based on data about each child's reading progress. There are forty-four levels of reading progress in the Diagnostic Reading Assessment, or DRA. All students should reach level 16 by the end of first grade and level 44 by the end of fifth grade. In this first-grade class, the actual levels of the students range from 4 to 32. As a result, the readers who need the greatest help are upstairs with the reading specialist, while the remaining students have been further subdivided into the Red and Blue Groups.

With a little effort on your part and the willingness of your child's teacher, you can quickly understand what the teacher is doing, and how best to help your child. If the teacher can't or won't explain this to you, you know there's a problem. In that case, you may need to talk to the principal.

8. How well organized is the teacher?

If Superintendent John Comer of New York were to visit the Sawyer Elementary School in Chicago, he would surely be impressed. The grounds are immaculate, the lawns are well kept and green, and an attractive fence provides security all around the perimeter of the property. The hard surfaces on the playground are freshly blacktopped, and there is an attractive mural on the walls.

Inside, Mrs. Pat Baggett-Hopkins has her fourth-grade class underway in their basement classroom. Mrs. Baggett-Hopkins is one of two teachers at Sawyer who have completed a set of rigorous federal requirements and are Nationally Certified Teachers. Today, she has twenty-nine students present. The students are seated at small tables of five or six, facing each other. It's October 31, Halloween, and she is in the spirit of things, with a pumpkin-colored sweater over her black pants.

The first thing you notice about Mrs. Baggett-Hopkins's classroom is that it is organized and disciplined. When visitors enter, the children do not look around but instead remain on task. The class is working on vocabulary words. The teacher has prepared ten definitions and has placed them on the wall. She hands Edgar a yellow slip of paper with the word "data" written on it. As he walks to the word wall, looking for the definition that fits his word, thirteen hands go up. The next word, "invertebrates," goes to Julio. The teacher has obviously gone to a lot of effort to prepare this exercise, writing out the words and the definitions on slips of paper. The students respond well—they're interested, eager to be chosen, and enjoying the drama.

The classroom is the picture of order and motivation. The children's work is displayed on the walls and from clotheslines that are strung across the ceiling from one corner of the room to the other. Clothespins hold cutouts of pumpkins and black cats that the children have colored. There is a large, comfortable rug in the reading area, which holds books, books, and more books. There is also a featured book of the month, *The Butterfly*. The blackboard at the front of the room clearly lists the schedule for today, so that the children know what to expect. It gives the homework assignment for tonight as well.

Fourth graders are on the cusp between childhood and preadolescence. Some of them still resemble the second or third graders, but others are nearly five feet tall. All of them are learning how to function independently at school. The teacher has the demanding task of encouraging their emerging sense of independence while maintaining discipline and order.

Mrs. Baggett-Hopkins conducts her class as if it were a symphony orchestra. The assignment now is to begin work on a two-week research project. Each child has chosen a book on the animal that he or she wants to study. The children are sitting at their desks, reading. One boy has a book on sharks, a girl has chosen to read about bats, and other choices include polar bears and whales. The teacher tells her class that she has arranged some Internet time for them later on so they can do more research on their animals. She has preset two Web sites for them but reminds them—no straying from those Web sites during research time!

After some time for individual reading has passed, she asks

each student to come up with three questions to research about his or her animal. Students volunteer their questions, and the teacher gently helps them to clarify. Here's a sample from one student: "When a snake bites a rat, the rat dies from the poison and the snake eats the rat, but the snake doesn't die. Why is that?"

Mrs. Baggett-Hopkins moves her class to their next topic, which is poetry reading time. She reads out loud one poem every day. Today the poem is "Goblin," by Jack Poluwski, one of her favorite poets. After poetry, the class lines up at the door to move to the next activity in another room. She gives them a silent hand signal, and they file out in an orderly line.

It's impressive to see a truly skilled teacher at work. It's difficult to take responsibility for twenty-nine children and treat each one as an individual. This teacher succeeds in large part because she is organized and has organized her students. Every minute is planned, the materials are prepared, and the students are never bored or fidgety, yet they're also not stressed or exhausted by too much activity.

9. ARE THE TEACHERS CONNECTING WITH THE CHILDREN AND THEIR FAMILIES AS PEOPLE?

In some neighborhoods, parents are present in the school almost to the point of wearing out their welcome. In others, the staff must go out of its way to make sure that the connection is there. At the Community Charter Middle School in Los Angeles, the outreach to families has a specific purpose—creating a supportive environment at home for each child's work.

Students are required to read for at least twenty minutes at home every evening and to write about a half page that summarizes what they've read—What was going on? What are the characters doing? for example. At least one parent must then read the child's work and sign the bottom of the page. The students bring in their signed homework the next day. Both parents and teachers sign a contract at the beginning of the year, pledging to do this reading assignment four nights each week.

If a student does not bring in the signed homework, the school's Connections program gets the word. A staff member makes an appointment with the parents to find out if something is wrong and get the reading back on track. Look for specific activities like this one that make the connection from school to home happen. Otherwise, it won't.

At the Caernarvon School, grades K–6, in Edmonton, enrollments were falling as the neighborhood aged and there were fewer families with young children. In order to build the enrollment back up, Principal Julia Elaschuk came up with several innovations, one of which was to attract Chinese families from nearby areas with a Mandarin language program. Today, she estimates that 40 percent of the students are of Asian descent, and the program has a waiting list.

Ms. Elaschuk keeps in constant touch with her families, and she's learned how to keep them at the Caernarvon School. Today, for example, eleven little girls—all in pink tights and white leggings—are participating in a Mandarin dance class in the school's gym after school that is run by an outside community group. Principal Elaschuk elaborates on what her families have told her they want: "I also have an after-school art class on Thursday. I do all these things—violin, dance, art—to keep my clients happy. I want to keep these Mandarin students. The more students, the more money the school gets."

Although it's an elite independent school, St. John's in Houston is an example from which you may be able to learn. If you don't have the same resources it does, perhaps you can improvise. St. John's starts out its kindergarten with a half-day schedule for the first two weeks of school. After that, kindergarten is a full day. Why? Because the school encourages the parents to gather informally with small parent-child groups in the afternoon (it could just as well be the evening, since most moms work nowadays), to get to know one another. They'll meet at a neighborhood park, a local restaurant, or in one another's homes. According to kindergarten teacher Donna Thomas, "We find that if parents meet each other very early in the kindergarten years, that camaraderie just seems to continue all the way through." If the families are comfortable with one another, it's going to be that much easier for them to relate to the school—at least they know they'll see a friendly face or two when they come to an open house.

10. IN A HIGH SCHOOL, LOOK FOR THE INTERACTION, NOT THE CLASSROOM LAYOUT

Most high schools are run on a departmental system. If there are enough classrooms, each teacher will typically have his or her own room, so that they can have books, supplies, and projects out and available to the students. In some districts, though, the building program has not kept up with the growth in enrollment, and then the teachers will have to travel to different rooms at different periods. Those classrooms won't usually have much personality, but that doesn't mean that the interaction that takes place there isn't productive.

Nonetheless, you can see a whole lot by walking through a high school. Here, in one unhappy example, are some of things that you hope *not* to see.

Los Angeles High School was once the flagship of the school system. Established in 1873, it is the oldest high school in the city. Principal Mary Kaufman is brand new, and she means to turn the school around. Students were drifting into the classrooms long after the morning bell had rung, and the teachers were angry, perhaps because of the management style of the former principal, who—some teachers say—rarely talked to them. No one in the central office has paid much attention to the school, even after the arrival of the new principal, although she says that her local area superintendent has been very supportive.

There are 4,471 students—75 percent of whom are Latino—but only 80 percent of the students show up for school every day. Los Angeles High has 1,750 ninth graders this year, but it will award diplomas to just 440 graduating seniors. If things continue this way, the dropout rate will reach 75 percent.

According to Principal Kaufman, the fire alarms go off constantly because the kids pull them as they walk by. If there really were a fire, they'd have to call the fire department on the telephone, she says, because it no longer responds to the alarms. It's not surprising that the students don't take pride in their school because it looks dark and old, much like a prison, although painters are working there today.

One group of teachers believes that standardized tests are racially biased, and with help from lawyers at the American Civil Liberties Union, they get students waivers so that they won't have to take the tests. The good news, so to speak, is that Los Angeles High is not considered to be the worst school in the city—it's considered to be the "best of the worst." Four others rank even lower.

Because Los Angeles has a centralized budgeting system, the principal has no control over how her school is staffed. She gets the formula-driven number of teachers, school psychologists, nurses, gardeners, office workers, and so on—no matter what she feels she actually needs.

Of course, you wouldn't know all of this as a visitor, but you can guess at it from what you *can* see, if you know what to look for. For example, the attitude here seems to be that a classroom is supposed to be an isolated place run by the teacher—and no one should visit. Some of the older teachers don't think they should have to post the district's learning standards where students and parents can see them.

At Los Angeles High School, some of the teachers teach a sixth period each day for extra pay. They are also supposed to stay after for an additional hour to talk to students, other teachers, or administrative staff, but almost no one does. Perhaps that's because no one checks to see who is around for that extra hour. Visit your school at the end of the day, and see if the teachers beat the students out the front door.

Gangs are a problem in this neighborhood, and the school has a strict dress code: no hats, no midriffs showing, no baggy pants. Unfortunately, the dress code appears not to apply to the teachers, and the union won't permit the principal to do anything about it. One teacher walks by with a baseball cap on backwards. Several other teachers are wearing blue jeans.

The classroom doors are locked, and the principal uses a key to gain entry to each one that she visits in her daily rounds— a practice that is new to these teachers, who are not accustomed to seeing their principal visit classes. In eleventh-grade history, the class is watching a video of *Dances with Wolves*. When the students are assigned papers for some classes, they are more often than not group papers, although an occasional individual paper is assigned. Group papers, of course, means less to read and grade for the teacher, but it also means less feedback for individual students.

A visit to Geometry A turns up eighteen students taking a test, and they appear to be intent on their work. In tenth-grade Honors English, the eighteen students are thoroughly engaged with their teacher, who has set up a game based on the TV show *Jeopardy!* to review their knowledge of Shakespeare. Then there's a class in science. The teacher immediately comes to the door, perhaps so that visitors won't have to walk all the way into the classroom to speak to him. They do walk in, though, and discover that the nineteen students are slumped in their seats watching a video on skateboarding. The teacher sheepishly explains that it's a reward for their hard work over the past few days.

It's painful, isn't it, even to *read* about a school this awful and to think about what is happening to most of these more than four thousand young people and their two hundred or so teachers every day. The silver lining is that the new principal is energetic, experienced, and tough. She displays an openness—she's not afraid to put her school's problems on the table, where she, her area superintendent, and the several dedicated teachers can work together on solving them. Remember, too, that medical students learn how to keep us healthy by studying pathologies—cancer, heart disease, and other infirmities. We can learn from Los Angeles High School, even if it's learning what to avoid. With any luck, the school will be able to look back on this one day and take pride in the turnaround it has created.

11. IS THE HIGH SCHOOL'S PROGRAM CUSTOM-DESIGNED, OR IS IT ONE-SIZE-FITS-ALL?

If you agree that every group of students is unique, it follows that every school should show the signs of custom design. We've seen how that looks in Edmonton's Jasper Place High School and in New York City's Edward R. Murrow High School.

Foshay Learning Center, grades K–12, is very much an inner-city school. It's on the tough south side of Los Angeles, in the middle of gang territory. Until 2001, Foshay had an extremely entrepreneurial principal in Howard Lappin. Lappin was among the first in Los Angeles to lead more than 75 percent of his teachers to vote to become a LEARN school, part of a reform movement that for several years enabled nearly four hundred schools to gain a real measure of local autonomy. After twelve years, Lappin became an executive in a charter school system. His school is an impressive example for other urban high schools. In the year 2000, *Newsweek* magazine picked Foshay as one of the 100 best high schools in the country.

If you'll take the time to ask about how the programs are set up at a high school, you'll soon see what makes it tick. Foshay has a total of 3,545 students in grades K through 12; 70 percent of the students are Latino and 29 percent are Asian; 92 percent are from low-income homes. Foshay has partnerships with the nearby University of Southern California and with several other school enrichment programs.

You might assume that all the grades at Foshay are roughly equal in size, but they aren't. The elementary school is very small, with about 170 students. The middle school is very large, with about 2,600 students; and the high school is middle-sized, at about 700. This distribution is the result of a school that has responded to the needs of the community.

The high school is further divided into three academies, and each academy is looped, which means that the group of students stays together for grades 10 and 11, with a set of teachers who teach only in that academy and only those fifty to sixty students, except for the math teachers, who specialize by course. In this way, the teachers are able to build a sense of cohesiveness with the students, with the result that attendance is a very high 96 percent. Even in the dress-permissive Los Angeles Unified School District, Foshay maintains a strict high school dress code (no gang colors, no cutoffs, shirts must have sleeves), with only one family having petitioned out of the dress code in twelve years. In recent years, the high school has had nearly three applicants for each place.

The middle school runs on Concept 6, with three tracks year-round, while the elementary and high schools each run on a traditional school year with a single track. In order to keep things organized, Lappin created a system of general managers in which he and each of his three assistant principals serves as general manager for one of the five tracks. Each track of students and teachers has a general manager who knows the people, the schedule, and the families.

It sounds a bit complex, and it is. But if you are going to offer a tailored education to a large number of students, you must come up with the organizational arrangements that fit the special needs of the situation. The organization of a school should be easy for students and parents to use. That often means it will be complex and difficult for the staff to manage, but that's how it should be. If your school's system makes sense to you, that's a good sign. If it's a large school with a diverse population but has no internal means of dealing with all of that variety and complexity, that's a bad sign. Not every high school has to have a complex organization, but every high school must have an internal flexibility and detail appropriate to its situation. If it doesn't, then your child may be lost in a sea of nameless students, or thrown into classes that don't fit her educational needs at all.

In some cases, as at the DeBakey High School for the medical professions in Houston, the solution is to admit only a narrowly specialized group of students. In that case, nearly every student has similar educational needs, and the school can thrive with a simple structure. Here's the rule of thumb: a school should have the internal variety and complexity that matches the diversity of its student body. A homogeneous student body matches up well with a simple curriculum and organizational structure. A diverse student body calls for complex organization. It's also true that the more complex the structure of the school, the more teamwork is required among teachers and administration—or else all will be infighting and chaos.

NOW THAT YOU KNOW WHAT TO LOOK FOR, YOU'RE AN INFORMED PARENT

There is a lot more to understanding schools than we've covered here, of course. You may not be an expert educator at this point, but now you are at least an informed parent and an informed consumer of education. You know some of what to look for, and you'll see your child's school with new eyes. Most important of all, you'll be better able to engage your child's teachers and principal in an intelligent conversation about the school. They'll be impressed that you've taken the time to learn something of their world and their language.

You have some advantages, too. First, you've heard from

some of the most experienced and highly respected educators in North America. You've gleaned lessons from some 223 schools—more than most teachers or principals have ever seen. Second, you've seen education systems from all three points of view—the classroom teacher, the principal, and the superintendent. That's a unique set of perspectives. Third, you've gained a perspective on the systems that make up a school—from curriculum design to teaching methods, to classroom layout, management and organization, to its financial workings.

If you are feeling a bit overwhelmed at the complexity of a school and at the enormity of the task of revolutionizing an entire school district, that's okay. You should probably feel some humility—after all, lots of smart educators have been suffering under their systems for a very long time, and they haven't figured out how to fix things. While humility is well and good, though, timidity is not. If you aren't going to be the one to attack the problems of your schools, who will be?

Just keep in mind a favorite old elephant joke that I first heard many years ago from my friend and former colleague Dr. Tom Hofstedt, who is an expert in helping big companies to change their ways, and who teaches courses on school finance. It will give you comfort as you move forward. How do you eat an elephant? One bite at a time.

11

What You Can Do to Improve Your School

So, where do you take the first bite out of the elephant? Is it the trunk, the tail, or a leg? And how do you get an elephant into a pot to cook it, anyway? Rhetoric about change is easy, but bringing about broad, lasting change poses practical challenges. You'll have to have a plan. In this final chapter, we'll address the practical issues that you will encounter as you set about to revolutionize your school and your school district.

We'll cover several topics that will help you to put together your blueprint for revolution. First, we'll review seven rules for change. These are time-tested lessons that come from several decades of experience of changing schools, businesses, and other kinds of organizations all over the world. There are some ways in which all large organizations are similar, and there are other ways in which schools are unique. These change processes have been studied by many people, and I've boiled them down into the essence that you need to know. Next, we'll go through three topics that will give you guidance on each of several strategies of change. First will be how to take on a revolutionary change of your entire school district. Second, we'll ask, what about the unions? Third will be some final thoughts as you struggle to cope with what you have while creating what you want.

You should keep in mind one basic distinction whenever you think about changing any organization. That is the difference between trying to change a *person* and trying to change an *organization*. Actually, it's even more basic than that. Ask yourself whether you believe that the basic shortcoming of your school is due to the inadequacies of the principal, the superintendent, or the teachers—or whether it's the *organization* that needs repair.

Most of us are tempted to blame the individual, and we miss the role that is played by the organization. We get angry that the darn principal is so pig-headed, that the teacher is too set in her ways, or that the bureaucrats are self-serving and narrow-minded. Let me ask you a question: When you've seen an inept or unqualified person get removed from their job, how good was their replacement? More often than not, the replacement fares no better. The reason is twofold: first, the system that picked the first incompetent also picked the replacement. It used the same faulty selection methods and probably drew from the same talent pool as before. Second, and more important, both employees had to work in the same, probably dysfunctional organization. Once in a great while, you will get lucky and find a new principal or teacher who is enough of an entrepreneur and contrarian to fight the system. That, however, is a long shot, because those people are rare. Most of the time, an able person will succeed when placed in a positive structure and will fail in a negative structure.

It's not possible to change the underlying character of an adult. That's not to say that all of the adults in a failing school system need to be thrown out because they can't change. But their basic values and predispositions were formed when they were children, and it is true that those won't change appreciably. However, as we've seen in Edmonton and elsewhere, these same people will rise to the occasion and become top performers when the system around them—the decentralization of control, the quality of the data on student performance, and the accountability systems—becomes positive rather than negative.

Some businesspeople are fond of saying that unless you have only A-class players, you can't have a winning team. I disagree. As one example, having top-class individual players didn't work for the Los Angeles Lakers until they got Phil Jackson as a coach. Then they became the NBA champions. In the second place, no one—not a company and not a school—can afford to hire only the best of the best. The key to success in building any organization is in teamwork. When you have teamwork—which means having a positive organization—*all* of the players soar, and you end up with an A team, which is what you want.

THE SEVEN RULES OF CHANGE

During the past thirty years, I've had the chance to serve as a management consultant to companies that wanted to achieve revolutionary change to become more successful. I've worked with companies as small as one hundred employees and as large as General Motors, IBM, and Amgen, the world's largest biotechnology company. Although I can't say that I succeeded entirely at my efforts, I did learn something from each of these engagements. More recently, I've worked with small school districts as well as some of the biggest ones in the United States. I've taught business school courses on organizational change, and I've studied the research of many scholars on how to change organizations. I've reduced my hard-won lessons into seven basic rules that I believe guide most successful attempts at change. Follow them, and you are more than likely to succeed, too:

Rule One: People don't fear change—unless they're kept in the dark

Rule Two: Revolutionary change requires the perception that there's a crisis

Rule Three: Structure must change before culture can change

Rule Four: Change must be top-down

Rule Five: Change must be bottom-up

Rule Six: Follow the money!

Rule Seven: School reform isn't partly politics—it's *all* politics!

Think about how each of these rules applies to your local situation and what you can do to start the process of change or help it along.

Rule One: People don't fear change—unless they're kept in the dark

Most of us aren't really opposed to change, contrary to what business books often assert. In particular, business gurus are fond of saying that the top leaders often advocate visionary change, but the middle managers gum up the works because they fear change. The implication is that the people at the top got there because they are a superior class of human beings—an assertion that, in the light of Enron, Tyco, WorldCom, and Arthur Andersen, is patently false. Based on personal experience, I conclude that everyone *favors* change as long as they're in charge of who and what will change. It's equally true that no one likes to be told to change without having had the chance to influence the new direction.

Seeing this point, if you agree with it, is easier than living it. Not only does it mean that you should include the targets of change in your discussion from the outset, it means that you have to listen to them. It doesn't mean that you have to accept all of their views, but it does mean that you'll have to listen to their views seriously, even when you've already decided that the targets of change are the cause of the problems. Often you'll find that the teachers, principal, and district staff will point out important facts that you didn't know, and you'll adjust your plans accordingly. Other times, you may end up simply agreeing to disagree, but at least you're not trying to sneak up on them, and they'll be more open to you as a result.

Business groups that get involved in the school reform process often stumble over this elementary point. They're accustomed to blaming their own workers' unions for their company's problems, so they assume that the teachers' union is at the root of the failure of the schools. Having reached this conclusion, they never invite the union leadership into their dialogue, and by leaving them out, they leave out one of the deepest wells of experience—not to mention a major potential ally.

In fact, if there is a favorite target for laying the blame for the failure of our public schools, it's the teachers' unions. Teachers are more universally unionized than are most other groups of workers. Stanford University political scientist Terry Moe estimates that 80 percent of all teachers, public school and private, are members of unions, compared to an estimate by Claremont Graduate School professors Charles Kerchner, Julia Koppich, and Joseph Weeres that only 11 percent of the private sector workforce is unionized.[1] Teachers' unions are blamed for corrupting the independence of state and local officials with their large campaign contributions, for supporting rules that protect bad teachers, and for handcuffing principals by denying them the authority to assign teachers to the schools and the classrooms where they are most needed. Some of that criticism is fair, but a lot of it is not.

Think about it this way: if the unions are running the school district, then what are the school board and the superintendent there for? It's true, as we will see in a moment, that unions have often become part of the problem, but it's simply not credible to argue that they should bear the lion's share of the blame. It's a truism that, in the United States, adversarial unions typically arise in response to abusive managements. Playing that countervailing role unfortunately places unions in the position of counterbalancing what is wrong, rather than helping to create what could be right.

To the typical principal, an all-powerful teachers' union often seems to have identified him or her as the enemy. The principal has not had an opportunity to visit Seattle and Edmonton, which have very strong unions of teachers and principals, or Houston, which does not, but has managed to create successful school districts. The typical principal has not had the chance to visit the University of Chicago Laboratory Schools, an independent school whose teachers are unionized. Instead, the principal sees only the trees that are just outside the window, not the entire forest.

Of the districts in our study, Los Angeles is the most centralized and bureaucratic. It's no surprise, then, to find that it also has developed the most contentious relationship between the teachers' union and the management. Over the past twenty years, the teachers' union has steadily increased its power over a variety of school-level decisions. Manual Arts High School has a required site council of twenty-one members. Eighteen of the members are from the teachers' union, along with one parent representative, one student representative, and one representative of the union that represents teachers' aides, clerical, and other noncredentialed employees. The principal is a nonvoting member of the council. The council must approve the appointment of assistant principals, program coordinators, and the expenditure of any discretionary funds. The principal has no say in the appointment of department chairs, and the teachers by seniority decide what courses they would like to teach.

At Garfield High School in heavily Latino East Los Angeles, there is an eighteen-member council that consists of the chapter chair of the teachers' union, eight teachers' union members, one noncredentialed union representative, six parents, one student, and the principal. Here, too, the teachers have a seniority right to teach what they want, and the principal has no involvement in the selection of department chairs. It's not unusual for a teacher with long seniority to demand a particular class even though someone else has a graduate degree and more training in that subject.

Many principals in Los Angeles said that they feel abandoned by the central office, and that conflicts between the central office and the head of the teachers' union are frequently transferred to each school. Both principals and the central office staff speak of the teachers' union as a powerful body that they simultaneously fear and resent. The result of this gordian knot of political interests is a system in which all of the parties—teachers' union, principals, parents, and central office—feel powerless.

If your district has descended into a negative relationship with the teachers' union, you'll hear lots about how the union is the real source of all problems. Be skeptical. Don't believe all that you hear from any one side. It is true that systems that grant budgetary and personnel control to committees of teachers and parents rather than to the principal are unlikely to work well. That's because parents and teachers aren't accountable for either student performance or budget performance. It's the principal who is accountable, and it's the principal who should have the final say in these decisions. As we've pointed out, though, that doesn't mean that the principal should be allowed to become an emperor or empress—he or she should be expected to consult with and listen to all parties.

Your teachers' union may well have become locked in a death grip with the school district, as was the case in Edmonton and Seattle. Don't be overcome by an apparently unsolvable problem. Just stick to the Seven Keys to Success. They will lead you to solutions that will result in a gradual melting away of the hostility and toward a mutually productive relationship with the unions.

So, as you begin your revolution, be truthful with everyone. Don't hide your intentions or desires, even from those you assume will oppose you. If the opposition won't come around to your view, at least you'll know in advance rather than finding out at the end. Don't be stopped by the worry that you'll be giving the enemy advance warning. They've been at this a lot longer than you have, and they already know what you're about. The only unknown in their minds is whether you are going to be open with them or try to sneak around them. If you are sneaky, they'll feel entirely righteous about being sneaky with you. The school board and the local and state politicians whom you'll ask for help will want to know that you've talked to all of the major parties. They won't insist that the principals and teachers' unions agree with you, but they're unlikely to agree to help you unless you've at least confronted all of these important players.

Rule Two: Revolutionary change requires the perception that there's a crisis

This is a tricky one. Generally speaking, people are skeptical of reformers. Even though they're not fully satisfied with their schools, they fear even more the chaos that your group might unleash. They're afraid that your idea of utopia could turn out to be their idea of hell.

Many observers find this situation puzzling. They think people are negative about all schools except their own. I don't think that's it at all. Instead, I'd argue that people are inclined to accept what they have if they don't believe that a better option is available to them. They don't want to be whiners. Rather than complain constantly about their school—which they don't believe can be improved from its current dismal state—they try to look at the bright side.

In order to get things moving, then, you've got to do two things. First, you need to gather together the detailed data on your school or school district, compare it to successful schools and districts, and make an undeniable case that your school is in crisis. Compare graduation rates, attendance rates, numbers of central office bureaucrats, test scores, and measures of teacher quality. Once you've done this, you'll be certain that every parent and teacher will react to your data with horror and anger and will demand revolutionary change. Unfortunately, you'll be wrong.

In order to motivate people, you'll need to prepare a detailed plan that has two elements. First, it will have to show what your school will look like after the revolution—present a *vision* of the future. How much local autonomy schools will have, for example, how they will be held accountable for student achievement and financial performance, and how their budget will balance within the existing budget limits. Second, you'll want to include an *implementation plan,* a step-by-step analysis of who will have to grant approvals, vote on your plan, allocate funds, and so on.

What you want to do is to get together the studies that arm the politicians with the facts that they can cite to support their call for revolution, then put together the plan that convinces the public that they *do* have a better option, that it's not just a pipe dream. Once your plan has visible public support, political support, and solid research, others will believe it could actually happen. At that point, the people who don't want to be seen as whiners will be roused into action. When you have all of these pieces in place, you'll in effect lead a mass parade of revolutionaries down the street to your school board. Everyone has the same innate response to a parade—they want to be part of it!

Rule Three: Structure must change before culture can change

Anthropologists define "culture" as consisting of a community's unspoken traditional ways of doing things. We learn what the culture of a school is by watching how the people in it actually behave, not by reading a set of rules about how they are supposed to behave. A negative school culture in which teachers are isolated, students are treated as objects rather than as people, and the principal hides in his or her office can be deeply embedded in people's habits and difficult to change.

A spate of books about leadership and management twenty years ago advocated learning the culture of a company and then changing it in planned ways. People don't listen to that advice any longer, because they've discovered what anthropologists knew all along, that while you can learn to analyze an organization's culture, you can't change it—at least not directly. For example, if the culture is one in which people avoid taking risks on behalf of the children, you cannot advocate more risk-taking and expect it to happen. If the culture is one of giving all children passing marks in order avoid difficult confrontations with their parents, you can't change that aspect of the school culture by attacking it.

However, culture is greatly influenced by the structure of an organization. If you alter the structural arrangements and then have patience, within a year or two the culture will begin to change. For example, Superintendent Angus McBeath eliminated all of his assistant superintendents in Edmonton who had schools reporting to them. He altered the structure of the school district by having all principals report directly to him. As a result, his central office staff has learned a new culture in which the principals are to be respected and served—in part because they have a direct line to their boss. Before, the central office staff treated the principals as low-level managers. Today, the principals are at least the equal of that staff in rank and influence, and they are treated accordingly.

You'll want to study the culture of your school and district to determine what needs to change and what should be preserved. The culture is the part that you can see, and it's more readily visible to you than the structure, so start with that. By including the teachers and the principal in your planning group, you'll have ready access to the natives who know the culture well. Once they've learned to trust you, they can tell you all about it. Because you've already decided that the problem is the system rather than the people, they will be inclined to trust you and to want to work with you. Your next step will be to figure out which structural elements have caused this culture to come into being. Focus your energy on changing the structures, and you'll see the culture change, too.

Rule Four: Change must be top-down

In Edmonton, Seattle, and Houston, the change came from the top. It was led by the school board and, above all else, the superintendent. Within a school, change comes from the princi-pal—whether it's at Mabel Wesley in Houston, Sawyer Elemen-tary in Chicago, or James A. Garfield in Seattle. In a sense, that's what a leader is supposed to do—lead change. Another way to look at it is that change that begins in the middle or at the bot-tom of any organization will sooner or later run into a lack of support or downright opposition from someone up above.

The only principle that you need to follow in evaluating the leader of your school and district is this: No excuses! It's their job to figure out how to overcome the obstacles that are in the way of improvement and to come up with solutions. If they can't do it, then they'll have to find another job. In school after school that we've learned about, the principal walked into an impossi-bly negative situation and successfully turned it around. In Edmonton, Seattle, and Houston, the superintendent did the same. It can be done—no excuses. This is the one exception to the rule (actually, rule #1 should be that every rule has an excep-tion) that it's the system rather than the person. The top leader creates the system in which everyone else will either succeed or fail. If he or she can't fix the system, you owe it to your children to put the pressure on until that top person leaves.

There's another very important subtlety to what happened in our three successful school districts. In each case, the new superintendent came into a situation in which a powerful coali-tion of citizens was willing to stand behind someone who had the courage to lead revolutionary change. If your community is broken into warring camps, you first need to heal those divisions and get everyone together.

Everyone means just that—*everyone*. For example, although the business community is a critical source of influence in almost every city, it cannot succeed in school reform if it shuts out the neighborhood associations, the parent organizations, and the ethnic leadership. If there are rival business associations or if the ethnic organizations are in conflict with each other, you've got to get them together for their common good, and for the good of the children. You'll never get everyone to back your moves, but you need to be willing to talk with all sides. In our democratic society, elected officials won't usually act on a controversial issue unless the proponents of change have made real efforts to include everyone, including their opponents, in the dialogue.

Every skilled top leader is in demand and has lots of options. No leader will accept the job unless the community is unified in giving him or her its full support. If you'll read the histories of revolutionary change by Don McAdams about Houston and by John Stanford about Seattle, you'll find that those communities had to go through a period of getting their act together before they could attract a real leader to the top job.[2] If you conduct a search for a new principal or a new superintendent with a divided community, the only kind of leader you'll attract will be one who either is so dense that she doesn't see the rift in the community, or so arrogant that he doesn't care what the community thinks. That's *not* what you're looking for.

As you lay your plans for revolution, reach out to the broader community. Don't assume that others have agendas that are in conflict with your goals. Talk to people, reach out to them, and listen. You'll have many positive surprises. You'll find that all of you want the same thing—a quality education for all children. You'll discover that differences of opinion often stem from incorrect assumptions about what each of you wants. Once you've reached a state of unity, you'll be able to attract the kind of top leadership that your children deserve.

Rule Five: Change must be bottom-up

This isn't really such a contradiction. A good superintendent knows that great ideas are out there in the schools. A revolution in your neighborhood school can ultimately influence the entire school district. It happens in business all the time. At Procter & Gamble during the 1950s, one factory experimented with self-managed teams of workers who ran a large, high-speed machine. The results were so outstanding that other plants adopted the idea, and eventually it became standard in all of the company's plants.[3] At the Chrysler Corporation during the 1980s, a parts-supply depot experimented with a radical approach to managing its workforce by giving people more autonomy, and it, too, spread to all of the parts depots in the company.[4] Edmonton experimented with a radical new way to manage a school district, and now that system is spreading to districts in the United States. In addition to Seattle and Houston, Cincinnati is implementing Weighted Student Formula, along with at least some of the other elements of the Seven Keys to Success.

It would be more accurate to say that change should be *initiated* bottom-up and *supported* top-down. That is to say that the central office should not be imposing new ways to run a school top-down on principals. Instead, a successful central office is one that gives principals the freedom to experiment for themselves. When a school comes up with an innovation that really works well, other principals and teachers will want it, too. At that point, the central office can provide the financial and other forms of support that will enable the schools that want it to get it. Seattle superintendent Joseph Olchefske said it best: "Every school's got to find its own way."

One final point in your favor: in a large, bureaucratic school district, the people at the central office visit the schools rarely, and they really don't know what your school is up to. That means that you have a lot of running room. If your parent group is united behind your principal and teachers, you can innovate in lots of ways, and it will be a while before the central office finds out. By then, you'll have had time to implement the innovations and produce some measurements that show that they work. Once you've got the data to show that what you're doing is helping the children, no central office bureaucrat will have the courage to tell you to stop simply because it's different. If they do, you've got the ammunition you need to go directly to the superintendent, the school board, the mayor—and the press.

Don't wait for new ideas to trickle down from the top of the district to your school. There aren't many good ideas there to start with. The good ideas typically come from principals, teachers, and parents who deal with students every day, and who are reading about new education ideas, going to conferences on education, and looking for creative new approaches. There are many, many more of you than there are people in the central office, no matter how bloated it may be. It stands to reason that you'll come up with more new ideas than they will. So go to it!

Rule Six: Follow the money!

Antonia Hernandez is president of the largest civil rights organization for Hispanics in the United States, the Mexican American Legal Defense and Education Foundation, or MALDEF. She's long been a school reform activist, because good schools are the key to a bright future for Hispanic children—as for all children. She's been through the school reform wars in Los Angeles, and her advice is worth hearing: "If you can figure out where the money goes—follow the dollars—then I think you'll be able to fix it."

That might sound like a tall order. But you don't need to plow through the school district budget, which is impenetrable even to the people who put it together. Hernandez is reminding us of the golden rule of education: She who has the gold makes the rules. What you need to do is to put tremendous emphasis on getting local control of the money. Then *you* can make the rules about how to run your own school.

Your school board and superintendent undoubtedly have told you that they support your local school councils, that they've long had school-based decision making, and that they even have student-based budgeting. It all sounds wonderful, but you've got to ask the question: So who has control of the money? Unless your school district means to follow the Seven Keys to Success, they'll hem and haw at this point. Either that, or they'll give you a rehearsed, smooth reply in an attempt to put you off.

You'll hear time and again from central office bureaucrats and some principals that they're in favor of creating local school decision-making councils, that they want parent input, that they're in a partnership with the community. Just smile, listen politely, and ask when they are going to give your neighborhood schools control over their own money. Without that local financial control, you gain nothing. Don't settle for the promise that financial control will move from the central office to an area superintendent. Don't accept the promise that principals will be included in the process of making up the district's budget. Seek out strong central office accountability over what you do with the money once you have control of it, but never, ever accept less than local control of the budget.

Sonia Hernandez is the former secretary of education of the state of Texas and former head of instruction of the California State Department of Education. Despite that background, she has always been a full-blown revolutionary. Sonia—no relation to Antonia Hernandez of MALDEF—cut her teeth on radical school reform programs in the late 1980s. She served as head of the main education reform group in Los Angeles, The Alliance. Here's her experienced view on the subject of getting straight answers to tough questions: "Every school district has on its staff someone who spins press releases for them—which is to say, they obfuscate the truth."

Don't bother to try to engage an experienced school district spinner in an argument. They've had a lot more practice at it than you have, and you'll just leave with your head in a fog. You don't need to argue with them, anyway. All you need to do and the one thing that you *should* do is to ask them when they're going to give your school control over its budget. My advice is that you pay no attention to anything else that they tell you on the subject of local control, because it's all smoke and mirrors. Only the money matters when it comes to local school autonomy. They know it, and they'll try to avoid the subject. Once they realize that you know it, too, they'll know that they're going to have to give up the head fakes and start planning for some real change.

Rule Seven: School reform isn't partly politics—it's all *politics!*

Keep one thing in mind—no school district has the ability to change itself from the inside. If the political forces that are acting on the district do not change, it will not change. The school district got the way it is by responding to the forces that are now in place. David Tyack and Larry Cuban put it succinctly in *Tinkering Toward Utopia:* "Educational reforms are intrinsically political in origin."[5] You and your allies have to provide the new force that will bring about the change. It won't be easy, and it won't be quick, but it will be worth the effort. Above all, be prepared for twists and turns in the road and for setbacks along the way. Know that success will ultimately be yours.

When you undertake revolutionary change, you're committing yourself to hand-to-hand combat. It won't be pretty at times, but you've got to stick with it. There's nothing magic about Edmonton, Seattle, or Houston. Mike Strembitsky sees it this way: "What happened in Edmonton could have happened I'm going to say in hundreds of other places on the continent. We had absolutely nothing going for us that other people don't have." Strembitsky points out that Edmonton has a conservative, agricultural population of immigrants who value stability and security. As far as he's concerned, if they could get the public support for revolution, you can do it, too.

One caution. Don't get kidnapped by the school reform industry or by the school district. When you begin to work with the schools, they'll see you as a potential source of new money. They'll try to co-opt you by convincing you that the problem is that they don't have enough money. If you're like most people who care about children, you'll feel sympathy for them and want to help. Many foundations have been led down that road and have put millions into paying for teacher training, books, or new curriculum. If you go along, the district will have succeeded at sending you on a wild goose chase. While you're off trying to help to solve a problem they already have the money for, you're out of their hair. Don't fall for it.

Stick to your goal. It is not to rewrite the curriculum or to choose a new reading program for the elementary grades. It is to get school authorities to implement the Seven Keys to Success. That means getting them out of their current patterns and into a set of more constructive habits. Your tools are not those of educational specialists but of politics. In our society, that means pulling together the majority of parents into agreement on one plan and then using your collective power to make the schools change their ways whether they want to or not.

It's also important to keep in mind the distinction between single-issue politics and the building of a political party. Your goal is not to gather together a group of people who agree on a wide range of issues, from the environment to tax policy to the death penalty. You have a single issue and a single goal: revolution in the way your school is managed. Many people who might not be your allies on other issues will be your allies on this one, and you need each other. You want to have a big tent, in which people who might otherwise be your opponents on a variety of issues can come together. For example, you'll find that the business community, the ethnic organizations, and the teachers' union will want to reduce central office bureaucracy, increase local school autonomy, and encourage the development of learning communities.

Ideally, you'll create a political position for your effort that has only one, or at most two, powerful opponents, the most likely of those being the central office bureaucrats. However, even some of them will be disgusted by how things run now, and even though they won't want to lose their jobs or their power, they'll be secretly sympathetic to your cause. Take care not to broaden the scope of your efforts beyond the Seven Keys to Success, which target changes in the relationship between the central office and the schools. If you broaden your scope much beyond those goals, you're in danger of picking up more opponents, which is to be avoided.

The concept of local school autonomy in a democratic society like ours is politically bulletproof. Opposing it would be like opposing the Boston Tea Party. No official or politician can afford to be against it. You can make use of this fact by making every attempt to push for local autonomy in the most public ways available—at school board meetings, in the press, and in letters to politicians. In private, these same people will want to keep centralized control and freeze you out; but if you can get them in public, they'll have to support your position. Eventually, you'll be able to corner them into making hard commitments to give your school its freedom.

When revolution begins, you can expect to see real progress in a school within a year, two years at most. It may take four or five years for the changes to be stable and resistant to unexpected hazards, but you'll see results pretty quickly. If your goal is to revolutionize the district, expect to be in a fight for two to four years, perhaps more. It may help to remember that you don't need to convert everyone in the district central office, just enough people that the new direction is perceived as permanent. That may mean as few as one third of the senior staff. The final rule, though, is *don't give up!* Even if it does end up taking fifteen or even twenty years to bring revolutionary improvement to your school district, don't you wish that someone had begun the effort twenty years ago?

CHANGING THE WHOLE SCHOOL DISTRICT MEANS CHANGING COMMUNITY ATTITUDES

In the end, a public school district belongs to everyone in the community, and thus the community must undergo a shift in its basic attitude toward the public schools if you are to succeed. As we've said, the first step in bringing about that change is to bring into sharp focus the crisis of the failing schools. That, in turn, means that your group needs to pull together the facts on student achievement and be ready to run a communications campaign to put those facts constantly before the public. The second step is to hold out a vision of achievable reform.

Nearly everyone already knows that the schools are in crisis. However, most people also believe that the schools can't be fixed on a districtwide scale. If your goal is to reform one school, your task will be to create confidence among the parents and teachers of that school that others have succeeded and that your group will, too.

It might be instructive to review what happened in the revolutions in Edmonton, Seattle, and Houston. In Edmonton, there was no widely perceived failure of the schools to educate the children. Instead, according to Mike Strembitsky, there was a constant sniping between the central office and principals, with each side criticizing the other in public. In the very weak schools, the families who were most dissatisfied decided to home-school their children. The conflict grew to the point, though, where the public and the school board wanted to see the fighting stop, and they pushed out the superintendent and reached down into the ranks for a young person who had not been involved in the controversy, Mike Strembitsky.

Thus, when Strembitsky took office, there was a crisis,

though it was not at quite the fever pitch that exists in so many U.S. school districts. Everyone acknowledged that things had to change, and Strembitsky had a vision clearly in mind: he would pass control of the money down to each school and transform the central staff from one that gave orders to principals to one that would assist principals when they asked for help. His vision was concrete; it was easy to explain and simple to understand; and it was pretty obvious that there would be a way to monitor progress, to determine that control of the money had actually been decentralized. Your plan would do well to have these same characteristics. You need to be able to explain its essence in simple terms, the public must be able to understand it, and there should be a simple way to measure the progress of your revolution.

In Seattle, as we've said, many families had fled the urban public schools by moving to the suburbs. People point to the consulting report commissioned by the state legislature as the straw that broke the camel's back. That report revealed, in stark terms and with corroborating data, the terrible failure of Seattle's public schools. The report had enough inflammatory specifics to feed the media for many months. After that, no one was willing to argue that change wasn't necessary.

When General John Stanford and Joseph Olchefske took over, they crafted a set of positions that they could present to families and teachers. They crafted ten shifts in philosophy; for example, "We would stop believing that some children would learn and start believing that all children would learn. . . . We would stop abandoning teachers and give them total support."[6] They also created a strategic plan which had six goals that were concise and straightforward, such as: "Goal #1: Increase academic achievement for all students . . . Goal #2: Close student achievement gaps."[7]

The Houston story is similar in several respects to that of Seattle. Years earlier, H. Ross Perot had led a citizens' group that widely publicized the failure of the public schools throughout the state of Texas. In Houston, the revolution began in fits and starts. The reformers suffered major setbacks, and the school board at first was not unified on the direction of change. Only after a united school board was elected and Rod Paige was persuaded to become superintendent did things really start to move. Like General Stanford in Seattle, Paige saw that until the entire community was together, the public schools could not undergo revolutionary change. I interviewed Dr. Paige in his office in Washington, D.C., after he had been appointed secretary of education in July 2001. This was his summary of what enabled Houston to succeed:

> The civic capacity must exist in a city to have a successful school system. You have all these interest groups—each with their own agendas—but for this one idea, like putting the Olympics in Atlanta or Los Angeles, they have to be willing to put those agendas aside for that one big idea. I tried to do that for education in Houston.

Because Houston had no experience at running a decentralized organization made up of entrepreneurs, Paige relied on local business leaders for advice. If you aren't part of the business community, you may wonder whether to trust its advice or not. Paige was unusual in that he had enough confidence in his own ability to judge people that he was willing to trust others. One of the people he decided that he could trust was the head of a Houston insurance company, Harold Hook. Hook played a major role in bringing to the school district business leaders who knew how to run large, complex organizations. Paige also had the conviction to decide for himself what advice to follow, what to modify, and what to discard. Often, a new superintendent is flattered by the attention that he gets from business leaders and makes the mistake of taking all of their advice, not realizing that what works in a business won't always work in a school system. Sorting through the many elements of the community takes a leader who has the rare combination of strength and willingness to listen.

The board appointed a three-person committee, with Paige as its chair, to come up with a vision statement that would let everyone know what the reformers wanted to achieve. The result was a simple, straightforward four-point plan: Beliefs and Visions. "I. HISD exists to support the relationship between the teacher and the student. . . . II. HISD must decentralize. . . . III. HISD must focus on performance, not compliance. . . . IV. HISD must require a common core of academic subjects for all students."[8]

These elements appear consistently across the cities that have undergone revolutionary change. Other aspects of the situation may be quite dissimilar, but there is always a widespread perception of crisis, and there is always a clear vision of the desired result. In large part, your success depends on your keeping the agenda tightly focused. If you give in to the pressures of the many interest groups, from the superintendent to the teachers' union and various parent groups, you'll end up with unfocused chaos. The public can spot the same old mess in a second, and they won't support an ill-prepared program.

If you do stick to your guns, though, you'll find that soon, the opposition will lose its steam. What you're proposing is largely common sense, and people will recognize it for what it is. They'll support your group, and they'll support your revolution.

SOME FINAL THOUGHTS

If parents, teachers, and principals don't want to put in the time and effort to figure out for themselves what their school should become, we'll remain in our present quagmire. The uncomfortable truth is that the world is constantly changing, and we've got to change with it. When it comes to designing any organization, schools included, no one way is best for all; school systems must allow for individual variation and flexibility. As we've seen, that doesn't mean that the central office should be all-permissive or that accountability should be lax. To the contrary, as with the proper governance of companies, so it is with schools. We need tough accountability from the central office *and* flexibility at the level of each individual school. These two forces are not incompatible; both are necessary for healthy schools.

What we see happening now is a dramatic increase in the number and variety of schooling options. In some states, home schooling is rapidly rising. Charter schools and voucher programs have appeared within the past decade. Around the country, reform is in the air, and future innovations such as cyberschools, privately managed public schools, and branded charter schools may each find a permanent place in the world of education. Independent schools have maintained their market share at about 10 percent, but that stability masks great internal changes. Over the past forty years, Jewish schools have increased in numbers while Catholic schools have declined. State governors are now running city schools—as the governor of Pennsylvania is doing in Philadelphia—while mayors in Cleveland, Chicago, and New York City have assumed the role of head of their public school systems.

Twenty years ago, these changes would have seemed unimaginable. Twenty years from now, we'll wonder how we ever could have had as few options as we do now. It's an exciting time. Whether as teacher, principal, or parent, you have an opportunity to be an active participant in what may turn out to be the great revolution of our times: to bring about a change in the way that we think about and run our schools. Education in America is about our children, it's about racial equality, and it's about the future vitality of our society.

When you embark on the path of revolution, you will be helping others to help their children, which is a plus because they already care deeply about the subject. It's a minus, though, because parents tend not to be rational about their children or to regard issues surrounding them in a calm, objective way. They're totally, irrationally committed to their offspring, and that's good. What an awful world this would be if it were otherwise! Keep in mind, though, that you, like everyone else, are not always the best person to think objectively about what your own child's school should become. You're passionate about having a great school. But remind yourself that you should listen seriously to the teachers, the principal, and the other parents with whom you may disagree on some points. They care about your children; but they also care about all children, including those not yet born who will someday attend their school.

Now you have the evidence that you need in order to be convinced and to convince others that your schools can be changed for the better. Others have done it, in large and small school districts, where unions are strong and where they are not. They've succeeded in mostly minority and low-income school districts and in largely white and middle-class districts. They've done it way up north, in Canada, and way down south, in Houston. They've done it in the Far West in Seattle, and in the East in District 2 in New York City. They haven't had to be perfect; they've only had to be persistent enough to get up after a setback, dust themselves off, and go to it again.

You've heard the best advice from reformers and from successful schools and school districts all around the country. Now it's up to you. Don't let your children down. There is no one to lead this change other than you. Go for it. Tell the bureaucrats that you're fed up, and you're not taking it any more.

Revolution!

Notes

1. The Best Schools in America—Problems and Solutions

1. According to the Program for International Student Assessment, in reading, U.S. fifteen-year-olds rank below fourteen countries such as Canada, Ireland, Belgium, France, and the United Kingdom, and above sixteen countries such as Brazil, Mexico, Portugal, and Hungary. The U.S. Department of Education reports that in our own National Assessment of Educational Progress, fourth-grade reading scores have been stagnant for the last several years. Does this make you angry? It should. It should make you so angry that you're ready for change, and not just plain change, but revolution!

International standardized tests in mathematics and in literacy enable each nation to gauge the standing of its school systems. In the Third International Mathematics and Science Study—Repeat (TIMSS-R), U.S. eighth graders ranked significantly below students in fourteen other countries, including Australia, Belgium, Canada, England, Japan, and Hungary. Our students' test results were comparable to students in Bulgaria, Latvia, and New Zealand.

2. See Jonathan Kozol, *Death at an Early Age* (New York: Plume, [1967] 1985); and Jonathan Kozol, *Savage Inequalities* (New York: HarperCollins, 1992). For statistics cited, see National Center for Education Statistics, *The Condition of Education 2002* (Washington, DC: U.S. Dept. of Education, 2002), p. 80.

3. See Eric Hanushek et al., *Making Schools Work: Improving Performance and Controlling Costs* (Washington, DC: Brookings Institution, 1994); and Diane Ravitch, *Left Back: A Century of Failed School Reforms* (New York: Simon & Schuster, 2000).

4. Los Angeles Unified School District, *Superintendent's 2001–2002 Provisional Budget, June 26, 2001*, pp. A-15, B-6. Operating cost figures include not only salaries for teachers and nonteaching staff but also such expenses as cafeteria expense, transportation, and school police.

5. *Los Angeles Business Journal, Private Schools,* August 7, 2000, pp. 34–35.

6. For a complete statistical analysis of the data, see the working paper by William G. Ouchi, Bruce S. Cooper, Lydia G. Segal, Tim DeRoche, Carolyn Brown, and Elizabeth Galvin, *The Organization of Primary and Secondary Schools* (Los Angeles: The Anderson School of Management, UCLA, 2002).

7. Arthur G. Powell, *Lessons from Privilege: The American Prep School Tradition* (Cambridge, MA: Harvard University Press, 1996), p. 71.

8. Allan Odden and Carolyn Busch, *Financing Schools for High Performance: Strategies for Improving the Use of Educational Resources* (San Francisco: Jossey-Bass, 1998), p. 27. For example, take decentralization of control over the money, which is one of our Seven Keys: "One problem with many approaches to education decentralization is that they have been conceived as ends in themselves. . . . The research shows, however, that this type of decentralization has little effect." It takes all Seven Keys to make a difference, not just some of them.

9. David Tyack and Larry Cuban, *Tinkering Toward Utopia: A Century of Public School Reform* (Cambridge, MA: Harvard University Press, 1995).

2. Three School Districts That Have Won the Revolution

1. Washington State House of Representatives, *Report of an Evaluation of the Seattle Public Schools, by Cresap, a Towers Perrin Company, November 15, 1990,* p. I-4.

2. Ibid.

3. Ibid., p. I-6.

4. Ibid., p. I-8.

5. Donald R. McAdams, *Fighting to Save Our Urban Schools . . . and Winning! Lessons from Houston* (New York: Teachers College Press, 2000), p. 1.

6. Linda M. McNeil, *Contradictions of School Reform: Educational Costs of Standardized Testing* (New York: Routledge, 2000), p. 192.

3. Key #1: Every Principal Is an Entrepreneur

1. Hanushek et al., *Making Schools Work,* pp. 85–86.

2. Diane Ravitch, *The Great School Wars: A History of the New York City Public Schools* (New York: Basic Books, 1974).

3. Anthony S. Bryk, Penny Bender Sebring, David Kerbow, Sharon Rollow, and John Q. Easton, *Charting Chicago School Reform: Democratic Localism as a Lever for Change* (Boulder, CO: Westview, 1998), p. 263.

4. See P. J. Robertson, P. Wohlstetter, and S. A. Mohrman, "Generating Curriculum and Instructional Changes Through School-Based Management," *Educational Administration Quarterly,* vol. 31, no. 3 (1995), 375–404; and Jane Hannaway, "Management Decentralization and Performance-Based Incentives: Theoretical Considerations for Schools," in Eric Hanushek and D. W. Jorgenson, eds., *Improving America's Schools: The Role of Incentives* (Washington, DC: National Academy Press, 1996), pp. 97–109.

5. Los Angeles Unified School District, *Superintendent's 2001–2002 Provisional Budget, June 26, 2001*, pp. A-15, B-6.

6. Los Angeles County Alliance for Student Achievement, *Student Achievement in the Los Angeles Unified School District, 1999–2001* (2001), pp. 32, 53. The calculation is that the district enrolls about 59,000 students in kindergarten each year and has about 28,000 in twelfth grade. Of those twelfth graders, only about 30 percent have taken the courses that they need to get into college. Of course, not all of those 30 percent will actually enter a two- or four-year college, but even if they all did, that would be only 8,400 per year, or 14 percent of the number who enter kindergarten. The Alliance assumes that some of those who leave the LAUSD transfer to other school districts and do eventually graduate and enter college, thus arriving at their estimate of 17 percent.

4. Key #2: Every School Controls Its Own Budget

1. Seattle Public Schools, *Budget Allocations to Seattle Schools for the 2001–2002 School Year* (2002), p. 5.

2. Paul T. Hill, Christine Campbell, and James Harvey, *It Takes a City: Getting Serious About Urban School Reform* (Washington, DC: Brookings Institution Press, 2000).

3. Odden and Busch, *Financing Schools for High Performance*, p. 19.

4. McAdams, *Fighting to Save Our Urban Schools . . . and Winning!*, p. 253.

5. Budget Services and Financial Planning Division, *Superintendent's 2001–2002 Provisional Budget* (Los Angeles: Los Angeles Unified School District, 2002), p. D-6.

5. Key #3: Everyone Is Accountable for Student Performance and for Budgets

1. Marc S. Tucker and Judy B. Codding, *Standards for Our Schools: How to Set Them, Measure Them, and Reach Them* (San Francisco: Jossey-Bass, 1998).

2. Ravitch, *The Great School Wars,* pp. 381–87.

3. Lydia G. Segal, "The Pitfalls of Political Decentralization and Proposals for Reform: The Case of New York City Schools," *Public Administration Review,* vol. 57, no. 2 (March–April 1997), pp. 141–49.

6. Key #4: Everyone Delegates Authority to Those Below

1. Clara Hemphill, *Public Middle Schools: New York City's Best* (New York: SoHo Press, 1999), pp. 92–94.

2. Hill et al., *It Takes a City,* pp. 154–62.

7. Key #5: There Is a Burning Focus on Student Achievement

1. If you are interested in probing more deeply into the pros and cons of standardized testing, one very good overview that isn't too long and is readable is Robert Rothman, "One Hundred Fifty Years of Testing," in *The Jossey-Bass Reader on School Reform* (San Francisco: Jossey-Bass, 2001), pp. 419–33.

8. Key #6: Every School Is a Community of Learners

1. W. Edwards Deming, *Quality, Productivity, and Competition* (Cambridge, MA: Center for Advanced Engineering Study, MIT, 1982).

2. Anthony S. Bryk, Valerie E. Lee, and Peter B. Holland, *Catholic Schools and The Common Good* (Cambridge, MA: Harvard University Press, 1993), pp. 69–78.

3. Raymond Domanico, *Catholic Schools in New York City.* New York University Program on Education and Civil Society, working paper, March 2001, p. 10A.

4. Bryk et al., *Catholic Schools and The Common Good,* p. 277.

5. Bruce S. Cooper and Marc N. Kramer, *The New Jewish Community, New Jewish Schools.* Fordham University Graduate School of Education, working paper, p. 3.

6. Ibid., p. 4.

9. Key #7: Families Have Real Choices Among a Variety of Unique Schools

1. Brian P. Gill, P. Michael Timpane, Karen E. Ross, and Dominic J. Brewer, *Rhetoric Versus Reality: What We Know and What We Need to Know About Vouchers and Charter Schools* (Santa Monica, CA: RAND, 2001), p. 53.

2. Ibid., p. 51.

3. Amy Stuart Wells, *Reactions to the Supreme Court Ruling on Vouchers: Introduction to an Online Special Issue*—www. tcrecord.org, 7/2/01.

4. Ibid., p. 4.

5. Ibid., p. 5.

6. Center for Education Reform, *Charter School Laws Across the States 2001* (Washington, DC: Center for Education Reform, 2001).

7. Gill et al., *Rhetoric Versus Reality,* p. xiv.

8. Ibid., pp. xv–xx.

9. See Samuel Casey Carter, *No Excuses: Lessons from 21 High-Performing, High-Poverty Schools* (Washington, DC: Heritage Foundation, 2001), pp. 85–86, 93–95.

10. Tony Wagner, *Making the Grade: Reinventing America's Schools* (New York: RoutledgeFalmer, 2002).

11. James Bryant Conant, *The American High School Today* (New York: McGraw Hill, 1959); Ravitch, *Left Back,* pp. 363–65.

12. Ravitch, *Left Back,* p. 363.

13. John E. Chubb, "The System," in Terry M. Moe, ed., *A Primer on America's Schools* (Stanford, CA: Hoover Institution Press, 2001), p. 32.

14. Center for Education Reform, *Public-Private Partnerships: A Consumer's Guide* (Washington, DC: Center for Education Reform, 2002).

10. How Good Is Your School?

1. William J. Bennett, Chester E. Finn, Jr., and John T. E.

Cribb, *The Educated Child: A Parent's Guide* (New York: Touchstone, 1999), p. 11.

11. What You Can Do to Improve Your School

1. See Terry M. Moe, "Teachers Unions and the Public Schools," in Moe, ed., *A Primer on America's Schools*, p. 152; and Charles Taylor Kerchner, Julia E. Koppich, and Joseph G. Weeres, *United Mind Workers: Unions and Teaching in the Knowledge Society* (San Francisco: Jossey-Bass, 1997), p. 9.

2. See McAdams, *Fighting to Save Our Urban Schools . . . and Winning!*, and John Stanford, *Victory in Our Schools* (New York: Bantam Books, 1999).

3. These changes at Procter & Gamble were described to me by former faculty colleagues at the Anderson School of Management at UCLA who had served as consultants to Procter & Gamble on those changes.

4. The innovations at the Chrysler Corporation were undertaken during the 1970s by Charles W. Joiner, Jr., who was general manager of the division involved. I had the privilege of advising him.

5. Tyack and Cuban, *Tinkering Toward Utopia*, p. 8.

6. Stanford, *Victory in Our Schools*, p. xix.

7. Ibid., p. 25.

8. Cited in McAdams, *Fighting to Save Our Urban Schools . . . and Winning!*, p. 8.

Index

9 781439 150450